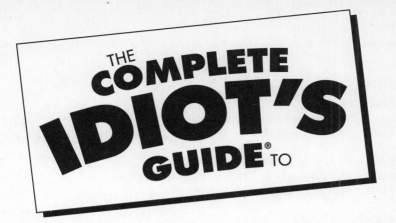

THE COMPLETE IDIOT'S GUIDE® TO

Project Management with Microsoft® Project 2003

By Ron Black

D1367173

ALPHA

A member of Penguin Group (USA) Inc.

This book is dedicated to the men and women who are creating a better world for all of us, one project at a time.

ALPHA BOOKS

Published by the Penguin Group

Penguin Group (USA) Inc., 375 Hudson Street, New York, New York 10014, U.S.A.

Penguin Group (Canada), 10 Alcorn Avenue, Toronto, Ontario, Canada M4V 3B2 (a division of Pearson Penguin Canada Inc.)

Penguin Books Ltd, 80 Strand, London WC2R 0RL, England

Penguin Ireland, 25 St Stephen's Green, Dublin 2, Ireland (a division of Penguin Books Ltd)

Penguin Group (Australia), 250 Camberwell Road, Camberwell, Victoria 3124, Australia (a division of Pearson Australia Group Pty Ltd)

Penguin Books India Pvt Ltd, 11 Community Centre, Panchsheel Park, New Delhi—110 017, India

Penguin Group (NZ), cnr Airborne and Rosedale Roads, Albany, Auckland 1310, New Zealand (a division of Pearson New Zealand Ltd)

Penguin Books (South Africa) (Pty) Ltd, 24 Sturdee Avenue, Rosebank, Johannesburg 2196, South Africa

Penguin Books Ltd, Registered Offices: 80 Strand, London WC2R 0RL, England

International Standard Book Number: 1-59257-308-8
Library of Congress Catalog Card Number: 2004113219

08 07 06   8 7 6 5

Interpretation of the printing code: The rightmost number of the first series of numbers is the year of the book's printing; the rightmost number of the second series of numbers is the number of the book's printing. For example, a printing code of 04-1 shows that the first printing occurred in 2004.

Printed in the United States of America

Note: This publication contains the opinions and ideas of its author. It is intended to provide helpful and informative material on the subject matter covered. It is sold with the understanding that the author and publisher are not engaged in rendering professional services in the book. If the reader requires personal assistance or advice, a competent professional should be consulted.

The author and publisher specifically disclaim any responsibility for any liability, loss, or risk, personal or otherwise, which is incurred as a consequence, directly or indirectly, of the use and application of any of the contents of this book.

Most Alpha books are available at special quantity discounts for bulk purchases for sales promotions, premiums, fund-raising, or educational use. Special books, or book excerpts, can also be created to fit specific needs.

For details, write: Special Markets, Alpha Books, 375 Hudson Street, New York, NY 10014.

Publisher: *Marie Butler-Knight*
Product Manager: *Phil Kitchel*
Senior Managing Editor: *Jennifer Chisholm*
Senior Acquisitions Editor: *Renee Wilmeth*
Development Editor: *Ginny Bess Munroe*
Production Editor: *Megan Douglass*

Copy Editor: *Keith Cline*
Illustrator: *Shannon Wheeler*
Cover/Book Designer: *Trina Wurst*
Indexer: *Tonya Heard*
Layout: *Ayanna Lacey*
Proofreading: *Mary Hunt*

Contents at a Glance

Contents

Foreword

If you are expecting this book to simply explain how to use Microsoft Project 2003 to schedule projects, you're in for a pleasant surprise. Ron Black shares my view that *projects are people*, and that Microsoft Project is a tool that can be used by those people to develop a plan to coordinate their work efforts. However, the software can't plan for you, nor can it tell you what to do! It is actually a program that performs calendar calculations that, admittedly, are difficult to do manually, and this makes it an invaluable tool, but a tool nevertheless.

Like any tool, it takes skill to get results. I have a friend who says that, "A fool with a tool is still a fool," and I might add that the more powerful the tool, the more dangerous a fool becomes. A saw does not make one a carpenter or perform carpentry for you.

Likewise, MSP does not allocate resources for you. It simply tells you when you have people or equipment overallocated, and it takes advantage of any slack in your schedule to relieve those overloads, but you must ultimately make decisions about whether these mathematical solutions are valid. In many cases they are not. They look good on paper, but in practice they often don't work.

I have long been disturbed by the fact that many managers believe that project management is just scheduling, and that if they give you a copy of MSP, they have turned you into an instant project manager. I call this Project Management in a Box. Just add water and stir. It's nonsense.

Because projects are people, project management is really about dealing with people, and I'm sad to say that many project managers know far more about the technology of things than they do the technology of people—and there is such a technology. It's called behavioral science, and while it isn't as precise as some engineering technology, it is a whole lot more valid than the kind of naïve psychology (call it guesswork) that is applied by too many project managers.

One thing is certain—if you can't get people to use MSP correctly, and then do their work as the plan prescribes, the only value of MSP is to help you document your failures with great precision!

My suggestion is that you read this book with special attention to Ron's down-to-earth advice on how to actually manage, and try to incorporate it into your manager's toolkit. Like me, Ron has a few gray hairs, gained no doubt through his experience managing projects, and that experience can help you avoid some of the more common mistakes made by project managers.

One good thing about this book—in spite of the title, you don't have to be an idiot to benefit from it! And if you take it to heart and apply it, no one can accuse you of being an idiot in your managing of projects.

—James P. Lewis, Ph. D., President, The Lewis Institute, Inc.

Introduction

Welcome to *The Complete Idiot's Guide to Project Management with Microsoft Project 2003*. This book is about success—yours! It was created to help you overcome the challenges of project management and achieve personal success on every project you undertake.

After all, project management is not for the faint hearted. At best, project management is an exciting and rewarding adventure in building the future. Without project management, there would be no new medications, no new schools, no new telecommunications, no new software, and on and on! In a large way, project managers are responsible for turning our best dreams into reality. On the other hand, at its worst—well let's not even consider the worst. As a project manager, you're here to succeed. And succeed you will! You've decided to use Microsoft's powerful Project software to help you get the job done. That's a good step!

The project you're currently engaged in may have been thrust upon you. Or perhaps you willingly accepted this project and all its challenges and responsibilities. Or maybe you're planning and implementing your own project. In any case, the project's successful completion is not the only thing at risk.

Intertwined with every opportunity is some level of threat. Your team's success may be on the line. In fact, your department or even your company's success may depend on your ability to get this project moving and keep it moving around, over, or through every problem that crops up, all the way to a successful conclusion. And yes, I know it's not nice to shout "fire" in a crowded theater, but you can't forget that your personal satisfaction and possibly even your professional reputation may also be at stake.

I wrote this book for those who have too much to do, too little time, too few resources, or all of the above. So the goal of this book is not to teach everything thing there is to know about project management, nor is it to describe every minor feature and function of Microsoft Project 2003. (Why kill all those trees when nobody could lift a book that size, or have enough time to read it anyway!) Instead, the goal of this book is to provide you with proven project management techniques and tools, in a format that is easy to learn, fast to implement, and powerful in use.

And so, here it is. The sum total of more than three decades of professional project management experience, combined with the world's most popular project management software (Microsoft Project 2003), tuned and tested by thousands of project professionals who have attended my seminars, all carefully condensed into a get-it-done-now format. Voilà—everything you need to make your project a huge success! (Of course you have to supply the project, attitude, and elbow grease.)

How to Use This Book

The Complete Idiot's Guide to Project Management with Microsoft Project 2003 is a ready-to-use success guide that steps you through a natural and effective management process. It blends the essentials of project management, with seasoned insight and advice from a real-world practitioner, and integrates the best ways to use MS Project, all with one goal: your project's success. With step-by-step instructions and an easy to use index, you'll want to keep this handy reference close by.

Users of Microsoft Project 2000 and Project 2002 will be happy to note that I haven't forgotten you! Naturally, there have been improvements and additions in each release, but for the average Project user, the most popular and useful functions have changed little. Microsoft has done a terrific job of maintaining consistency in the user interface. The big changes are easy to spot and easy to use (like expanded help files, explanatory Smart Tags, and additional wizards for common tasks). Rest assured that I'll call your attention to any important differences and provide any extra guidance that you might need.

The book is divided into five parts and two appendices.

Part 1, "Focusing On Your Success," provides a jump start on initiating a project, gaining buy-in and commitment from stakeholders, making your project's success measurable, and identifying problems before they arise. It explains key concepts, provides proven strategies, and translates your new-found knowledge into action with ready-to-use checklists.

Part 2, "Planning Your Project," takes you through the thinking and the mechanics of building an effective project plan. From the first question (what needs to be accomplished?), to a workable baseline plan, you'll master the work breakdown structure, duration estimating, modeling workflow, and assigning resources.

Part 3, "Optimizing Your Plan," sharpens your project planning success skills. You'll learn time-tested techniques and how to apply them with Microsoft Project 2003 to deal with resource shortages, overly aggressive timelines, or both.

Part 4, "Managing for Success," keeps you in control of even the most difficult project. You'll learn how to measure true progress, identify problems, analyze options, and take timely, effective action.

Part 5, "Beyond the Basics with Project 2003," teaches you how to manage multiple projects with ease, keep virtual teams perfectly in sync, share information with other programs, and (when you need to look your best) present project information with credibility, confidence, and persuasive clout!

Appendix A is a glossary of important project management terms, concepts, and techniques that will help you sound, think, and communicate like a professional project manager.

Appendix B provides a listing of my favorite project management resources, websites, professional organizations, and user's groups. You'll find a link to my website where you can download all the forms and checklists provided in this book.

Conventions

The information in this book is formatted to help you find what you need as rapidly as possible. A variety of visual elements are used to make you aware of potential hazards, supporting information, project management terminology, software shortcuts, planning tips, and good ideas. At the beginning of each chapter you will find a listing of the major topics to help you locate the information you want. The end of each chapter includes a listing of the concepts covered. You can use these to test your knowledge and select those areas that you may want to learn a little more about.

Communication skills are an important aspect of project management. Wherever possible, I have taken the time to point out how project managers use an otherwise common word or phrase in a special way. In addition, new terms are indicated with an *italic* typeface. And there is a complete glossary, "Words at Work," that is compliant with the Project Management Institute's *Project Management Book of Knowledge*. You've got easy access to all the project management terminology you need to communicate effectively throughout the profession.

When entering data into your computer, a **bold** typeface is used to indicate text that you type. A `monospace` typeface indicates onscreen messages or text that appears onscreen.

Pointing and clicking with the mouse is usually the fastest and easiest way to make the program do what you want it to do. So although there are usually other ways to accomplish the same task in Microsoft Project 2003, I focus on those methods that help you get the fastest results.

Along with plentiful screen shots, examples, and annotated figures, you'll notice several other elements I've used to speed your mastery of project management:

Words at Work

Learn how to speak the language, understand the short-hand, and cope with the countless conventions that project managers have created over the years. The secret language of project managers is revealed. You'll learn why stakeholders don't hold stakes, why noncritical tasks are essential, and why crashing the project may be the only way to success.

Secrets of Success

You'll find key concepts and special techniques to make your job easier, faster, and more enjoyable. These bits of sage advice and tricks of the trade are the stuff you usually learn only after years of hard knocks! Both rookies and seasoned project managers will find these secrets helpful.

More Good Stuff

These notes provide additional information, pointers, and good ideas that are important and useful but not absolutely essential. If you want to delve a little deeper into project management or Microsoft Project 2003, watch for these notes and dig in!

Project Pitfalls

If you hate being blind-sided, watch for these cautionary tips. They're designed to help rookies survive and to help veterans relax. You'll avoid pitfalls and problems, and learn to navigate safely around potential disasters.

Acknowledgments

No project is ever successfully completed alone, and this book is no exception. It has been a pleasure to work with so many excellent professionals, all of whom have been essential to this book's success. I am in debt to the stellar Alpha Books team who guided, nurtured, and graciously facilitated the process. It's been a delight to work with senior acquisitions editor Renee Wilmeth, development editor Ginny Bess, technical editor Michael Campbell, project editor Megan Douglass, copy editor Keith Cline, and proofreader Mary Hunt. You've all been terrific! And a special thanks goes to illustrator Judd Winick.

Trademarks

All terms mentioned in this book that are known to be or are suspected of being trademarks or service marks have been appropriately capitalized. Alpha Books and Penguin Group (USA) Inc. cannot attest to the accuracy of this information. Use of a term in this book should not be regarded as affecting the validity of any trademark or service mark.

Part 1

Focusing On Your Success

It's that last line item in the job description that gets us into these fixes: "and other duties as assigned."

You were caught doing well, and the next thing you know, someone slaps the project of the century down on your desk. Let's face it, whether you are a project manager by choice or chance, project management responsibilities place you in a high-profile, high-risk position. No matter how poorly conceived, inadequately resourced, or overly optimistic the project may be, it's up to you to make it a success.

Part 1 of this book is about project success and personal success. The two are inseparable. You'll learn how successful project managers think, what tools they use, and how to build your professional reputation. You'll see why it's essential to understand the project from the stakeholder's point of view before you ever start planning, how to get and stay in control of any project, and how Microsoft Project can it all a little easier.

Surviving and Thriving in a Project World

In This Chapter

◆ Why project management is one of the most important skill sets you can learn

◆ How project management is different from everything else you do at work

◆ The essential skills you need on every project

◆ How Microsoft Project 2003 can help you manage successfully

◆ How to create a reputation just short of miracle worker

As the world changes, so does the way the world works.

Not long ago, the only place you saw project management in action was in the development of high-technology products or in heavy construction. Outside of the aerospace, defense, electronics, and building industries, project management tools and techniques were rarely encountered and then only in fragments. Even though project management methods were well developed, mainstream enterprise had not widely embraced this proven approach to achievement. Experienced project managers and skilled project teams were relatively rare. Much has changed in the past few years! This chapter provides the perspective, strategies, and tactics you need to thrive in this new world of work.

Changing the Way the World Works

From geopolitics to technology, the world is changing before our very eyes. Widespread change has been the way of the world for decades, and there seems to be no respite in view. Virtually every industry, organization, and profession is impacted by this onslaught. It has been said that the only constant is change. Today we might add that the only constant is accelerating change!

Managers, leaders, and professionals of every ilk are seeking new ways of coping in this dynamic environment.

Changing the Way Organizations Work

To survive and thrive in turbulent environments, organizations must be able to take an initiative or product from conception through to delivery, in a timely and effective manner. They must bring expertise together on short notice and focus on the right problems and opportunities. They must be able to choose effective implementation strategies within the inevitable confines of short timelines and resource scarcities. Above all else, organizations must be able to rapidly adapt and deliver results on queue.

More Good Stuff

An illustration of the growing reliance on project management methodology is the growth of the Project Management Institute, the world's largest professional organization for project managers, consultants, and educators. Founded in 1969 with fewer than 100 members, by 1979 membership was still only 2,000. It took until 1990 for the group to reach 8,500 members, but by the turn of the century membership had swollen to 50,000. The organization now boasts over 125,000 active members residing in 140 countries.

For all these reasons, the project management approach is gaining widespread acceptance. Its growth is not just because it is a new (at least to some) and effective way of *dealing* with problems and *pursuing* opportunities. More important, the project management methodology is a proven way of *creating* change, and doing it *rapidly*.

Changing the Way You Work

Demands placed on the organization naturally affect an individual's approach to work. To survive and thrive in changing environments, individual workers must be effective in both their fields of expertise (their ordinary work) as well as in their ability to rally with others and effect change (their project work).

Project skills are therefore no longer relegated to a few key, highly trained individuals in a handful of industries. Project skills are now in demand throughout most industries and most professions. More and more, the skills of project management are a prerequisite to success in jobs from the top manager to the lowest supervisor, from scientist to engineer, technician to clinician, in large organizations and in small. The ability to collaborate, communicate, and authentically participate in a project environment is no longer optional. It has become an essential survival skill.

Project Management and Your Organization

Project management has been described as the ability to create the impossible, with the unwilling, against insurmountable odds, under budget and on time, and I like to add, while singing the Battle Hymn of the Republic and drinking a glass of water. But it's really not that bad. Project managers are rarely asked to sing while drinking.

Successful project management requires a broad range of technical, managerial, and social skills, as well as the ability to tolerate ambiguity, accept risk, and not infrequently, deal with high-pressure situations.

Call It What You Want, It's Still a Project

Many industries and organizations have their own names for project management. You hear the terms *product management*, *construction management*, *director of initiatives*, *program management*, *change management*, and others. Don't let the titles mislead you. Regardless of what you call it, if it has the attributes of a project, it is a project. Moreover, you can expect that the project management methodology will be an effective approach. In general, a project is a sequence of activities, with a beginning and an end, intended to create specific outcomes.

Words at Work

The term **program** or **program management** describes a group of projects related to a common initiative and managed in a cohesive manner.

Projects always have a degree of newness to them. To some extent, what you're doing hasn't been done before, at least not with this team, or with this strategy, or with this set of resources. With newness comes unknowns, and with unknowns, there is always risk.

In comparison, consider the work you were originally hired to do. We'll call it your ordinary work. (In retrospect, you may realize that by doing such a good job and earning upper-management's trust they decided to give you a reward—projects!) In our ordinary work we know what to expect. We know what works and what doesn't, who we can trust and who we shouldn't, how long things take, and where the problems might lie. We've done the work more than once, so we've created systems and improved them over time. In short, we know what we're doing.

Compared to ordinary work, projects have greater unknowns, complexity, newness, and risks. They are temporary in nature. People assigned to the project must quickly come together and morph into an effective team. To succeed, they must deal with issues, problems, and work activities that at the outset may not be understood.

Simply put, projects are anything you do one time, or for the first time. Applying the principles of project management will ease the journey and hasten your success.

The High-Stakes, High-Visibility Job

There are two things you can count on as a project manager: high stakes and high visibility.

Let's consider the high-stakes project environment for just a moment. Every project that reaches the planning or implementation stage is, by definition, important. As a rule, organizations don't fritter away scarce resources on projects that are not worthy. (Careful now, I know what you're thinking.) Somewhere along the line somebody (the originator) spotted a problem or opportunity, thought of a solution, and decided to implement it (or convinced a sponsor to). The decision was made to invest precious time and resources, put off other competing uses for the resources, and to assume any risk inherent to the project. From that point forward the investment and exposure grows (as more and more time, money, and resources are consumed), until hopefully, the project is completed and its presumed benefits are realized. Failure is not an option. In projects, the stakes are high!

That's why effective organizations give this special high-stakes work special status, special treatment, and special people. High-stakes projects are given to the best people we have. People who can be counted on to get the job done. Pat yourself on the back—that's why your project got you!

Secrets of Success

Surprisingly, adoption of the project management approach to work often meets the greatest resistance at the highest levels of management. Those dealing directly with implementation issues often are perplexed by upper-management's resistance to invest or participate. Even when the benefits are obvious to you, don't expect to gain support until you can clearly validate the benefits in their terms. Find what is in it for your boss, and you'll gain a convert.

Projects Are a Team Sport

In projects, you can't be successful alone. It takes an effective team with a variety of skills and expertise to succeed on even small projects. Like all effective work groups, project teams are most effective when goals, roles, and responsibilities are clearly understood, in sync, and fully committed to.

In the broadest sense, all stakeholders (everyone who can impact the project or who will be impacted by the project) are members of the project team. This includes the owner, end users, planners, implementers, and depending on the project, many others. If your projects are state or local government projects, every voter and alleged voter is a project stakeholder! I'm not recommending that you attempt to manage at this level of detail, but I am recommending that you're aware of all stakeholder groups, their points of view, and their potential influence. Mice do occasionally roar!

Table 1.1 lists the stakeholder groups you'll want to carefully interact with. Project success requires coordinated, effective contributions from each of these stakeholder groups.

Table 1.1   Primary Stakeholder Groups

Stakeholder	Roles and Responsibilities
Originator	Spots an opportunity to make things better and proposes the idea. Originators can hold any position within or even outside of the organization.
Sponsor	The project's upper-management advocate. This person influences planned outcomes, authorizes resource expenditures, helps set project deliverables and priorities, and often selects the project manager. Serves as representative, supporter, and liaison within upper management.

continues

Table 1.1 Primary Stakeholder Groups (continued)

Stakeholder	Roles and Responsibilities
Project manager	The project's team leader, whose primary responsibility is to ensure project success. Usually involved from the earliest phases of project initiation through planning, execution, and closure. Provides leadership, facilitates communication, exerts control, and has overall authority as set by the project sponsor and upper management.
Core team	Project participants with a high level of involvement during execution. Often helps in project planning, especially in their own areas of expertise. Likely interacts frequently with many members of the project team. Responsible for achieving specific tasks, outcomes, or deliverables as directed by the project manager.
Extended team	Project participants with little involvement during execution but whose contribution is nonetheless essential. The extended team might include budget approvers, specification submitters, data providers, vendors, and various internal or external customers.

Project Team Peculiarities (and Problems) Are Predictable

Experienced project managers remain alert for potential problems so they can eliminate or mitigate issues before they arise. Some problems are inherent to the project team approach and can be expected on most projects. When undertaking a project, it is often necessary to assemble a group of technically diverse (and often geographically dispersed) individuals, to create a *cross-functional* project team. It's not surprising that effective communications are a critical success factor. Many of the difficulties and potential pitfalls within team communication and collaboration are easy to predict. Projects and people vary, but human nature does not!

For example, extended teams are typically difficult to manage because their ordinary work dominates most of their time and energy. Your project is just an interruption to what they believe is most important—keeping their direct supervisors happy! When it comes to making you happy or keeping their bosses happy, you can count on who's going to lose.

Having extended team members' responsibilities "slip through the cracks" is a common lament. Short of a good crack sealant, frequent communications and careful control is the best approach when dealing with extended teams.

Intuition, common sense, and personal experience validate a finding by Murphy, Baker and Fisher (1974) in their *Determinants of Project Success*. Taken together, the communication elements accounted for more than 75 percent of the factors that enabled project success. These included such items as coordination, interpersonal relations, communication of the project's importance, and consensus on the success criteria. Clearly, a key success strategy is to improve stakeholder interactions and communications throughout the project.

Now that you're armed with an awareness of issues common to extended teams, you're probably wondering if Microsoft Project 2003 can help. You bet it can! But let's not get ahead of ourselves. There are two more key points you'll want to think about.

Consider your core team members. I'll bet you know what to expect from these people. Chances are you're familiar with the content they provide and the technology or methods they use. And you're probably aware of the inherent risks and typical problems that arise in their work. Furthermore, if you've worked with some of these same individuals on other projects, you'll have a pretty good understanding of who you can trust, and perhaps, who you shouldn't. In any case, core team members have significant involvement, contact, and interaction with each other and with you. This provides many opportunities to learn their styles, skills, and expertise, and it gives you many more opportunities to organize, direct, and orchestrate their efforts. If weaknesses or problems arise, you're in a good position for discovery and preemptive action. Compared to extended teams, authentic participation is much easier to attain within the core team.

Secrets of Success

Whenever possible, project team members should be collocated. Their ability to interact professionally and personally allows the team to bond in ways that e-mail, instant messaging, web access, conference calls, and even videoconferences can't match. If they cannot collocate, provide a common project room where they can gather and use as their own. If physically separated by doors, floors, buildings, time zones, or continents, get them together as early and as often as possible. Whenever core team members are isolated, maintain a disciplined, aggressive communication schedule.

Central to your project's success is this group's ability to identify all required work, participate in the development of an effective plan, commit to an agreed-on course of action, integrate their work activities effectively, maintain a state of forwardness during implementation, and honor the project's deadlines. As you probably noticed, effective communication is a prerequisite for each of these items. All these issues can be improved and many can be eliminated with the skillful use of Microsoft Project 2003.

Secrets of Success

Carefully consider the project's stakeholders. The better you understand their views, issues, concerns, and power, the more capable you will become in managing their interactions and facilitating communications. Even on simple projects, identify the stakeholders thoroughly. I use a large flip chart and sticky notes. Begin by brainstorming the type of stakeholder groups you'll encounter and list them on the flip chart. Then list each individual (or a representative of the group) on a sticky note and arrange those notes in clusters of important attributes (project proponent, resistor, end user, remotely located, doesn't speak the language, and so on). After they are identified and arranged in this manner, potential issues and opportunities are easier to spot. You can then prepare and execute communications strategies accordingly.

I've left what can be the most important, frustrating, and decisive project team peculiarity until last: the working relationship between the project manager and the project sponsor.

Ultimately, the sponsor is your most important teammate. The sponsor establishes your project responsibilities, your access to resources, and your level of authority. Ideally, the sponsor, the project manager, and possibly a few of your core team members will collaborate early on, working together to mold the proposed project's implementation approach with the organization's resources and objectives. Early collaboration can broaden implementation options, facilitate the best use of resources, and help to minimize every project manager's worst nightmare, your boss's over-optimism!

If conflicts arise with other departments or project managers over resources, priorities, or approaches, the issues are best resolved at the project sponsor level. Left to the managers, whoever has the most power will likely prevail, even if it's contrary to the overall best interests of the organization. Effective project sponsorship is good for you, the project, and the organization as a whole.

Unfortunately, communication and collaboration between the project manager and sponsor is rarely as good as it should be. On most projects it falls into the range somewhere between "nonexistent" and "strained." Making important decisions requires trust, respect, and genuine rapport, all of which takes time to develop. Many projects just don't last that long. In addition, the ability to communicate project status meaningfully requires a common project language, an understanding of fundamental project management tools, and an agreed-on basis from which to evaluate (goals, schedules, baselines, and so on). Throw in the high stakes, the high visibility, and a few mixed signals that you'll find on any project, and you've got the makings for high drama! When problems inevitably arise, the results can be tragic (or comical depending on you sense of humor and vantage point). If you'll allow me to continue the (albeit overworked) metaphor, projects can get theatrical ….

The drama begins when the project sponsor hands the project over to you with all major assumptions and expectations having been set without your input. With little or no discussion, you're handed the microphone, stage, cast, script, and, oh yes, the bright lights. With all of its problems, ill-conceived ideas, and overly optimistic claims, you're now the one in charge. As of that moment, you're responsible for everything on the project including the weather and postal strikes, and an occasional emergency appendectomy. Worse yet, the team doesn't report to you, you didn't get to pick them, and they all have other projects and responsibilities.

At this point, the sponsor steps off the stage, but sponsors don't always leave the theater. This can be good or bad. Sometimes they remain in the wings, working with you, offering words of advice or encouragement, helping you set the stage with all the resources you'll need, working issues you can't reach, and doing whatever they can to help you succeed. Isn't that nice! There they are, out of your way and tactfully out of sight, but close by if you need them. Even if they handed you a mess, you've got to love a project sponsor who's genuinely trying to help.

On the other hand, some sponsors plop themselves down in a front row seat. There they remain overly vigilant, occasionally hurling directives and criticisms at your team, endlessly editing, adding, and changing the script. In a case like this, I hope you're good at ignoring stupidity and dodging tomatoes.

Meek project sponsors are found in the back row, close to an exit. These are the ones who like to see and to be seen, but who are ready to dart out at the first sign of fire, smoke, and in some cases, even a little friction. When the going gets tough, these folks have long since left the premises.

And that brings us to the corporate magician. These sponsors have an amazing ability to entertain the majority views, disappear when the going gets tough, and reappear just in time for the awards ceremony.

In the end, good sponsors are like all good bosses. It takes high levels of trust and two-way communications to work together effectively. To get the best from your sponsors, honor their points of view, keep them informed, present your ideas credibly, remain logical and forthright, and finally, if they give you all the responsibility and none of the authority, speak up! Take whatever time and energy is required to teach them how to help you serve their needs. (They may be new at projects, too.) And yes, you guessed correctly, we'll use Project 2003 to make your ideas clear, credible, and persuasive.

Project Management and You

In my training seminars, I like to ask participants to write down the first things that come to mind when they hear the words *project manager*. There's usually a good laugh or two in the answers: "the guy who forgot to duck," "what happens to you if you miss a meeting," "how to get rid of someone you can't fire," and so on. The message is clear. Project management can be a grueling experience. But it's also clear that these same project managers take pride in their work. Even though the work is challenging and the risk can be high, some sense of satisfaction keeps us coming back for more.

Here's another revealing exercise: Write down everything you can in 30 seconds that a project manager does. Well?

Here's what I've discovered in my seminars. The lists are easy to group into two categories. There are those that are long with a detailed view and those that are short with an obviously big-picture view. Would it surprise you to learn that beginning project managers almost always create long, detailed lists? They're great. You'll see things like planning, Gantt charting, creating work breakdown structures, finding the critical path, estimating durations, statusing, tracking, reporting, managing, organizing, holding meetings, and on and on.

Project Pitfalls

Before you accept an additional assignment (again!), carefully consider your workload. Everyone has a limit, no matter how much we hate to admit it. The next responsibility, no matter how small, might be one too many. Ask yourself whether doing one more thing is worth the risk of failure on them all.

The seasoned veteran's lists are markedly shorter, but no matter how they say it, their obsession with results is clear: Deliver results on time and on budget; satisfy the stakeholders; achieve success; get it done what ever it takes, and my personal favorite, work yourself out of a job.

Let's consult the Project Management Institute (PMI), the largest professional organization for project managers, for the formal definition. According to their Project Management Body of Knowledge (PMBOK) guide, project management is "the application of knowledge, skills, tools, and techniques to project activities to meet the project requirements." The nine knowledge areas they include are managing project initiation and integration; definition of scope; estimating and controlling time; estimating and controlling costs; quality assurance; human resource management; the creation, collection, and distribution of information; risk management; and procurement. Whew! That is a lot to know and do.

No one will likely have to perform all those functions on any one project, but it does show how easy it is to be distracted from what might be the critical success factors in your project. One thing remains certain for rookies and veterans alike: First and foremost, focus on delivering results, and make sure your people do the same thing.

The Qualities of High-Quality Project Managers

One of the most important determinates of project success is the effectiveness of the project manager. The relative importance of each of the criteria listed here might vary from project to project, but to some extent, all are important on every project:

◆ **Personal ambition and motivation.** Enthusiasm on the part of the project manager, although difficult to gauge, consistently proves to be a precursor to project success. Negotiating the inevitable challenges that befall every project, and leading others to do the same, requires a positive point of view.

◆ **High tolerance for ambiguity.** In projects, authorities are rarely clear-cut. Project managers must persevere even with unclear requirements, uncertain results, untested team members, and stakeholders who send mixed messages.

◆ **Coalition-building skills.** Gaining results in difficult situations, across department lines, throughout the stakeholder groups, without direct reports or clear-cut authority requires a consummate coalition builder.

◆ **Technical competence.** Although project managers don't have to know everything the technologies embodied within the project, technical competence improves their ability to judge the merit of conflicting views, relate to the project team, and make timely decisions.

◆ **Business orientation.** Project decisions often have far-reaching effects. Understanding the organization's scope of operations and core business, maintaining a focus on objectives and strategies, and being able to weigh the implications of options is crucial.

◆ **People skills.** Project managers achieve results through other people. The ability to identify interests, motivations, strengths and weaknesses, and to build authentic participation is fundamental to achieving results.

Project managers with high marks in all these attributes are undoubtedly rare. Perhaps an equally important attribute is the ability to recognize our own short-comings. With awareness comes the opportunity to improve or compensate effectively.

The Project Manager's Many Roles

On any given day, project managers have ample opportunity to display their many talents. Moving from role to role is impossible for some, even over the course of a career. The project manager must be able to shift into a new modality as the situation requires.

> **More Good Stuff**
>
> Effective project managers champion the success of their teams. Meredith Belbin (1996) noted in his research on effective teams that the single most important influencer of team success was an effective team leader, whom he describes as fair, firm, trustworthy, and able to realize and utilize the abilities of others.

Think of a detailed-oriented professional you've known. Someone adept with managing facts, figures, specifications, down to the smallest detail. Asking that person for situation overviews, pervasive trends, or big-picture implications may be asking too much! Conversely, it's the rare visionary who is good with the details. Project managers must be able to keep both ends of the spectrum in focus. Good decisions can't be made without broad perspective and an understanding of the supporting detail.

In any given project, some roles prove to be more important than others. Table 1.2 lists the project manager roles necessary in most project environments.

Table 1.2   Key Roles of the Project Manager

Role	Description
Visionary	The ability to see what can be and describe it to others with such persuasive clarity that they, too, can believe it is possible
Team builder	Cheerleader, coach, counselor, and teammate who is skilled at helping individuals succeed for the good of the whole
Planner	Identifying needed resources and tasks, scheduling activities, and orchestrating efforts
Estimator	Accurately forecasting time, money, and resource requirements of a project
Meeting chair	Making meetings productive and ensuring that people and ideas are respected

Role	Description
Collaborator	Creating an environment of trust, respect, and cooperation to produce appropriate decisions that everyone supports
Negotiator	The ability to influence, persuade, or otherwise manifest lasting agreements
Manager	Administrator of organizational policies, procedures, and controls
Communicator	Keeping the information flowing throughout the entire stakeholder group
Problem solver	The ability to see what everyone else sees and come up with a better solution
Leader	The ability to gain willing followers even in the face of adversity

Project management can be a demanding profession requiring many skills and talents. However, for those who enjoy challenges, value teamwork, and want to make a difference in the world, you've found your dream job!

For Aspiring Project Management Professionals

If you're seeking professional growth and career advancement, hone your project management skills. Success on projects depends on talented and motivated project managers who are willing to lead the way. People like that are hard to come by, and most organizations know it. Opportunity abounds for those who can consistently bring projects in on time and on budget. Taking on a project and proving your mettle can put your career on the fast track.

However, there's an easy trap for the aspiring rookie to fall into. More than once I've seen a project management opportunity that a department head decided to give to a talented subordinate. Sounds good, right? The subordinate gets exposure, gains experience, and if needed, the boss is there for assistance.

Here's the catch. In both of these situations, the rookie project manager continued reporting to the department head, not the project sponsor. The project manager was completely isolated from the project sponsor. Beyond the obvious communication problems, the project manager in both cases was set up for the fall. If the project went well, the department head gets the credit. If the project goes poorly, the rookie project manager takes the hit.

When the opportunity arrives to manage a project, make sure you're working directly for, and closely with, the project's sponsor. Anything less than a direct, personal connection reduces your effectiveness and can put you, as well as the project, at risk.

For the Accidental Project Manager

You may be an engineer, executive, scientist, teacher, programmer, administrative assistant, entrepreneur, and so on; but given the responsibility to accomplish a project, you become a project manager no matter what your title says. At that point your personal success, like it or not, depends on project success. If you could do everything by yourself, there wouldn't be a problem. But you can't. You'll have to rely on the expertise of many others. Some of them you'll know and some of them you won't. Some of them will have good ideas and some them ... well, you know. Here's my first tip for accidental project managers:

◆ If you don't know everything there is to know about the project, know who you can trust.

And while you're continually taking on more assignments, who's doing your ordinary work? The natural response is to work a little harder, faster, and longer. Obviously, these tactics have diminishing returns. Sooner or later, harder-faster-longer will fail. If you take on more and more responsibility without giving something away, you're choosing to fail. Here's my second tip for accidental project managers:

◆ For everything you take on, give something away.

Another common malady plagues new project managers: They are intent on doing the best job possible. This is especially true for technical professionals. We all like doing our best work, and we take pride in a job well done. But even though perfection is a good goal in many arenas, in the project environment this quest can cause time and budget problems, or even complete failure.

Project management defies perfection. If you're having a difficult time knowing when good is good enough, you're not asking the right question. Instead of asking, "Can we make this better?" ask, "Is this fit for the intended purpose?" In projects, going beyond fitness for purpose is probably a luxury you can't afford. Which brings us to my last tip for accidental project managers:

◆ Focus on success, rather than perfection.

Establishing a Reputation as a Project Pro

In the corporate world, you win more points for results than for style. Success, no matter how easy it is, carries greater influence, prestige, and reward than the best fought, but unsuccessful battle. And because anyone can get lucky occasionally, establishing your reputation as a project pro requires more than one successful project. By the time you're on your third or fourth project, you will have had plenty of opportunities to prove your mettle.

To build your project reputation, start out easy and stay there as long as possible! Carefully and gradually, move up the difficulty scale. The last thing you want is for people to think you're a miracle worker. Stay just short of that lofty title—you don't want them to assign you only the impossible projects!

In the process, be careful not to fall victim to this common misconception:

◆ Small projects are safer than large projects.

Although it's true that large projects have higher stakes, more visibility, and offer a greater potential for problems, little projects may actually harbor greater professional risk. When things go wrong on large projects, you have more options. There are more resources to work with, more expertise to draw from, and more time to sort things out. When things go wrong on small projects, you have fewer resources, less expertise, and less time to sort things out. Failure on either can ruin your career.

Furthermore, most organizations carry an overly optimistic project portfolio. This in turn causes resource scarcity. When a small project and a large project compete for resources, who do you think will prevail?

Here's another misconception to avoid:

◆ Adequate time and resources are enough to succeed.

Adequate time and resources are never quite enough. No matter how well you identify work, estimate requirements, and do the math, "adequate" falls short of what is actually required. I ask you, have you ever seen a perfect plan, a project without a problem, or a team without a bad day? You'll always need a little more than just adequate. How much more is a judgment call, but if you cut it too close, you're designing failure into the project from the very beginning.

Why I Manage Projects with Microsoft Project 2003

I have learned to love all kinds of software programs over the years, because basically, I'm a lazy guy. If a machine can do it, why not let it? There's no shortage of tasks in my workday and there probably isn't in your workday, either.

Like any good tool, Microsoft Project 2003 performs wonderfully in skillful hands. Expecting too much or using it in the wrong situations can be frustrating and counterproductive. An overview of what Microsoft Project 2003 can and can't do will help you choose what's important for your project. First, let's take a look at Figure 1.1 and see how project management software works.

Figure 1.1

Microsoft Project 2003 simplifies the collection, processing, and reporting of project details, allowing you to focus on information evaluation, decision making, and project implementation.

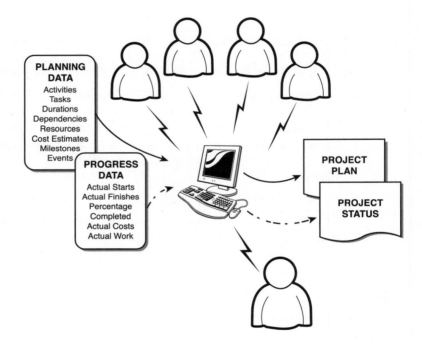

Outside of the processing speed and ability to communicate electronically, there's nothing magical going on in Project. It's just third grade math at warp speed (and without the errors).

When I first learned scheduling methods, we did most everything Project does with a stack of graph paper, a number two pencil, and one large, extremely soft eraser. (About the third mistake you'd have to scrap the now holed chart and start over.) Don't get me wrong, I wouldn't go back to managing projects on graph paper any more than I'd trade in my spreadsheet for an abacus.

Think of Microsoft Project as a highly efficient factory that takes raw materials (data) and produces products (information) that are custom tailored for each and every customer (stakeholder). Other than for doodling, my graph paper days are long gone.

What Microsoft Project 2003 Can't Do

Some people think that successful projects are packed inside every Microsoft Project box. (I hope your boss isn't one of them!) You've probably observed this: An important project starts up, so someone runs out and buys Microsoft Project. With typical project manager's zeal, they install the software, enter data, create a schedule, and shortly thereafter drown in a sea of detail, options, views, and unexpected results!

Obviously, installing Project 2003 won't make anyone a successful project manager any quicker than Microsoft Word could make them a successful playwright. Lots of good stuff comes inside the box, and most of it is automatically installed. Unfortunately, project success isn't a standard feature! Here are a few reasons why:

- It can't make up for a poorly conceived project concept.
- It can't make up for fundamentally inadequate resources.
- It can't remove or reduce external risks.
- It can't identify any of the required work.
- It can't make decisions, inspire people, take corrective action, or facilitate a team's authentic participation.
- It can't determine which of it's many options and features are best for your project.
- And it sure can't make up for your boss's overoptimism!

However, there is much that Microsoft Project 2003 can do, and much that will help you with the issues and problems discussed thus far.

Creating a Perspective for Project Success

"Not being able to see the forest for the trees" is a common problem for anyone who has ever planned a project. Even on simple projects, the project manager and the planning team is torn between having enough detail to plan and execute, and being buried in so much detail that they lose perspective. Individual team members awash in information overload can easily lose sight of their objectives, schedules, and responsibilities. Thousands of pieces of data can make up a project plan. However, data is not information until it arrives in the hands of the person who can use it, and in a format that person can understand.

To better communicate, project managers have created and refined many powerful tools and techniques. They include the work breakdown structure, the chart of activities, resource tables, network diagrams, roles and responsibilities charts, and many others. (You will learn to create and use each of the key tools in later chapters.) Because there are so many interacting relationships within the data, even the smallest change or update previously required a huge amount of effort on the part of the project manager. Consequently, on the old, paper-based systems, plans were less flexible, showed less detail, and were almost always out-of-date!

Microsoft Project 2003 gives you a multitude of information viewing options so that even the most complex project can be brought easily into focus:

◆ At almost every point, you can drill down to greater depths of detail or zoom out for the big picture.

◆ You can use predefined reports detailing tasks, resources, assignments, schedules, costs, and progress, or create your own custom documents.

◆ You can use filters and autofilters to limit what you see (or let others see).

◆ You can use traditional and intuitive sheet, graph, form, and calendar views as well as more refined and informative Gantt and network diagram charts.

Every one of the views can be printed on paper, sent electronically, posted on a website, or just stared at in the glow of your monitor and the tranquility of a darkened, after-hours office.

With Microsoft Project 2003, you are able to gather and control a greater amount of detail, maintain a better perspective, and stay abreast of changes more easily. Microsoft Project 2003 cannot make decisions for you, but it can provide you with the right perspective, at the right time.

With a working knowledge of how to actually use Project 2003, an understanding of project management fundamentals (Chapters 1 through 4), the discipline to adhere to an effective process (Chapter 3), a good team, and quality leadership, you'll be on your way to project success!

The Least You Need to Know

- Projects are strategic tools of change that enable organizations to rapidly adapt, solve problems, and pursue opportunities.

- To advance in their careers, many professionals must become more proficient working in a project environment.

- Many problems are predictable and avoidable given an understanding of the project stakeholder environment.

- Microsoft Project 2003 is a powerful tool, but it can't replace your leadership, judgment, or project management skills.

- Above all else, stay focused on achieving results and make sure your people do the same.

2

The Project Management Process

In This Chapter

- ◆ Getting in control of even the most difficult project
- ◆ Scaling and adapting the process model to your needs
- ◆ Using checklists to get your project off to a running start and to keep it on track
- ◆ Controlling scope creep and changing requirements
- ◆ Improving coordination and collaboration between stakeholder groups

Not long ago I was called into a turnaround situation as a replacement project manager. The project had seemingly progressed smoothly for the first 18 months, but as they approached the 95 percent completion point, progress had slowed to a grinding halt. Deadlines had been missed, budgets were bashed, and tempers had long since reached the vaporizing point. The few team members that weren't arguing were in hiding! The situation was beyond grim.

A colleague of mine, Matt DuPlesis, coined a name for out of control projects. He calls them vampire projects—you wish you could kill them, but you can't; meanwhile, they're sucking the life out of you and the entire project team.

Vampire projects don't produce job satisfaction. The experience falls somewhere between despair and remorse, with maybe just a hint of panic hanging overhead. You'll do about anything to finish the project, but there just aren't any good options left. In a project's late stages the good choices have already been made, missed, or ignored. Every remaining course of action has undesirable consequences: Kill it and admit defeat; ask for more time and more money (again?); start over with new people; try a different approach; dust off the resume, or …?

In the final days of a project, you know exactly what worked and what didn't, which assumptions were right or wrong, and what might have been a better approach—in fact, your vision is terrific: 20/20 hindsight! Unfortunately, early in the project when maximum options and choices are available, your vision is at it's worst. At best, you've only a fuzzy idea of where you're going, how you'll get there, what you might expect along the way. This chapter solves the dilemma (and helps you avoid nightmarish experiences), with an effective process model.

Secrets of Success

Projects don't fail at the end; they fail at the beginning.

Getting in Control of Any Project

To deal with this vision-versus-options control conundrum, project managers have developed a systematic approach—a process model—to guide project management activities. The process model corresponds with the typical life cycle, from concept to completion, of a typical project. Although no project process model is a perfect fit for all projects, the fundamentals are highly applicable to a wide variety of projects and situations. Like all tools, the skill with which the process model is used is at least as important as the tool itself.

The most widely accepted process models are based on the Project Management Institute's (PMI) Project Management Body of Knowledge (PMBOK) discussions of project life cycles, and the integration of the project management processes: initiating, planning, executing, controlling, and closing. Overall, the process model guides stakeholder participation, facilitates learning, structures communication, and greatly improves collaboration. Table 2.1 lists each of the processes and describes their function in achieving project success.

Table 2.1   The Project Management Processes

Process	Description
Initiating	Activities in the initiation process screens project concepts, defines the project's intended purpose, describes known constraints and assumptions, summarizes the work, and upon stakeholder agreement, assigns a project manager and authorizes planning to proceed.
Planning	In general, planning validates the assumptions made in the initiation phase, models the proposed execution approach, identifies and communicates essential elements, and if necessary, revisits earlier decisions in order to create the most appropriate project execution plan. The decision to proceed to project execution is carefully considered, and then authorized or denied by the key stakeholders. From this point forward costs increase rapidly, as do the consequences of failure.
Executing	Execution of the project commences in accordance with the baseline plan that was established in the planning phase and approved by the key stakeholders.
Controlling	Controlling occurs throughout the project life cycle, but more so in the execution phase. During execution phase, we monitor progress and expenditures, compare actuals to the baseline plan, evaluate performance, and take action as required.
Closing	There are many administrative tasks in this phase such as formal acceptance and signoff by the stakeholders and customers, final billing, inspections, reassignment of project staff, archiving of information, and assessing lessons learned. However, stakeholder satisfaction (the primary indicator of success) is best gained as the natural outcome of an effective, concept-to-conclusion, integrated process.

Figure 2.1 illustrates the relative importance of each process as a determinant of project outcomes. As implied by the illustration, small efforts in the initiation and planning processes can have significant impact later on. If you have uncooperative stakeholders (perhaps your boss or customer) who believe they have no time to plan and that the best course of action is, "hurry up and get started," this illustration may help alter their perspectives. More than once I've scratched this diagram on anything handy—from white boards to napkins—and made the appeal, "The little time we take now will make a big difference in your satisfaction at the end of this project."

At each transition between life cycle phases, the playing rules change. Options deteriorate and the consequences of a stalled or failed project increase. Each transition point is, therefore, a natural decision point, or *phase gate.* Manage them carefully.

Figure 2.1

The ability to impact success rapidly deteriorates as the project life cycle progresses.

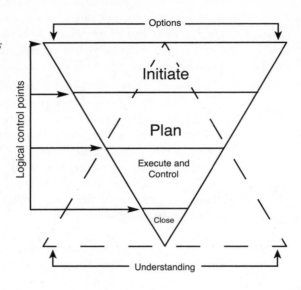

Secrets of Success

Own the process model; don't let it own you.

You will get the best results from using the process model when it is adapted and scaled for the needs of each project. For example, a simple project with little risk requires less structure, control, and analysis than does a large project with greater complexity or risk.

Even though I wish it could, the process doesn't give us the power to see into the future. However, it does the next best thing. An effective project management process expands, refines, and sharpens what we currently know, it keeps the all-important outcomes in clear focus, and it brightly illuminates our choices. With a good process, you can move your project forward faster and safer than ever before.

If you dislike vampire projects, (or want to succeed on your projects), only the foresight provided by an effective process model can keep you out of trouble.

By the way, I took on the stalled project mentioned at the beginning of this chapter. It would obviously be risky, but I knew and trusted the principals and they knew and trusted me. After some energetic negotiations, they conceded to my "never take on anyone else's project unless" rules. We were eventually successful, and the organization was stronger for it. If you're ever in a similar situation, here's the strategy I use:

Step 1.   Save whatever progress, deliverables, or knowledge has thus far been gained. If all there is to show for the effort is what not to do, at least that's something. Only if the major stakeholders are willing to concede defeat with the current approach, will you have a chance of accomplishing the next step.

Step 2.   Now you can kill the project. Allowing it to continue will waste already thin resources, send mixed messages to the project team, and create false hopes within the major stakeholders. As long as this project is kept alive, it will continue sucking the life from the project team and make the next step impossible.

Step 3.   Here's the big one, save the people. The team didn't make this mess. The organization as a whole made this mess with no process, poor stakeholder participation, overoptimism, and probably a host of other core issues. This team has probably learned some very expensive lessons (or at least they'll be more receptive to a better approach). If you keep them and treat them with dignity, they'll likely respond with renewed determination and authentic participation. By saving them, your organization can benefit from the lessons you've already paid for. Finally, perhaps most important, the way people are treated in times like these sets the stage for staffing and teamwork in all your future endeavors.

Step 4.   Now start the project over. Do it this time with the structure, discipline, and benefits that come from using an effective project management process.

The project management process can lead you to success in many difficult situations. It is especially useful when projects include new teams, high-risk endeavors, complex work, challenging timelines, untested methods, new technologies, widely distributed stakeholders, or a lack of focus and consensus. As you'll soon see, the process doesn't provide *answers*; rather it provides the right *questions* at the right time. And when you know what the right questions are, solutions aren't far behind!

Secrets of Success

You don't have to understand the project—you have to understand the process.

The Secrets to Success Are in the Process

There's no shortage of theories on the secret to success. Philosophers of every age have counseled that it's attitude, perseverance, or one of dozens of other like profundities. There's probably an element of truth in each.

The secret to success in projects isn't easy to pin down. The fact is more can go wrong in a project than can go right. Although one thing can make a project fail, one thing can't make a project successful.

The truth about projects is that they're all different and most of them are difficult. Regardless of whose research you cite, both the numbers and experience validate that project failures are commonplace. There are just too many unknowns, flaky vendors, overworked teams, unreliable systems, fickle customers, and overly optimistic senior managers to be successful on every project. To improve the odds of project success, we need a system that helps us make fewer choices that are wrong and more choices that are right. In effect, we need a *decision* management system.

Secrets of Success

If you manage project decisions, you'll manage project success.

The secrets to project success (and project failure) are more likely to be discovered if we effectively integrate all five project management processes. Figure 2.2 shows the processes as a block diagram flowchart with initiating and planning as distinctly preparatory activities carried out in a linear fashion. In contrast, execution and control are shown as interrelated activities that freely cycle as needed. When the threshold of execution is crossed, the project team takes whatever force may be necessary (within project constraints) to gain project completion and closure.

Figure 2.2

The project management process is a systematic approach to managing decisions throughout the project's life cycle.

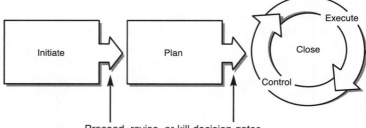

Proceed, revise, or kill decision gates

The activities in each phase produce decisions and information that will be used in the next phase. Asking the right questions in the right order allows us to explore options and make better decisions. The transitions between phases are natural decision points, typically called *phase gates* or *stage gates*. At each gate the consequences of inadequacies or failures increase dramatically. The decision to proceed, revise, or kill the project at each phase gate should be carefully considered and formally signed off on by at least the sponsor and project. Depending on the project and organizations involved, other key stakeholders such as the design engineer, customer representative, or finance officer may also need to sign off at each phase.

To be an effective process, the organization must have both the will and the discipline to control each of these major decision gates. Directives to revise, proceed, or kill should accommodate signatures (for the improvement in commitment that signatures provide), and should become a part of the project's official documentation.

Manage Decisions to Manage Success

Figure 2.3 diagrams the relative activity level, timing, and interactions among the five processes over the course of the project life cycle.

Notice the treatment of the closing phase. In reality, close is not the final step. This phase actually begins the moment stakeholder expectations begin to form, possibly establishing unendorsed but nonetheless anticipated outcomes. Without formal decision management, every stakeholder could have different and possibly opposing project expectations. (Did a troubled project you know of just come to mind?) This is a serious issue and unfortunately, it is quite common.

Similarly, control encompasses the entirety of the project from concept screening through completion and after-project evaluations. We typically think of control in terms of schedule, quality, risk, and costs. It is helpful to expand your thinking of project control to include the control of the process, of decisions, and of expectations, as well.

Secrets of Success

Expectations set in the beginning establishes the finish line you must eventually cross. Manage stakeholder expectations carefully.

Project initiation includes much definition, preliminary design, and discovery work. Rightly or wrongly, assumptions are made (such as time allowed and resources required) that carry a significant impact to project success. Assumptions must therefore be identified, so that they can be validated, revised, or rejected in the planning phase. The process best serves your needs when it reveals errors before they can do damage. Be especially alert for these common and potentially deadly initiation and planning phase errors:

◆ **Errors of omission.** Much project failure is caused by not understanding what's required for success.

◆ **Faulty assumptions.** All projects have assumptions and some are larger than others. Explore your assumptions and you'll better understand the risks.

◆ **Overoptimism.** Have you noticed that the further you get from work, the easier it looks? What looks good in the boardroom may be impossible in the real world.

◆ **Overcommitment.** In our attempts to succeed in hectic environments, organizations and individuals tend to overcommit. Choose your undertakings with great care.

In Figure 2.3, initiation and planning are shown with large overlaps indicating that an early incorporation of planners with the sponsors can improve outcomes in both phases. The step-by-step planning approach as laid out in Part 2 of this book makes Project 2003 an effective tool when shaping the sponsor's project expectations with the planner's project realities.

Planning and execution are shown with a minimum of concurrency, indicating that the baseline plan should be well developed and formally approved before mobilization is authorized and execution proceeds. Once started, stopping or redirecting a project is both difficult and expensive.

Figure 2.3

Manage process activities, interactions, and transitions carefully for maximum process effectiveness.

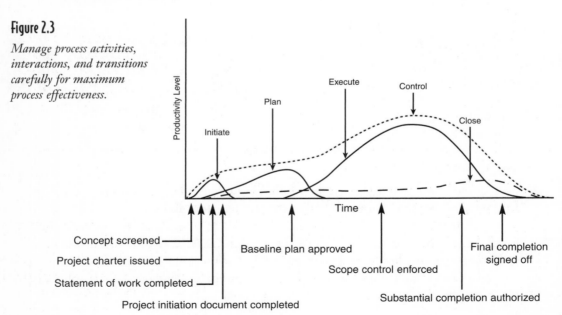

Control Documents and Checklists

The merits of an effective project management process can't be fully realized until the organization has adopted, usually through trial and error, an appropriate set of documents and checklists to provide structure, detail, and convenience. The documents and checklists included in this section are not industry specific. They are necessarily general in nature and represent a minimum control baseline from which you may add, delete, and edit as appropriate for your projects and situation.

You're encouraged to copy and use the documents and checklists presented here as a starting point. You may also download these documents from the author's website. The address is listed as an additional resource in the appendix. Each is designed to fit on a single page for handwritten notes and small projects. For larger projects, each heading can expand as required when using the files on a word processor. In Chapter 21 you'll learn how to insert these documents into your project plan.

Secrets of Success

To promote the use of your project process documents and checklists, keep them as simple as possible and place them where everyone has access. Many organizations set up a project section on their networks where information, templates, procedures, and checklists are readily available.

When considering which documents and checklists are best for your project environment, keep in mind that brevity encourages thinking. In contrast, complexity reduces thinking (if it were important, there would have been a box for it), and reduces the chances that the documents actually will be used. Think of the documents and checklists as suitable for most small to medium-sized projects and as a way to "prime the thought-process pump" on larger projects.

By the way, please don't resell these documents. If you do, the publisher and I will have to come looking for you.

Table 2.2   Process Control Documents and Checklists

Document	Figure	Description
1. Concept checklist	2.4	The concept screening checklist helps to ensure that only viable projects that support the organization's goals and objectives are allowed to proceed. Screening criteria may include preliminary investigations,

continues

Table 2.2   Process Control Documents and Checklists (continued)

Document	Figure	Description
		feasibility studies, evaluation of merit, strategic fit, viability, delivery of real benefit, risk level, project portfolio fit, and whether it would detract from ongoing operations, other projects, or capacities. Project prioritization begins at this point.
2. Project charter	2.5	The charter establishes the authority for a project manager to undertake the project and sets the limits of responsibilities and power. It serves as a formal notification and alerts stakeholders that project initiation will proceed.
3. Statement of work (SOW)	2.6	This document helps the originators and sponsors to clearly describe and document their expectations of the project. It includes goals, measures of success, constraints, deliverables, and the project's intended outcomes. It eases the handoff from upper management's vision to the planning and execution team's realities. It will likely be challenged, negotiated, and modified as various stakeholder groups interact with it. Prior to moving forward, consensus on the SOW content with all significant stakeholders should be reached.
4. Project initiation document (PID)	2.7	This document is a one-page aggregation of all early phase decisions for smaller projects. Ease of use and brevity is weighted heavily in its design. It can readily serve as a preliminary document, when considering how much process structure and control is suited for a given project. This document and the listed abbreviation is not recognized in the PMI PMBOK.

Document	Figure	Description
5. Scope statement	**N/A**	The scope statement takes on a project specific format. Its purpose is to describe in great detail everything that the project includes and conversely, everything that the project does not include. It helps manage stakeholder expectations and provides the planning team with a starting point for identifying the work activities, materials, resources, and others items necessary for achieving the project's outcomes.
6. Baseline plan	**N/A**	This term is used to describe what might need to be many documents. They could include the project's schedule, resource requirements, budget, finalized scope, communications plan, and others. In the context of the process model, the baseline plan is the agreed-on approach and formally signed-off notice to proceed to the execution phase of work. The baseline plan is used in conjunction with measured progress actuals to track progress, evaluate results, and judge the effects of corrective actions. Strategically, the baseline plan should be a safe, simple model that supports all project constraints and objectives and is deemed highly likely to succeed by the planning and execution team.
7. Scope change request	**2.8**	This control document identifies requested changes and helps manage alterations to the scope of the project. It describes the change; its purpose; any important background information; the proposed approach; and the impact on progress, cost, time, and resources. The document

continues

Table 2.2   Process Control Documents and Checklists   (continued)

Document	Figure	Description
		can serve as a formal notice to proceed, revise, or kill the proposed change. Signature lines should be included to signify authorization and agreement. From the project manager's point of view, it provides the information and sets the stage so that they are able advocate properly for or against the requested change.

This listing of process documents is representative of a typical small to medium-size project, with average risks and complexities. It provides the basic structure necessary to manage and control the project management process. It also can serve as a starting point to scale or refine the process for the specific needs of a project, organization, or industry.

You may find some new terms and concepts within the documents in the illustrated in the following figures. Chapter 3 thoroughly covers all the concepts important to the initiation and planning phases. A quick check of the glossary should resolve any overwhelming curiosity, for now.

Project Concept Checklist

Project

Originator   Sponsor   Project Manager

Project Summary - Major objectives, scope, and relevant background information.

Business and Strategic Fit

☐ Is the strategic fit clear?
☐ Is the opportunity attractive?
☐ Will the organization's mission, goals, and objectives be served?

Accountabilities

☐ Has a project sponsor been identified for the investigation phase?
☐ Has a project manager been assigned for the investigation phase?

Operations and implementation

☐ Will the project resource requirements fall within the current organization's capabilities?
☐ Will the project's technical requirements fall within the current organization's capabilities?
☐ Is the technology feasible?
☐ Is there access to additional funding for this project?

Describe Potential Risks or Issues

Recommended Action (kill, revise, proceed)

Authorized by   Date

Figure 2.4

Screen all proposed projects as to merit, fit, feasibility, and priority within the organization's project portfolio.

Project Charter

Project   Date

Purpose, Scope, and Objectives

Defining Conditions, Constraints, and Assumptions

Project Manager Designation, Responsibility, and Authority

Budget Sources and Uses

Project Personnel / Core Team Members / Steering Committee

Communication and Reporting Requirements

Project Authorization   Date

Figure 2.5

The project charter signals go ahead to initiation, issues responsibilities, and establishes authority levels to conduct the project.

Statement of Work

Project

Purpose Statement

Prioritized Objectives

Key Outcomes and Deliverables

Scope of Work and Limits

Working Assumptions

Known Constraints

Preliminary Cost Estimate

Preliminary Estimate of Resource Requirements

Key Stakeholders and Roles

Project Authorization   Date

Figure 2.6

Used by the controlling stakeholders to describe the project and its intended outcomes to the planning and execution team.

Project Initiation Document

Project   Date

Goal Statement and Scope of Work

Business Case / Project Validation

Objectives   Related Deliverables   Time Frame

Project Assumptions

Triple Constraint Ranking: Importance ◄-------------------------------------► Flexibility

Time

Resources:

Outcomes:

Threats / Risks / Opportunities

Sponsor Approval   Date   Project Manager   Date

Figure 2.7

The project initiation document is an easy-to-use composite of several documents for smaller projects.

Scope Change Request

To   From

Project

Background of Request

Approach or Methodology

Estimated Impact

Communication Routing List

Attachments

Requested by   Date

Sponsor Approval   Date

Other Approval   Date

Project Manager Approval   Date

Figure 2.8

The scope change request is used to control alterations to the project's scope during the execution phase.

The project management process improves stakeholder collaboration, project management effectiveness, and your odds of success. To reap maximum benefit, the process must exist beyond the files, documents, and checklists of the project manager's office. For best results, the process must live in the thoughts and actions of the entire project team, from the top executive to the most remote team member. Ideally, the project management approach becomes part of the organization's culture—the culture of accomplishment.

The Least You Need to Know

- ◆ Project success or failure is determined in the beginning, not at project completion and closeout.

- ◆ You cannot effectively manage or control a project without a project process and supporting control documentation.

- ◆ Scale and refine the process documentation to meet the needs of your project and organization.

- ◆ An effective process model improves decisions, helps manage expectations, and improves collaboration throughout the project's stakeholders.

3

Rig Your Project for Success

In This Chapter

- Get your project off to a good start

- Learn how to protect your project from unknown problems and issues that can crop up

- Determine how much detail you should have in your plan

- How to ask and get your sponsor to answer your toughest questions

Using Project 2003 to create a *good* plan is fast and easy when you start "slow" and understand your project. Using Project 2003 to create a *bad* plan is fast and easy when you start fast and don't understand your project. Unfortunately, no one can tell the difference … well, at least not for six months.

This chapter shows why preparation is essential, what must be done, and how to make it happen.

Start "Slow" to Finish Fast

When dealing with aggressive timelines, a frequently made error is to ignore project definition and planning activities and rush into execution. It's difficult not to when the boss or customer is ranting, "More! Sooner!

Faster! Experience shows that starting a little slower and fully exploring the project's "physics of success" doesn't cost—it pays! However, trying to slow a stampede, even of corporate lemmings, can be a risky endeavor. Once it begins, few can escape the stampede to disaster.

Experience validates that taking a little time to understand the project enables better planning, which provides better communication, which enables better control, execution, problem solving, and speed. Starting "slow" creates the understanding, a catalyst if you will, that facilitates effective project management. If you're forced to start too fast, you'll likely be working harder, taking greater risks, and having less to show for it.

Consider the following scenario:

A multinational conglomerate has just purchased our hero's company and rumors are running wild. To make matters worse, the big boss is flying in and no one knows why she's coming. It's late in a typically hectic day, when our resident MS Project 2003 expert hears a large group marching down the hallway. Arlie realizes it can only mean one thing—the boss and her entourage are coming! It dawns on him that his cubicle looks more like a recycling bin than a workspace, and he leaps into action. As he drops the remnants of a lunch (yesterday's?) into the trash, he realizes he's not alone.

"Jones? I'm Laura Henderson. I understand you managed the Transpod project last quarter on Microsoft Project."

"Yes, Ma'am."

"Grab a notepad and meet us in the executive conference room in 10 minutes. We've got a project for you. It's big. Can you handle it?"

"Yes, Ma'am!"

As if on command, the group vanished down the hallway and Arlie was alone with his thoughts. "… Wow! I can't believe she knew my name … I guess this means I'm not going to get laid off … Oh my, what did I just get myself into?"

Victor or Vanquished?

No project professional gets up in the morning and chooses to fail. Like most of us, our hero took on the challenge as if by instinct, long before knowing anything about it. Organizations suffer from the same overoptimism. Projects are committed to and deadlines are set long before understanding goals and objectives, considering resource requirements, or identifying risks.

Emerging from the conference room less than an hour later, Airlie realizes he's in trouble. Upper management loaded him down with responsibilities, expectations, and a supreme sense of urgency. The future of the division rests on our hero's project management abilities.

"The whole project's moving too fast—it hasn't even started and it's out of control!" he grumbles to a colleague. "I was enthusiastic about it in my office, but by the time they told me the goal and everyone around the table just kept adding more to it, I was getting a little disillusioned. So I asked about the resources and they told me I didn't have to worry about them—what few they could muster had already been assigned— I didn't even get to discuss it! I was sinking into despair when they off-handedly mentioned the timeline. That's when it hit me … the panic attack. Six months into the project, I can see the project and my career in total ruins. I just sat there dumbfounded, nodding with a blank stare on my face. They want a project schedule by Friday. I've got to do something, but I don't know where to start."

> **Secrets of Success**
>
> Organizations often try to cover too much with one project. By breaking large projects into subprojects, they become easier to plan and control, reducing risk and making success more likely.

Our hero is right. When given responsibility without authority, project managers must take action. In projects it's how we respond to situations like this that separates the victors from the vanquished. Arlie could go with the flow, create a great plan in Project 2003 (at least it would look good), and hope for the best (or perhaps a miracle), but unless he could actually get the control and information he needed, all was lost. He took action the next day with a one-page checklist and a 20-minute phone call.

"Hello, Ms. Henderson? … Thank you for this project responsibility and for placing your trust in me. I won't let you down … I've implemented a fast start and I need some information to make sure we're on solid footing. Do you have a few minutes right now? …"

With one call Arlie has taken control of the project, initiated his project process, shown he supports her sense of urgency, facilitated sponsor participation, and proven he'll do what it takes to get the job done (even go straight to the top).

If Arlie's approach seems too aggressive, let me ask: If it were your project, who would you prefer to manage it, Arlie or a corporate lemming? One more: Who would you prefer as a team member, Arlie or the lemming? Encourage your work group,

"If you have bad news or an unpopular view, speak up. We'll deal with it as a team." Encourage is the correct word here. You must draw out their courage. That, after all, is what heroes are made of, doing the right thing, even when it's not easy. Or as I say in my seminars, "If you've got to go ugly, go ugly early, while there's still a chance it can do some good!"

How "Slow" Should You Start?

What might seem like a slow start to your stakeholders is, in reality, the fastest way to start any project—that is, any project you want to succeed! The question is how much effort to put into these early process activities.

The amount of effort spent defining and planning a project is always a judgment call. As illustrated in Figure 3.1, it's best to think in terms of diminishing returns. At the onset of definition and planning activities, every dollar or minute spent returns itself many times over. However, in most projects the overall benefit diminishes at an increasing rate, depending on a host of factors. These typically include the project's overall size, complexity, and anticipated risks. At some point, additional effort poured into planning no longer makes any appreciable improvement in the lowering of risks, time, or costs.

Figure 3.1

Early on, planning dramatically reduces overall project costs and durations. At some point, the cost of planning begins to outweigh the benefits.

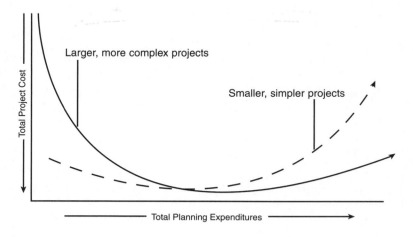

Obviously, a small, simple project with little or no risk won't need as detailed of plan as would a large project with high complexity and severe risk. MS Project 2003 speeds many aspects of the planning process, which in turn produces better returns on our planning investment. The caveat, of course, is the tendency when using Project to include excessive detail. The quest for the perfect plan (no matter how well you computerize the process) may add costs and time that you can't afford. Knowing when good is good enough requires insight, intuition, and experience.

To maximize your return on planning, consider these factors:

◆ The overall complexity of the project

◆ The risk of the project

◆ The team's experience with this type of project

◆ The team's experience working together

◆ Potential technology issues

◆ Confidence in vendors

◆ Experience with extended team members

◆ Availability of key resources

◆ The number and complexity of your other projects

◆ The overall timeline

Figure 3.2 correlates complexity, size, and risk with an appropriate amount of planning detail.

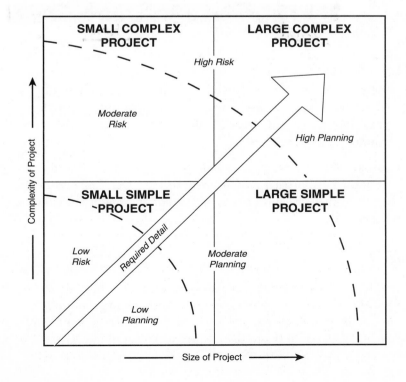

Figure 3.2

The time and detail required for effective planning varies with the project's size, risk, and overall complexity.

Complexity can be a real "gotcha." Seemingly innocuous events can dramatically increase a project's difficulty. Be wary anytime your standard approach is modified in any way, such as using a different vendor, substituting "or comparable" items, being forced to do work out of sequence, adding or changing team members, increasing the number of workers on a task or in an area, and speeding (or slowing) your normal pace.

In the end, when pushed hard to start faster, trust your intuition and experience. To finish faster, "start a little slower. "

Think Like a Project Pro

Project professionals are especially adept at keeping their teams focused on results. One of the ways they manage this is with skillful use of common concepts. For example, most everyone uses the terms *goals* and *objectives* interchangeably—the intended results or outcomes. Project professionals are careful to discriminate between the two, and for good reason.

For the project manager, the goal is *what* you will have when the project is completed (the outcome). The objectives are the strategy or approach you'll use to make it happen, the *how* you'll get results. Project goals are realized when project objectives have been achieved.

As an example, assume your project's goal is to improve the quality of your organization's customer service. Thinking in terms of objectives (the how), we might decide on a strategy that embodies a combination of objectives: increase the number of customer service representatives on staff; rewrite the user's manual to better address common problems; or my favorite, get rid of the dumbest customers. (Go ahead and confess, that last one sounds pretty good, doesn't it?)

The point is there are always multiple ways to accomplish anything. The set of objectives undertaken is your strategic approach to delivering success. Carefully examine the objectives. Make sure that they are appropriate and are the best approach for your project, resources, and timeline.

How SMART Is Your Goal?

It is difficult to overemphasize the importance of using an effective project goal. It sets expectations; provides a basis for planning; helps identify all the required resources, activities, and budgets; and becomes the standard by which we measure achievement, outcomes, and ultimately the project's success. If you're too busy to develop a solid project goal statement, you're too busy to lead. Don't try to go forward without it.

To build a good goal statement, use the SMART approach. This acronym will help you remember that every goal needs to be specific, measurable, agreed on, realistic, and time-bound.

Making Your Goal Specific

To create a SMART goal, focus on the essence of what the project will achieve and describe it with only two words, an *action* and an *outcome*. This narrow and precise communication will cut through the day-to-day clutter, and keep you and your project team focused on the core issues.

Let's return to the scene when Arlie contacted the big boss. "Ms. Henderson, we covered a lot of ground in our first meeting and there are many outcomes this project will produce. Help me understand in your own words what you want this project to accomplish."

"The short answer is this," she replied, "the division's profits have been down for five consecutive quarters. I want you to design, build, and deliver a new product that will turn the division around and return it to its former glory days of growth and profitability. You know Arlie," she added, "a lot of people's jobs depend on the success of this project."

Even from the top, straight answers are sometimes hard to get. But to be successful, project managers must be able to see the big picture and still bring the right detail into sharp focus. What is the best focus for Arlie's project? Given this same information, you'll get many opinions, with potentially very different results. Should the project focus be to: Design a new product? Enter a new market? Manufacture a new product? Market a new product? Increase profitability? Return the division to glory? Or perhaps, save our jobs!

> **Secrets of Success**
>
> As a project manager, your professional reputation is no better than your least-successful project. To keep your career on track, identify the criteria you will be held responsible for. Make sure you can demonstrate measured success on every point.

If I were responsible for this project, I'd focus the team's attention on the action and outcome "increase profitability." In my judgment (and it is a judgment call), this focus will set the tone and direction for the entire project, making it clear what needs to happen. With a focus on "build a new product," the team may be encouraged to let costs swell or allow timeliness to languish (building an unprofitable new product or getting it done late would just add to the company's problems). "Save our jobs" is too broad to provide direction and would probably scare half the team away, making success all the more difficult.

The first two elements of your goal statement, the action word and outcome, funnel your team's attention. Moreover, if problems arise (and they usually do) better decisions can be made. Tight, bright, and laserlike, a specific goal magnifies importance, enables decision-making, and maintains a narrow, achievable project focus.

Measuring Your Way to Success

Now its time to make the outcome "measurable." Don't worry about grammar at this stage. If you must, it is okay to create the world's longest run-on sentence. Describe exactly what your project will accomplish. Use as many descriptors and numbers as you can. Leave nothing to the imagination. Describe the intended outcomes as empirically as possible.

In our example, "increased profitability" can be measured in several ways: a net amount, a percentage of sales, or perhaps an amount per unit. Because an increase in overall company profitability is needed to save the company, the net amount would be a good measure. The better the goal can be measured, the easier it is to determine the project's level of success. Remember, goals that can't be measured are impossible to prove they were achieved.

Agreeing On the Goal While It's Still Possible

Next, ensure that all stakeholders agree on the outcomes and their measures. You can plan brilliantly and execute flawlessly, but without consensus on the goals and their measures, someone will not be satisfied—your project will not be a success.

Consider how the various stakeholders might judge success for the project goal "improve service." Key stakeholders might include the chief financial officer, the sales manager, the customer service manager, and the big boss. You may have completed this project exactly to specification, before the due date, and under budget—you're delighted with the outcomes. And, the customer service manager has fewer irate customers. However, what if the sales manager doesn't see sales growth, or if the chief financial officer can't see a return on the investment, or if the big boss can't see increased profits, strength, or growth—were you successful?

Your project's success and your personal reputation requires gaining the substantial satisfaction of all major stakeholders. Identify the key stakeholders and deliver success measurable in their terms.

Where Are the Realists When You Need Them?

You've come to the biggest judgment call in the goal-setting process: Is this specific, measurable, agreed on, time-bound goal realistic? Can we make it happen? Generally,

I'm a proponent of optimism, but when it comes to goal setting, optimism can be deadly!

Here's a simple truth I bet you've experienced: Work always looks easier before you start it.

Before committing to a goal, ask yourself and your project team, "In average conditions, with our average people, on an average day, can we do this?" Too many teams set themselves up for failure from the very beginning. Innate optimism clouds their thinking.

At this stage of planning, do yourself (and everyone involved on the project) a big favor. Be a realist!

> **CAUTION**
>
> **Project Pitfalls**
>
> Stakeholder overoptimism is a silent threat to your project's success. Make sure all expectations are clear before planning and executing the project. Resist the temptation to say yes to all stakeholder requests. Freeze the scope with stakeholder signatures prior to planning. And when change is needed, use the scope-change process unfailingly.

Time for Action

The precursor to all action is a sense of urgency and timeliness. Nothing seems to motivate people more than an approaching deadline!

Project goals are typically time-bound with a deadline. More formally, this is the time constraint known as an FNLT (finish no later than). But as you'll see, the FNLT is not the only date constraint that is important. Obviously, a project can't finish on time unless it is started on time. One might then ask, which is more important, the latest day you can finish the project—or the latest day you can start the project? Many of the techniques within the Project Management Body of Knowledge (PMBOK) help us identify and manage time constraints.

When we understand the flexibility, or lack of flexibility, in the timing of work, our ability to manage and control progress is greatly improved. The core function of Project 2003 is this scheduling of work. It helps you find the most time-effective way of using resources and structuring workflow.

Make sure you set time constraints on every goal you want to achieve. Whether little goals or big goals—goals for the project, milestones, activities, or tasks—only with a sense of urgency and timeliness can we drive achievement.

Understanding the Physics of Projects

There is a wonderfully useful project management concept known as the triple constraints that I like to compare with the physics of fire. You'll recognize them as the three basic components of every project: performance (the quality and quantity of the outcomes), time (how long we have to accomplish the work), and resources (money, people, materials, and so on). All three exist in every project, they're interconnected, and they must be in kept in balance for your project to succeed.

We all learned in elementary science that there are three requirements to start and maintain combustion: fuel, heat, and oxygen. Remove any one of the three and the fire goes out. Add any one of the three to an existing fire and it gets larger.

Projects are similar. Over a given amount of time, with a given amount of resources, a certain amount of outcomes can be achieved. Take away time or resources, and less can be achieved. Add required outcomes, and either it will take longer or it will require more resources over the same timeline. But you knew all that, right? So why doesn't your boss? It seems that sponsors, customers, and end users are constantly asking for more, and they want it faster, and they want it cheaper. As a project manager, you are tasked with creating as much as possible as soon as possible with the fewest number of free sources—that's the physics of it. Your ability to produce is constrained by science, and still the onslaught comes: Change this, add that, move in the delivery date, let me borrow a few of your resources—it's a constant battle to keep your project's triple constraints in balance.

Let me ask you this: Which of the triple constraints do you think is most important on your project? That is, if you can't do everything in the allowed time with the available resources, what should be done to get the project into balance? Reduce the outcomes? Go over the allocated time? Add more resources and go over budget? Of course, none of these are desirable, but if something had to give, what is least important? What is most important?

If you're thinking that it varies project by project, you're right! But here's the problem, it usually varies not only by project, but also by every stakeholder on that project. The sponsor might think that time is most important, so he would have you spend more resources or do less, but get it done on time; the end user might prefer a later delivery, but don't cut outcomes or spend more; on the other hand, the project manager probably prefers fewer deliverables to produce, and more resources and more time to make it all happen! On every project, every stakeholder holds a legitimately selfish opinion. So if something has to give, how can the project manager achieve success?

Two key strategies help you maximize your chances for success on any project:

♦ Identify and prioritize the stakeholders. It's not possible to satisfy everyone, all the time, on all your projects. Therefore, know who the most significant stakeholders are, and fully understand their points of view. The difference between failure and success largely depends on who's happy and who's not. Project success is best described as the substantial satisfaction of the significant stakeholders.

◆ Prioritize the triple constraints and own at least one of them. Your ability to deliver project success is in direct proportion to the control you're able to exert over the triple constraints. If you own, that is control, at least one of the triple constraints, you have options. If all constraints are fixed (that is, out of your control), you have few options and little control.

Let's use an example to further illustrate: You're going to a conference next week and because you'll likely meet some new colleagues, you decide to check your stock of business cards. Alas, only a few shop-worn cards remain, and furthermore, your e-mail address has changed. You decide to visit a printer and order some new cards. Arriving at the printer's counter, you order 500 cards with your new e-mail address and a four-color logo, for delivery as soon as possible, and you want rock-bottom pricing. You want to have your cards fast, good, and cheap. Unfortunately, you've ignored the physics of project management. As the old printer's adage says, "You can have it fast. You can have it good. You can have it cheap. Pick two."

The physics of project management (the triple constraints) restricts choices and decisions. Each one affects the other two. If you want greater performance (the four-color logo), it will cost more and likely take more time. If you want them faster, you may have to spend more and cut out the fancy logo. To spend less, cut out the logo and let the printer fit it into their workload conveniently. Although the printer (the project manager) doesn't get to choose in order to be successful, he must remain in control of the balance. To be successful, make sure that you can exercise control over at least one of the constraints. Help the project stakeholders understand what is and is not possible.

How would you like your next project: Good and fast? Fast and cheap? Good and cheap?

Prioritizing the Triple Constraints

The triple constraints set the tone for every decision you'll make as a project manager. It is therefore important to understand which of the constraints is most flexible and which is least flexible. By definition, the driving constraint (the least flexible) must be achieved or the project is a failure. Successful project managers make sure they identify and achieve the driving constraint on every project.

The weak constraint is by definition the most flexible. Although it may be very important, it is not as important as the driver. And, of course, the constraint that falls between these two extremes is called the middle constraint. Its importance and flexibility falls somewhere between the driver and the weak constraints, although not necessarily equidistant from the two. Figure 3.3 illustrates constraint flexibility from key points of view.

Figure 3.3

Understanding the triple constraints helps you understand the project's difficulty, risk, and options throughout the project's life cycle.

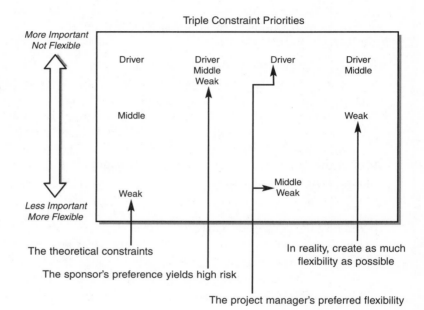

The constraint prioritization can and does change during a project. Not long ago, I planned to replace my company's computer system. There was no urgency. I was willing to settle for less than the latest hardware performance to save a little money. We planned on catching some items on sale and installing the new system ourselves, as our workloads allowed. Cost was the project's driving constraint. I wanted to get as much performance as possible on a targeted budget. Performance was the middle constraint and it was only slightly less important than cost. Because I was in no rush replacing the existing system, time was the weak constraint, the most flexible of the three.

Then one sunny summer afternoon, a thunderstorm blew over and changed all that. With one bolt of lightning, our existing system was destroyed. Before the thundering crack had rumbled away, the triple constraints were turned upside down: To stay in business, we needed to get a system up and running fast. Cost was no longer the driver; it was now the weak constraint. Performance jumped into the driver status.

Time followed closely in importance and became the middle constraint. In a flash, the project's original constraints of cheap and good had changed to good and fast!

I hope lightning never strikes your project. But be forewarned, the triple constraints are important and they can change quickly.

Good? Fast? Cheap? The constraint that drives the success of your project must be protected, even at the expense of the weak and possibly middle constraint.

Who's Really in Control Here?

After you understand the triple constraints, it becomes evident that the project manager's role is to achieve the project outcomes while protecting the driver, and if possible, the middle and weak constraints as well.

There are three problems with this strategy (and probably what drives most project managers nuts). First, as we have seen, the prioritization of the triple constraints is not in the direct control of the project manager. Although you may recommend an appropriate balance of time, resources and outcomes, ultimately the project sponsor controls the final decision.

Second, usually other key stakeholders don't control or even participate in the prioritization. Although their take on this issue is important, we often rely on the project sponsor to accurately identify and communicate everyone else's point of view. Unfortunately for the project manager, all the other stakeholders retain complete and full rights of project rejection. If their needs aren't served, they can and will be vocal!

Last (and perhaps, most absurdly), it is the rare project sponsor who knows what the triple constraints are, has fully considered their influence on the project, and will "admit" what may be flexible and what is not. Even though they can control the triple constraints more than any other group, they all too often opt out and use the ill-advised approach of demanding that everything is a driver. They want it all. They're rightfully trying to get as much as possible for their time, money, and resources! This issue brings us to the following important skill.

Questioning the Boss and Remaining Employed

Ask the project sponsor (the boss), "What is most important on this project, achieving the cost, the performance, or the time constraints (real good, real fast, or real cheap)?" You know what the boss will say, "They're all essential! Give me all three, or else!"

Beware of projects where all three constraints are drivers. These projects provide few alternatives for recovery if, and more likely when, you run into problems. Breaking any of the constraints makes the project a failure, and punches a major dent in your reputation.

If you look closely enough, there is usually some continuum of importance within the three constraints. Each may be important, but they are rarely equally important. Find out how each compares by asking the project originator a series of guiding questions. Try to find out what choices they would make, given a set of circumstances.

By asking questions, you will assist their understanding of the project, reveal their constraint priorities, and make it easier to achieve their idea of project success. You cannot be effective at planning or decision making unless you understand the project goals and the triple constraints.

Here are some of my favorite ways of interrogating the boss (or customer). This first set of questions is open ended:

- Why are we doing this?

- What is the worst thing that could go wrong?

- If we had plenty of time, money, and resources, what would this project look like?

- If everything goes smoothly, what is the best possible outcome we can expect from this project?

- If everything went badly, what is the least acceptable outcome we must achieve with this project?

- In your opinion, what is the order of importance between the project's performance (describe this in their terms), the project's budget, and the time that is available to get it all done?

The next set of questions is designed to force a choice and extract the sponsor's preferred prioritization. Use project-specific examples and compare two of the constraints at a time.

Here's the format I use: Describe a scenario, state two alternatives, and then ask for their preference. Make sure your stakeholders know that you are exploring *theoretical* scenarios. With this technique, you can establish the priorities of even the most incommunicative project sponsors. Here are some examples:

- If there are not enough resources to fully staff this project until project XYZ is completed, what would you want me to do, wait until resources become available or stop XYZ?

- If it cost an additional X dollars to complete the project within the targeted time line, or no more to finish two weeks late, what would you prefer we do?

- If to meet the deadline we could either finish X weeks late or not deliver objective Y, what would you want us to do?

Understanding the triple constraints sharpens your problem-solving tools to a fine edge. Planning becomes more effective. Execution becomes easier. When problems arise, you'll be ready to cut, slash, or hack your way into the clear with the least amount of trouble.

Speaking of trouble, have you met my friend Murphy?

Murphy Joins the Team

Several decades ago, a courageous U.S. Air Force project manager (Dr. John Paul Stapp) was testing the physiological effects of acceleration and deceleration on the human body. The test subject (often John Stapp himself) was strapped into a rocket sled, blasted down a set of railroad tracks (at up to 632 miles per hour), and purposefully slammed into a water braking system. In the process, tremendous forces were sustained. If anything went wrong, somebody could easily be injured, or worse.

It was shortly after a failed trial of four new electronic measuring devices that the most important, and now famous, law of project management was born. Each of the four devices could only be wired in one of two ways, yet despite the 50 percent chance of success, all four had been wired backward, consequently failing the test.

Upon hearing of the failure, the frustrated designer of the device, Edward A. Murphy Jr. commented about his assistant's apparent error, that if there was any way of making a mistake, he would. Dr. Stapp and his project team, no doubt unhappy with Murphy's blaming a subordinate, shaped the original comment into a memorable witticism that seems to hold a universal truth for project teams everywhere: *If it can happen, it will happen.*

More Good Stuff
Links to additional information about the story of Dr. John Stapp's rocket-sled research projects and Murphy's law are available on the author's website at http://www.ronblack.com.

This playful but pessimistic point of view (although some consider Murphy to be an optimist) allowed the project team to maintain an amazing success record during a long and hazardous project.

Ask any project manager today and you'll find Murphy's law alive and well, even embellished a bit: *If anything can go wrong, it will go wrong. Furthermore, it will go wrong at the worst possible moment!* As this tradition of "optimistic pessimism" lives on, it reminds us that perfect projects do not exist. Flexibility in the triple constraints is not an option, rather it is essential to success.

Preplanning Checklist

As you've no doubt deduced, I encourage the use of checklists. I buy into the notion that a short list is better than a long memory, especially for project managers! When you have to keep the big picture in focus, it's easy to lose sight of a few details. But as you know, the success of the entire project might reside on a tiny detail.

The preplanning checklist shown in Figure 3.4 was created to expose omissions, focus attention, and summarize what has been learned before sitting down with Project 2003 and creating a plan. You'll find this checklist as a Word document at the author's website. Freely download it and edit or modify as your projects require.

Preplanning Checklist

Project   FNLT date

Goal Statement (SMART)

- ☐ Reviewed and agreed upon by key stakeholders.
- ☐ Is clearly realistic.
- ☐ Is realistic given:

Key Objectives

- ☐ Is agreed upon by all stakeholders?
- ☐ Do they fall within our areas of competency?
- ☐ Is there a priority within the objectives?
- ☐ Can they be broken out into smaller stand-alone projects?
- ☐ Are there other objectives that might deliver the same results?

Assumptions

- ☐ Have assumptions been listed and discussed by all significant stakeholders?
- ☐ Should contingencies be identified and included in the planning process?

Triple Constraints

- ☐ Is there agreement on the prioritization of the triple constraints by all stakeholders?
- ☐ Is there sufficient flexibility in the triple constraints?
- ☐ Is control of the triple constraints negotiable?
- ☐ Are the resources required for this project in abundance, adequate, or scarce?
- ☐ Is there access to additional funding for this project?
- ☐ How flexible is the timeline?

Risks

- ☐ Have risks and potential issues been candidly discussed by all stakeholders?
- ☐ If this project fails or cannot proceed, have options been identified?

Staffing and Administration

- ☐ Will existing administrative systems suffice for this project?
- ☐ Are all lines of authority and responsibility clear to this point?

Prepared by   Date

Figure 3.4

Thoroughly review this checklist before beginning to plan the project.

The Least You Need to Know

- ◆ Never begin your project without a well-written goal statement.

- ◆ The priority of the triple constraints—time, money, and performance—affects every decision you'll make as a project manager. To be successful, achieve the goal and protect the driving constraints.

- ◆ Identify the project's stakeholders and understand their measures of success.

- ◆ Begin planning only after you have a thorough understanding of the project's goals, objectives, stakeholders, assumptions, and flexibility within the triple constraints.

Part 2

Planning Your Project

You've arrived at the heart of the planning process; to succeed, you'll need a set of tools. Part 2 is just that—your very own collection of planning power tools. So let's plug them in, turn them on, and build a schedule!

We begin by making sure you can get around in Microsoft Project 2003. With the program basics covered, you'll learn how to easily identify every single task that must be done to make your project a success. Then you'll learn the tricks of the trade for estimating how long each task will take to complete. Then you'll enter the workflow sequence, set up and enter your resources, and before you know it, you've got a complete schedule! You'll know the start and finish times of the whole project and every task in it. You'll be ready to communicate everyone's roles and control their participation. All the whats and whens of your project will be lined up and ready to execute.

Chapter 4

Getting Started with Microsoft Project 2003

In This Chapter

◆ Installing and starting Microsoft Project 2003

◆ Moving around in the program, starting a new project file, and saving and retrieving your files

◆ Finding help and additional information when you need it

◆ Modifying the program to suit your needs and preferences

Microsoft Project 2003 is a powerful program with many features designed to help you manage projects effectively. Its rich set of functions provides almost everything the majority of project managers could ever want. The first time you look at the screen, it can be rather intimidating; after you've entered a few tasks, added some durations, and set their work-flow dependencies, however, you'll be amazed at how fast and easy scheduling can be.

Users of Microsoft Project 2000 and Project 2002 will notice that some features have been added or expanded in Project 2003, but the core structure, function, and interface remains wonderfully intact. After you're acquainted with the basics, you'll find transitioning from one version to another is easy.

More Detail or More Results?

Congratulations, as a user of Project 2003 you're now able to track just about anything and everything you'd like! But, please don't. Attempting to control every detail of your project is a common error, especially if you're new to the project management game. The quest for perfection has been the undoing of many. What seems like more control often turns out to be less control. And even though Microsoft Project makes it relatively fast and easy to track copious amounts of detail, it still takes your time and your attention. Excessive detail can keep you busy doing the wrong things—entering data, running reports, and updating charts—when you should be monitoring progress, communicating with people, and controlling their results. When using a feature-rich system like Project 2003, it's easy to start managing the plan instead of managing the project.

Secrets of Success

Good project managers know what to manage. Great project managers know what to ignore and they have the courage to ignore it.

Plan projects with the minimum detail possible. If something is clearly necessary, make sure you include it and that you give it close attention. If it's not clearly necessary, think again before diluting your efforts. I'll help you be more selective on what you choose to manage throughout the book. (For more information on how much detail you need, see the section "Keeping It As Simple As Possible" in Chapter 5.)

Likewise, don't assume you must master every detail of this feature-rich program, although it is nice to know that these capabilities are available if you need them. To help maximize the return on your time and energy, I've ordered the techniques in this book based on their usefulness. It starts with the essentials and moves on to the exotic, staying focused that the goal is *project management* success, not *managing Project 2003* success. If you have some experience with Microsoft Project and want to jump ahead, simply review each chapter's "The Least You Need to Know," and go for it!

Installation and Program Basics

This section assumes that you're familiar with at least one of the Microsoft Office family of applications, but have little or no experience using Project 2003. Here you'll

learn how to get the most out of it for your specific needs, by mastering the fundamentals of operating and modifying the program.

Installing and Starting Project 2003

If you haven't already installed Microsoft Project 2003, you're in for a pleasant surprise; it takes only a few minutes. Most of that time, it does all the work while you
watch. (That's the kind of work I like!) To avoid installation problems, close all other
applications, including virus protection. When you're ready, follow these steps:

1. Place the Microsoft Project 2003 CD into your computer and close the drive.
   The dialog box should appear shortly after the CD drive closes. If it doesn't,
   click **Start** (found at the lower-left corner of your desktop), click **Run,** and type
   in **D:\SETUP.EXE** (assuming D: is the name of your CD drive).

2. Locate the product's 25-character key code on a label attached inside the CD
   storage case. When the Setup dialog box appears, type in the characters (omit-
   ting dashes). The dialog box is shown in Figure 4.1. When finished, click **Next.**

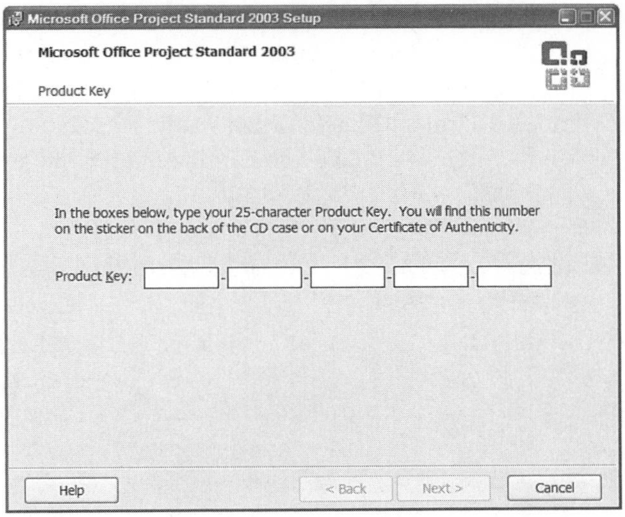

Figure 4.1

*Type the product code found
inside your packaging materials into the fields provided.*

3. Type your name, initials (optional), and organization (optional) into the fields
   provided as shown in Figure 4.2. These will identify you as the author of the
   files you create and store. Click **Next.**

Figure 4.2

Your username, initials, and organization will appear in the Properties dialog box for files created with this application.

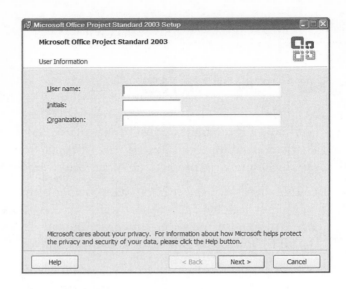

4. When the License Agreement dialog box appears, check the box next to **I accept the terms in the License Agreement** and click **Next** to proceed. Select an installation option in the Type of Installation dialog box shown in Figure 4.3. The options are described in Table 4.1. Keep in mind that you can change your installation options at anytime by double-clicking **Add or Remove Programs** in the Windows Control Panel. When ready, click **Next**. Now's a good time to get up and stretch—it'll take a few moments for the application to be installed.

Figure 4.3

The recommended option for new users is Typical Installation.

Table 4.1   Project 2003 Installation Options

Option	Comments
Upgrade	Appears only if you have a previous version of Project installed. Removes earlier versions but keeps your settings and project files intact. (Project 98 and earlier versions cannot be opened by Project 2003 unless they are converted to the MPD file format.)
Complete Install	Installs all features and tools and requires the most space. Installs many items that are not normally needed for most users.
Minimal Install	Use when drive space is limited.
Typical Install	Recommended for most users. This option installs the most commonly used features and tools.
Custom Install	Recommended for advanced users or those who want to keep an earlier version of Project on their computers.

5. When the Setup Completed dialog box appears, installation is almost finished. If you have access to the Internet, select **Check the Web for updates and additional downloads** as shown in Figure 4.4. Do not check **Delete installation files** unless you have limited hard drive space. Keeping these files will save time later, when you update or maintain the application.

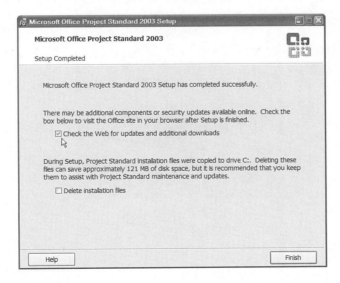

Figure 4.4

Check the web for program updates to complete the installation.

6. After installation finishes, the application opens to its default view, the Gantt Chart view, and an Activation Wizard appears. The first 50 times you start Project 2003, it will remind you every time to complete the required activation before it restricts use. You may activate over the phone if you don't have web access. The message no longer appears after you complete the activation process.

To start the program in the future, click the Windows **Start** button, point to **All Programs,** and click **Microsoft Project.**

Congratulations, Project 2003 is ready to go! Before you move on, remember to take the application CD out of the drive and store it in a safe and easily accessible location. Occasionally, you may need the CD to maintain or repair Project 2003.

Installing Project 2002 and Project 2000

Installing Project 2002 or Project 2000 is almost identical to the process described for Project 2003. For either program, begin by inserting the CD as in Project 2003 and follow the onscreen instructions, entering product key codes, name and organization, and confirming acceptance to the license agreement. Installation options for Project 2002 are shown in Figure 4.5 and described in Table 4.2. When installing Project 2000 refer to Figure 4.6.

Figure 4.5

*The Project 2002 installation dialog box will show **Upgrade Now** if an earlier version of Project is installed.*

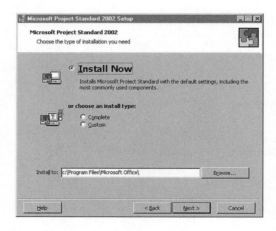

Table 4.2   Project 2002 Installation Options

Option	Comments
Install Now	Recommended for most users. This option installs the most commonly used features and tools.
Upgrade Now	Appears only if you have a previous version of Project installed. This choice enables you to keep the existing version or completely remove it. Project files are not removed.
Complete	Installs all features and tools and requires the most drive space. Installs many items that for most users are not normally needed.
Custom	Recommended for advanced users.

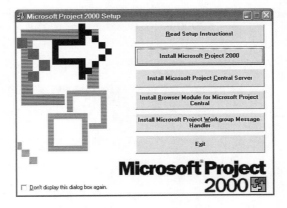

Figure 4.6

*Select **Install Microsoft Project 2000** and follow the onscreen instructions.*

Finding Your Way Around the Program

If the program isn't currently running, start it up and we'll take a short tour of the workspace. If this is your first look at Microsoft Project 2003, don't be alarmed at all the buttons and menu items. It really is easier than it looks.

First of all, if you've used any other Microsoft Office products, such as Word, Excel, Access, Outlook, Visio, or PowerPoint, you already know many of the basic commands. Second, the most frequently used commands are available several ways: pull-down menus, shortcut keys, and toolbar buttons. Consequently, there really aren't as many commands to learn as it looks. And third, it's easy to hide items you don't use and make those you frequently use more accessible. After using the program for a while, you'll develop your own favorite methods of accessing each command.

When learning a new program, some people find it's easier to remember where commands are in the pull-down menus, whereas for others it's easier to remember icons on the toolbar buttons. I, however, can rarely remember anything (as my colleagues will attest). Fortunately, no command memorization is required. There are plenty of descriptions and clues to help you navigate Microsoft Project 2003's commands. For example, place your mouse pointer over any button, hesitate for just a moment (as if you can't remember whether this is the choice you want), and notice what happens. Instant recall! A description of the button pops up, guiding your selection. I wish they could do something like that with my car keys.

When Project 2003 starts, it opens an empty project file in a view known as the Gantt chart. The workspace is divided into two main areas in this default view, the Entry table on the left side of the vertical divider and the Gantt chart background on the right side. This is shown in Figure 4.7. If you use any other Microsoft Office 2003 products, you'll recognize the large Getting Started pane on the left side of the workspace. In it you can search for help on the Microsoft website and get assistance starting a new project.

Figure 4.7

The opening view is the Gantt Chart view with no project data entered.

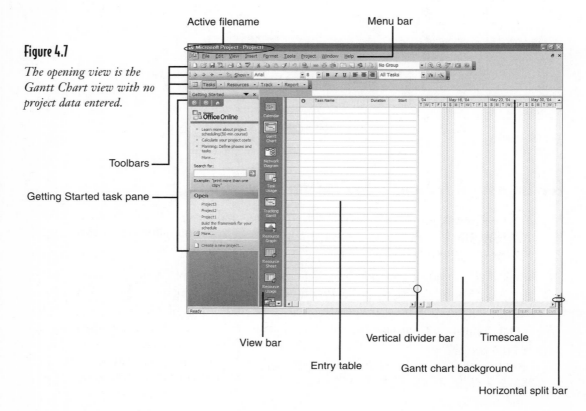

As soon as you start a new project the Getting Started pane is replaced by the Task Pane and the view bar moves to the far left, as shown in Figure 4.8. The task pane is a goal-based help system that walks you through common planning, tracking, and reporting tasks. The goals in the task pane cycle as you complete each step. Clicking the Project Guide toolbar changes each set of tasks displayed in the task pane.

Project Guide toolbar

Project Guide
task pane

Entry table
field headings

Drag divider to see all fields

Click to Hide task pane

Caution. Do not enter data
in Start or Finish fields

Figure 4.8

The Table view acts like a spreadsheet, enabling you to view different sets of fields depending on the table selected.

The vertical divider can be dragged right or left, revealing more or fewer field headings. To drag, point at the item you want to move, click and hold, drag to the new location, and then release the click button to drop it.

You can think of the Table as a spreadsheet view of different sets of data that are available in the project file. Other tables are ready for various scheduling and tracking tasks such as for tracking actuals, comparing variances, entering progress, or working with cost data.

CAUTION

Project Pitfalls

Don't enter dates into the Start and Finish fields of the Entry table. These fields are calculated by the scheduling engine in Project 2003 based on the task's duration, workflow relationships, and resource availability. Placing dates in these fields overrides Project's calculations and creates inaccurate schedules.

In Figure 4.8, the vertical divider bar has been moved to the right, revealing all the field headings on the Entry table. Double-clicking a column divider adjusts the column's width to the widest data in the field.

Customizing Your Workspace

You can adapt the workspace to your needs and make it more productive with a few simple techniques. Don't be afraid of experimenting. As long as you've saved your project files, you can always reset Project 2003 to the original menus and views by reinstalling it.

Changing Views

You can select from eight popular views in the view bar by clicking an icon of the view you want. To create more working space you can hide the view bar by right-clicking anywhere on the view bar and unchecking the bottom item. Right-clicking the resulting narrow blue area will reverse the process when you want the view bar back. The view bar is identified in Figure 4.7.

You have 27 other predefined views to choose from besides the Gantt chart. All of them are available by selecting **View** on the menu and scrolling down to **More Views.** If you don't find what you need, you can create a new view or modify an existing view and save it with a new name. Figure 4.9 shows the More Views dialog box and the View Definition box that pops up when you want to edit an existing view. For easy access to your new view, attach it to the View menu by selecting **Show in menu.**

Figure 4.9

You can select from 28 pre-defined views or create your own.

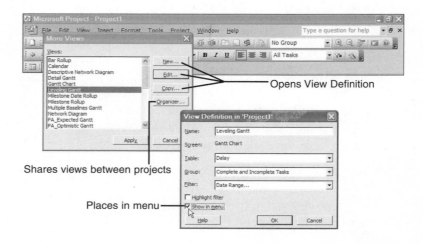

Opens View Definition

Shares views between projects

Places in menu

Changing Tables

To display a different set of fields in the table, select **View,** scroll down to **Table,** and select a table from those shown in Figure 4.10. You can create a new table or edit an existing one to suit you needs by choosing the **More Tables** option.

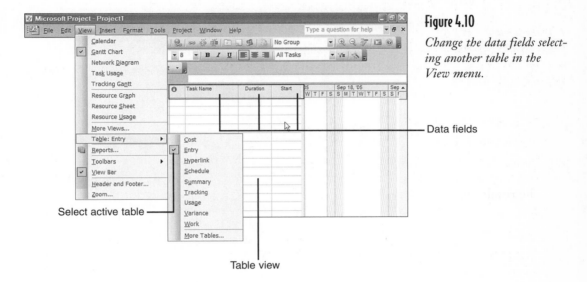

Figure 4.10

Change the data fields selecting another table in the View menu.

Changing Toolbars

All of the toolbars can be moved, hidden, or displayed, and their buttons can be added or removed. To move a toolbar, click and hold the vertical line on its left edge. Adding and removing buttons is also easy; just click the small down arrow on the right edge of the toolbar, as shown in Figure 4.11. Select the buttons to be added or removed by checking beside the item.

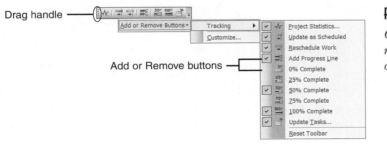

Figure 4.11

Click the down arrow on the right edge of a toolbar to add or remove buttons.

It's fast and easy to add or remove toolbars from your workspace. Select **View, Toolbars,** and check the toolbars you want and uncheck those you don't want. You can also get the Toolbar menu by right-clicking the toolbar area. Figure 4.12 shows the available toolbars.

Figure 4.12

To reduce clutter and increase your workspace area, it only takes two clicks to hide or reveal a toolbar.

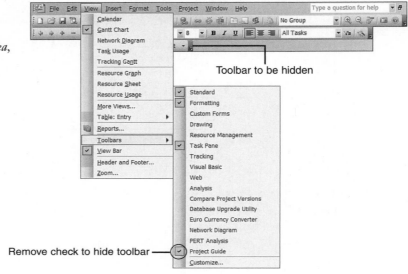

In an attempt to tailor menus for each user's specific needs, Microsoft has included a dynamic menu starting with Project 2000. Your menu usage is monitored, and the most popular items are placed conveniently near the top of each menu. Items you haven't used for a while remain hidden, but can be revealed by clicking the Show Full Menu icon. Figure 4.13 shows the Tools menu before expanding, and Figure 4.14 shows the full menu.

Figure 4.13

Dynamic menus hide unpopular items.

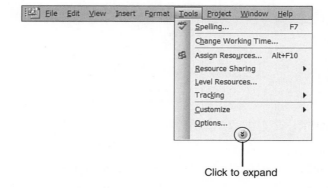

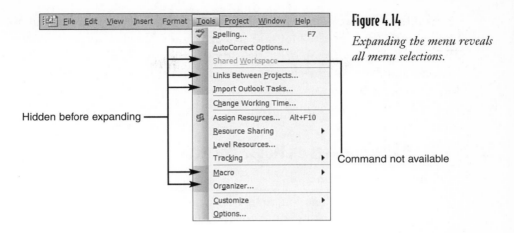

Hidden before expanding ———

Command not available

Figure 4.14

Expanding the menu reveals all menu selections.

If you find the ever-changing menus confusing (I do), you can turn this feature off in the Customize dialog box. On the menu select **Tools, Customize, Toolbars** to open the Customize dialog box. Figure 4.15 shows the Customize dialog box. Select the Options tab, if it isn't already, and place a check in the **Always show full menus** check box. You can also pick which toolbars to show in this dialog box under the Toolbars tab. And under the Commands tab, you can select the individual buttons that appear on a toolbar.

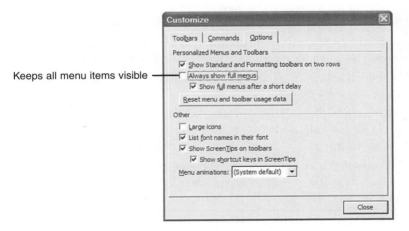

Keeps all menu items visible ———

Figure 4.15

Use this dialog box to modify toolbars, menus, and command accessibility.

Mousing Around the Program

It's helpful to understand how the mouse pointer changes depending on it's current function. Check out Table 4.3, take hold of your mouse, and make some tracks! (Forgive me, it had to be said.) See how many different mouse pointers you can make appear. Try clicking, pointing, and hovering on fields, lines, buttons, and menu choices. And while you're mousing around, try double-clicking items. Whenever available, dialog boxes pop open, providing speedy access to additional information, options, and detail. Right-clicking opens context-sensitive submenus. You'll learn to love the mouse buttons in Microsoft Project—they're the fastest way to access many useful features.

Table 4.3 A Few Pointers on Mouse Pointers

Pointer	Function
⬉	What you see is what you get. The default pointer for selecting, clicking, dragging, and pressing on date spinners.
✛	Indicates your pointer is over a field in a table view. Clicking selects that field for data entry or editing.
I	Shows the location of the cursor in text, numeric, currency, or date fields.
◄╫►	Indicates that the pointer is hovering over a vertical window separator and by pressing the left mouse button, you may drag it to adjust the size of the split.
▲╪▼	This does the same as the pointer above except it adjusts horizontal splits. When in the Task Table view, this indicates that you have selected a task for moving up or down within the task list.
◄╬►	In field headings, drag this pointer to adjust the width of columns or double-click to automatically adjust column width to fit data.
▲╪▼	In row headings, drag this pointer to adjust the height of rows.
◄╬►▼	This pointer shows that you have selected an object, such as a network diagram node or a toolbar, and are ready to drag it to a new location.
∞	This pointer can be tricky, so be careful when you see it. It creates new links, and sometimes new tasks, in the Gantt and PERT Chart views.

Starting and Saving Project Files

Before using Microsoft Project 2003 to plan an actual project, let's make sure you can create, save, and open project files. This way, you can be confident that your work is safe.

To create a new project, open the **File** menu and select **New.** In the window that appears, select **Blank Project**. (Later, in Chapter 18, I show you how to make and use project templates.)

In Project 2003 and Project 2002, the task pane will appear to guide you in setting up a new project. We won't be using it right now, so you may either ignore or close the task pane. If you're using Project 2000, the Project Information dialog box pops up, but just close it for now.

CAUTION   Project Pitfalls

If you're accustomed to using the undo features in Microsoft Office applications, you may be disappointed with this feature's lack of power in Project. Unlike MS Word, where you undo many actions and recover work, in Project you're lucky if you can undo the very last command! Get in the habit of frequently saving iterations of your files, using sequential names. Then when you're done working in project just open your working directory and delete any unnecessary files.

To save your new file, click **Save As** in the File menu. A File dialog box opens similar to the one in Figure 4.16. Select an appropriate folder for your project files. You'll have easy access to them if you select the **My Documents** icon, click new folder, and name the folder **Projects.** Double-click the folder to open it. Type the name of your new project file at the bottom of the dialog box and click **Save**. If a dialog box appears regarding saving with or without a baseline, select without. You'll learn about baselines in Chapter 13.

All you need to do to open this project file is select **Open** on the File menu, navigate to the appropriate location, and double-click the file you want.

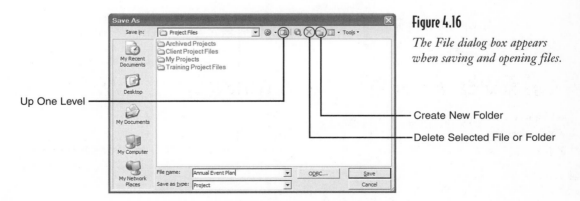

Figure 4.16

The File dialog box appears when saving and opening files.

Getting Help in a Hurry

With such a robust set of commands and options, it's nice to know there's help available no matter where you are in Project 2003. Microsoft has continually improved the ease of use and the quality of Project's help resources. From the moment you start to the moment you exit, there's ready help on everything from project management practices to the details of printing a report.

Locating the Help You Want

Navigating through all this information is easy with Project 2003's new Assistance pane. To access it, select **Microsoft Project Help** in the Help menu or press the **F1** key. If an online connection isn't present, Assistance searches the help files on your computer only, resulting of course in fewer results.

The Assistance pane, shown in Figure 4.17, takes quite a bit of workspace, but it's easy to hide and retrieve, and it provides convenient navigation throughout many topics and sources. With it you can find information not only on how to use the features and commands in Project, but also an assortment of articles on project management concepts, sources of additional training, the opportunity to interact with other users, and downloads for product updates, templates, and newly released information.

Figure 4.17

Project 2003's new Assistance pane provides convenient access to a plethora of topics, resources, and discussion groups.

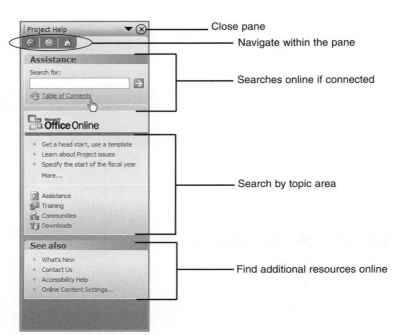

To access the Help dialog box in Project 2002 and Project 2000, select **Help** on the menu, and then select **Contents and Index.**

Figure 4.18

The Contents and Index box in Project 2002 and Project 2000 (Project 2002 is shown) provides easy access to help information, references, and tutorials.

The following list describes the Help menu options:

◆ **What's New** helps you learn about the new features in Microsoft Project 2000, in case you've used a previous version.

◆ **Project Map** is a good overview of using the program. It enables you to quickly navigate to the points you want to learn more about.

◆ **Tutorial** steps you through the process of entering project information, creating a schedule, tracking, and reporting progress. If you have a little time, these lessons are a good way to increase your program knowledge.

◆ **Reference** is an encyclopedic listing of the features and functions of Microsoft Project 2000 and Project 2002. You'll find help on views, tables, filters, templates, troubleshooting, glossary items, features for disabilities, technical specifications, mouse and keyboard shortcuts, and more.

Meeting Clippit, Your Personal Tutor

Perhaps the easiest feature to use (and certainly the most entertaining) is your personal computer tutor, Clippit. To put him to work, click **Show the Office Assistant** in the Help menu.

Figure 4.19

The energetic and somewhat interruptive Clippit retrieves information and warns you of possible mistakes.

Type in any words or phrases (it doesn't have to be a complete sentence), select **Search,** and Clippit retrieves a list of subjects for you to pick from. You'll be amazed at how well he gets the job done.

When you aren't using Clippit, he waits patiently, although not always quietly, for your next question. It can sometimes get a little disruptive, so if he distracts you, just give him the boot by right-clicking him and then selecting **Hide.** He doesn't seem to hold a grudge—he'll be back whenever needed, cheerful and eager as ever. Don't you wish you had the same control over interrupters at the office?

Smart Tags Lend a Helping Hand

Smart Tags are a content-triggered help system that helps guard against common errors. Beginning in Project 2002, Smart Tags have helped by clarifying choices and helping users avoid common mistakes. A small warning icon pops up when a potential error or the need to clarify an action is detected, as shown in Figure 4.20. Clicking the icon reveals available options and explains their implications. The user can thereby reconsider or reaffirm the action.

Figure 4.20

Smart Tags provide clarification for easily made mistakes.

Congratulations! You've mastered the controls for Microsoft Project 2003, so it's time to put it to work planning one of your projects. Pick one out and let's focus on success!

The Least You Need to Know

◆ You can easily modify all the program's workspace, views, toolbars, and menus to improve convenience and productivity.

◆ Creating, saving, and opening project files in Microsoft Project 2003 works like other Microsoft Office programs.

◆ The mouse pointer changes shape in different locations of the program window to indicate its current function.

◆ Getting help is quick and easy with the new Assistant pane, the Help home page, and help on the web.

Thinking of Everything, Even If You Don't Know What You're Doing

In This Chapter

- ◆ Identify every task that must be accomplished to make your project a success
- ◆ Subdivide your project into logical, manageable segments with a work breakdown structure
- ◆ Translate your project strategy into tactics you can implement
- ◆ Make your project more manageable with summaries, sublevels, and milestones

To accomplish a project goal, hundreds or even thousands of individual tasks must be identified and successfully completed. The process of identifying all required work is called project decomposition. This can be a chaotic process unless you understand the tricks of the trade.

Identifying What It Takes for Success

Perhaps the most daunting challenge project managers must resolve is how to identify every activity required to accomplish the project goals, not leave something out, and not burden the project with unnecessary work.

Missing even a seemingly minor item can blow the project's chances of success. For example, which bolt, nut, or screw could be left out of out the space shuttle? I wager none of them could be—they're all essential. And yet, every additional ounce of structure reduces the payload capacity. To be successful, what's in the project and what's left out of the project are extremely important decisions.

The worst project error I've ever made was an error of omission—one line item slipped past our checks and rechecks of the bid we'd been preparing for weeks. The problem was found moments after our bid had been announced publicly as the "lowest responsive bidder." We had won the project, but as we realized the omission, our excitement turned to despair. You see, somewhere along the line we (my chief estimator or I) had accidentally changed the spreadsheet cell holding our bid bond factor from 1.75 percent to 0.0 percent. The net result was a cost of more than $65,000 left out of the project bid! Neither of us noticed it until we were victoriously scanning down the printout looking for our profit margin. Fortunately, we were both too young to have heart attacks. We survived our mistake and grew from it, but it was an expensive lesson. From that day forward, two sets of eyes checked every project estimate. The success of your project, and your success as a project manager, largely depends on how well you choose the line items in you project plan.

Secrets of Success

There's a notable difference between rookie and expert project managers—rookies seek bigger and better tools; experts seek big and better skills. Some of the most effective project management tools, like the work breakdown structure, are conceptually very simple. Don't dismiss simple tools. In the hands of a consummate expert, simple tools are powerful tools.

Introducing the Work Breakdown Structure

To create order out of this chaos, project managers use a concept known as the *work breakdown structure* (WBS). Like a safety net, the WBS helps you include every activity essential to achieving the project's goals and objectives. In addition, it helps protect your project from the nonessential activities that undoubtedly will try to creep in.

The WBS is a simple, flexible approach—a thought process. It can take on several different forms, depending on the project manager's personal preferences. The traditional and most popular metaphor is shown in Figure 5.1. Notice that it resembles an organizational chart. What's important about this metaphor is that it shows a hierarchy of work. The presumption is that it's relatively easy to think of the large elements of the project and that by breaking the elements into smaller and smaller pieces the project manager can a) think of everything, and b) understand how it all fits together.

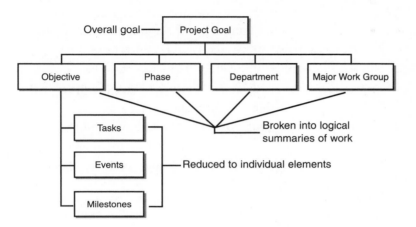

Figure 5.1

The WBS subdivides the project into smaller, more manageable components. Use as many levels as needed to organize and describe the work that must take place.

Another conceptual model that is used to decompose the goal into smaller and smaller units is the outline. This format fits into any table or listing nicely and is consequently how we enter the work into Microsoft Project 2003.

An accurate WBS is fundamental to project success. Creating it reveals how a project's major outcomes are supported by key objectives or strategies, and in turn, what tactics or activities are needed to implement these strategies. No matter what conceptual model you use to help you understand the hierarchy of the work, the list of activities you end up with becomes the backbone of all other planning, monitoring, and controlling decisions you'll make.

How to Create a Work Breakdown Structure

Trying to think of every task that must be completed on a major project is enough to push even seasoned project managers to the verge of a nervous breakdown. However, you can remain cool, calm, and collected by using the procedure outlined in the following sections. (Later in this chapter I'll show you how to enter the WBS data into Microsoft Project most effectively.)

To create a WBS, you must have a clear understanding of the project's goals and objectives, the

CAUTION **Project Pitfalls**

Although it may be tempting, never skip or shortchange the project initiation phase. Planning is worthless unless you have a clear understanding of the project's goals, objectives, stakeholders, assumptions, and constraints. The quality of your WBS depends on the output of the initiation phase.

triple constraints, and the project assumptions. You probably already gathered this information when in the initiation phase. (See the section entitled "Preplanning Checklist" in Chapter 3.)

Begin by focusing on the goal—the "what" will be accomplished. Next break the goal down into its major elements or supporting objectives—the "how" it will be accomplished. This thinking process is modeled in Figure 5.2. When properly done, the second level describes a project implementation strategy. This strategy can then be broken down into the separate tasks required for achievement.

For example, if the project is to create a new product, begin your WBS with its goal: To design and manufacture a new product that will increase market share by year end to 15 percent in the European division while maintaining a minimum margin of 32 percent.

Obviously, there are as many strategies as there are project managers for implementing this project. I use a simplistic approach for illustration purposes.

Figure 5.2

Brainstorm the tasks required for each phase of work.

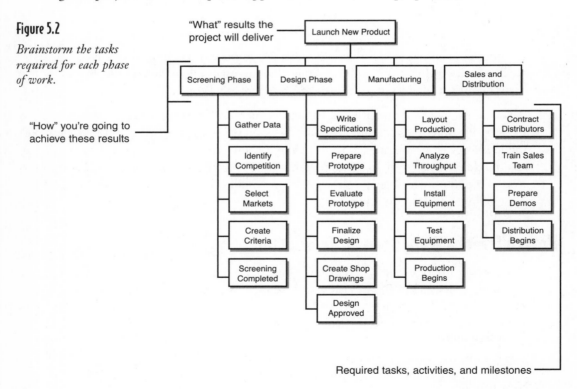

Transferring the WBS Hierarchy Concept to an Outline Format

You've just seen the thought process of decomposing a project's work modeled as an organizational chart. No matter how we think through and list the elements of work, ultimately we want it in an outline format that can show the hierarchy in a project plan created in Microsoft Project. In the outline format, indentation indicates each level in the hierarchy.

For example, a generic project plan could be indented similarly to this:

Project goal

    Major objective 1

        Phase of work

            Work task A

            Work task B

            Work task C ...

        Phase of work completed milestone

    Major objective 1 completed milestone

    Major objective 2 ...

        Etc.

Project goal completed milestone

For the new product example, the hierarchy when outlined might look something like this:

New product launch

    Design phase

        Write specifications

        Create prototype

        Conduct user review

    Design approved

    Etc.

New product shipped

Although each project manager has a favorite way of thinking through the hierarchy of work and identifying all the work elements, the information will be entered into Microsoft Project 2003 in an outline form. You'll learn more about this process later in the "Organizing Your Project Tasks with Microsoft Project 2003" section.

Going It Alone for Simple Projects

When the project is simple and you fully understand its nuances, the WBS can be created without assistance.

However, creating the WBS is a learning process, and you want to uncover the best implementation process you can. As you proceed, alternative methods or approaches may appear. Don't reject anything yet. Now is the time to turn your creativity meter on high and your judgment meter to low. Let the ideas roll!

When you think you've got it all, take a break and let your ideas soak in. It helps to regain a balanced perspective before continuing. When time allows, sleep on it. If you're in a time crunch, step away from your desk for at least a few minutes. Better yet, take a break or go to lunch.

Then, with a fresh set of eyes, review your WBS and ask yourself these questions:

- Are lower-level items both necessary and sufficient for completion of project goals?

- Are there any items that are not essential to the project's success and that can be removed?

- Can adequate cost and duration estimates be developed at this level of detail?

- Is each element described in tangible, verifiable results?

- Can each item be appropriately scheduled, budgeted, and assigned?

Remember that planning is an iterative process. As you plan, you learn. Don't hesitate to return to a previous step in the planning process to improve your plan. Continue refining your WBS until you are confident that it adequately and as simply as possible describes the project. A minute spent now can save much frustration and many hours of implementation later.

When the Going Gets Tough, Call for Reinforcements

As the project manager, you are ultimately responsible for the success of the project, so it falls on you to facilitate the development of a good WBS. However, in a complex project environment, no one person can possibly have all the experience, training, and knowledge needed to create a viable WBS alone.

Fortunately, your role as a project manager is not to think of everything, but rather to make sure everything is thought of by someone!

> **Secrets of Success**
>
> In project management, if you want something done right, *don't* do it yourself. Allow, encourage, or insist on participation throughout initiation and planning. This is particularly true while creating the WBS. Involve those who do the work. When you facilitate participation, you facilitate buy-in. When you have buy-in, you don't have to do it yourself!

Using Cross-Functional, Experienced Experts

The first step is to gather a team of "experts." Chances are no one is an expert on this project or he or she, rather than you, would be the project manager! However, what you can do is bring in people who collectively represent all the skills, knowledge, experience, and techniques your project requires. A group like this is called a *cross-functional team.*

Individuals who are willing and able to work in collaborative environments are most valuable. Some people prefer to work alone or are unwilling to work as part of a team. You'll make life easier on yourself and on them, and you'll improve your chances of success, by honoring each individual's work-style preferences.

Choosing how much detail to place in your WBS is an important decision. Excessive detail bogs down communications and control; inadequate detail misses important work elements, overlooks potential problems, or puts too much faith in the wrong people. Keep your plan as simple as possible when it's a new type of project for you or your team. When the team hasn't worked together before, when there are high levels of risk, or when there's a scarcity of time or resources, drill into the detail until you're comfortable!

Entering the WBS into Microsoft Project 2003

After you've established an initial WBS for your project, it's time to use the awesome power of Microsoft Project 2003 to organize, analyze, and further sharpen it. This step also paves the way for the next stages in planning: estimating task durations and sequencing the work. To create a WBS in Project, follow these steps:

1. With your WBS nearby, start Microsoft Project 2003 and open your project file. Make sure the Gantt chart and Entry table are shown. If not, select the **Gantt Chart** view from the view bar.

2. Click the first empty field under Task Name. When selected, the field is highlighted with a dark outline, showing it is ready for data entry.

3. Enter the first item that makes up your WBS. This might be the project name, a phase of the project, a major workgroup, or perhaps a task. After typing its name into the selected field press **Enter.**

   Notice that Microsoft Project automatically sets the task's duration to 1 day. It also sets the start date to today's date (or to the project start date you may have entered earlier). The start and finish dates automatically calculate as you enter tasks, durations, and workflow sequences, and the availability of resources. Don't worry about (or try to change) the dates for now.

4. Continue entering all the items that make up your WBS until you're satisfied that all the required work is listed.

5. Check your list for content and clarity, making sure that nothing has been missed and others will understand your descriptions.

Inserting, Deleting, and Moving Items on the Task List

Inserting an item that you may have missed, or adding one you just thought of, is easy to do in the Entry table of the Gantt Chart view. For example, you might decide that inserting a short description of your project as the first line would help others understand the work breakdown structure. To do this, select the field where you want to insert the item and press the **Insert** key. Presto! Everything is magically shifted down and an empty row appears. Type in the description and you're finished. Notice—no eraser dust!

Deleting an item or several items is also simple and fast:

- ◆ For one item, click it anywhere in the Table view and press the **Delete** key.

- ◆ To delete a continuous series of items, click an item and move to the last item in the series and click it while pressing the **Shift** key.

- ◆ Alternatively, by holding down the **Ctrl** key as you click items, you can select a noncontinuous list.

> ### More Good Stuff
>
> By right-clicking anywhere on a task and selecting **Task Notes,** you have a handy storage place for any information you want, even pictures! A Task Note appears in the Information column so that you won't forget it's there.

Be careful! Both the wanted and the unwanted can vanish with equally blinding speed.

Reorganizing your list is a breeze in Microsoft Project 2003, as shown in Figure 5.3. Click once on the row header to select the entire row. Now click and hold the mouse button down and drag the task to its new location in the list. Wow! Now that's living! (If you have trouble with this, be sure to pause just a moment between clicks so that the computer doesn't interpret it as a double-click.)

You may edit field data here

Defaults to today

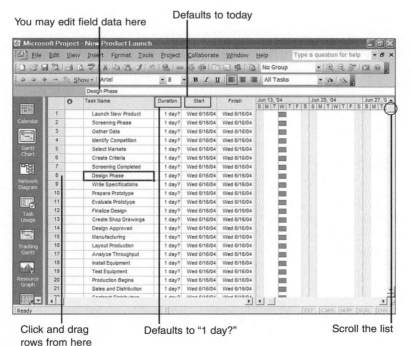

Figure 5.3

Enter each major work category, task, and milestone event from your WBS into the Gantt Chart view in general order of workflow.

Click and drag rows from here

Defaults to "1 day?"

Scroll the list

Making Your Task List Easy to Understand

Your project plan needs to be easily understood by everyone who relies on it for information. To get off to a good start, here are some things you can do (as discussed more fully a little later):

◆ Use consistent naming conventions throughout your task list.

◆ Use an indentation system that visually communicates the WBS hierarchy.

◆ List the tasks in their general sequence of workflow.

◆ Add summary tasks and milestones to the task list to make the project easier to understand and easier to manage.

Using Consistent Name Formats

Review your WBS naming conventions for consistency and clarity. Not only will your WBS communicate the strategy and tactics of your project more clearly to everyone who uses your plan, clear names will make many planning chores, such as structuring workflow logic, estimating costs, and estimating durations, much easier. Use these guidelines and examples when naming:

◆ **Tasks.** Tasks are the heart of your project. Describe tasks with clear and unambiguous wording in units that allow accurate cost estimates, accurate time estimates, and clear delegation of responsibilities. An *action outcome* format is effective. Examples include excavate footings, survey users, issue purchase orders, debug code.

◆ **Milestones.** Arrival at a milestone confirms that all tasks it depended on have been successfully completed. An *outcome achieved* format is a good way to communicate a milestone's importance. Examples include testing completed, users trained, approval received, system operational.

◆ **Summary tasks.** These items are subheadings within a task list. Tasks may be rolled up into the summary task, thereby greatly simplifying complex projects. Include a *grouping term* in these items. Examples include mobilization phase, needs assessment section, training category, production department.

Adding Milestones

These events measure your progress and help you monitor and control the project. The careful placing of milestones in a large project can make it much easier to understand and manage.

Milestones are created in the task list exactly like tasks are with the exception that the task duration is set to zero. All zero-duration tasks are considered milestones in Microsoft Project 2003 (see Figure 5.4). In the Gantt Chart view, they are denoted with a small diamond symbol.

You may occasionally want to use a task with a nonzero duration as a milestone. To do this, from the Gantt Chart view right-click the task to select it, click **Task Information,** and then select the **Advanced** tab. In the Duration box, enter the task duration and click the **Mark task as a milestone** check box (found in the lower-left corner of the Information dialog box).

Showing Work Phases with Summary Tasks

Another method used to make a large task list more readable is the summary task. Major workgroups or phases are effectively communicated when shown as summary tasks in the task list. Lower levels can be rolled up into the summary task and hidden from view. Now you see it, now you don't!

You create summary tasks in Microsoft Project 2003 by indenting a task or group of tasks in the list. The item immediately above the indented items becomes a bolded summary task. The summary task's duration is automatically calculated as the time required to complete the subtasks.

Using Indentations to Convey WBS Hierarchy

Outlining your task list with indents and outdents has two main benefits. First, a graphic representation of WBS levels enables you to more easily spot which items are tasks, summaries, milestones, and the like. Second, task information may be compressed or expanded section by section with a click of the mouse. This enables you to focus on a group of items and hide the rest from view.

To indent or outdent single items, go to the Gantt Chart view, as shown in Figure 5.4. Select the item you want to indent. On the Formatting toolbar, click the **Indent** or **Outdent** button.

Indenting a summary task or a task consisting of lower levels (such as subtasks) may cause the lower levels to indent one level too far. This can be rectified by selecting the effected tasks and clicking the **Outdent** button.

You can display or hide any indented group of items in the task list. This proves helpful in several situations.

Figure 5.4

Make your project easier to understand by indenting and outdenting items according to your WBS hierarchy and by using meaningful names. To illustrate, compare this WBS with the one in Figure 5.3.

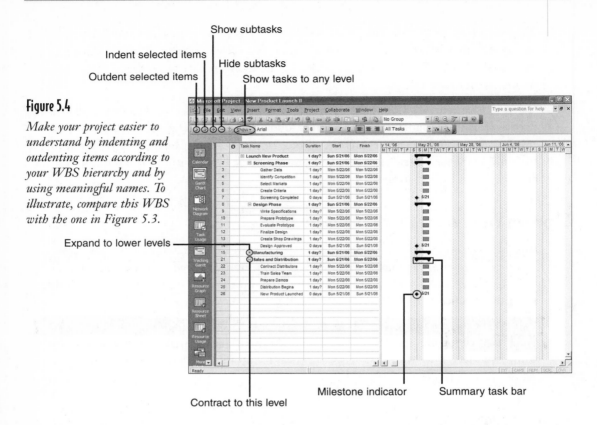

For example, you want to call attention to a team member's area of responsibility, you want a report without potentially confusing detail, or you want to limit what is displayed on your screen when working on large projects.

To expand or contract your list, select the **Gantt Chart** view. Click the **minus sign** or **plus sign** icons next to the name of the section you want to expand or contract. You can also select an item, and then click the **Show Subtasks, Hide Subtasks,** or **Show All Tasks** buttons.

Printing Your List and Checking It Twice

A printed copy of the WBS listing is sometimes needed for the project's archives, for reports to management, and as part of contractually required documentation. While creating the WBS, I like having a fresh printout in my hand to mark changes on with a brightly colored pen.

A printout can also help determine whether the WBS accurately and effectively describes the project's implementation. One way of facilitating this is to mark a copy "Final Review" (a bright red font is best) and circulate it for comment among your team members.

If you created the WBS alone, solicit comments from one or more knowledgeable colleagues. Successful project managers are adept at picking other people's brains! Unfortunately, Microsoft Project 2003 can't help you with the brain picking, nor can it print anything but a rather blasé rendition of the WBS listing.

However, if your printed listing doesn't need to be pretty, you're in luck! With just a few keystrokes, you can print the view that appears on your computer screen. The caveat is that you can't easily remove unnecessary columns, legends, or other items you might not want to appear. (If it needs to be pretty, check out the section titled "Presenting with Persuasive Pizzazz" in Chapter 21 to see how to print it in Word, PowerPoint, or Visio.)

To print a quick review copy of the WBS, follow these steps:

1. Save your project file before you make any of the following adjustments. After you've finished printing, save the modified view with a new name in case you need it again, and then reopen the unchanged original.

2. In the Gantt Chart view, drag the vertical divider to the far right.

3. Select all the column headers except the task name and right-click. Then select **Hide Columns.**

4. Drag the column width to the right so you can see the complete tasks names.

5. Select **Page Setup** on the File menu and change your page orientation to **Portrait.**

6. Now you can click **Print Preview** and check out the results.

7. Choose **Header** in Page Setup and type in the project's name. When you're satisfied with how it looks, print it.

Figure 5.5 is the result of our work! Okay, okay. I know I promised you quick and easy. You didn't have to resort to white out or scissors, did you? (See Chapter 22 for a presentation-quality WBS printout.)

Figure 5.5

A well-thought-out and well-presented WBS is an essential step in planning a successful project. Hide unrelated or potentially confusing information before distributing it.

The Least You Need to Know

◆ The work breakdown structure (WBS) is the best approach for identifying all the tasks needed to make your project a success.

◆ Eliminating unnecessary tasks will improve your odds of success.

◆ Using Microsoft Project 2003's Gantt view, you can easily insert, delete, or rearrange tasks.

◆ Make your plan easy to understand with summary tasks, milestones, and sub-levels to communicate the WBS hierarchy.

Chapter 6

Estimating Durations with Science, Skill, and Fourth-Grade Math

In This Chapter

- ◆ Why accurate duration estimates are important to the success of your project

- ◆ Six methods project managers use to estimate the amount of time required to complete a task

- ◆ How to enter estimated durations in Microsoft Project 2003

- ◆ How Microsoft Project 2003 handles project time and calendar time

As a project manager, you're asked to see into the future on every project: How long will it take? How soon must we begin? Will we be done on time? Ever wish you had a crystal ball? Well now you've got something better. You're about to replace superstition with science, skill, and fourth-grade math. You're about to see into the future with amazing accuracy. Allow me to explain.

How Long Will the Project Take to Complete?

One of the key questions on almost every project is, "How long will the project take to complete?" To effectively estimate the project's duration, you must know four things:

◆ What tasks must be accomplished?

◆ How long will each task take (given appropriate resources)?

◆ What resources are required?

◆ In what order will the tasks be accomplished?

If it is not obvious why order of task accomplishment is important, consider the following: Some tasks can begin only after others have been completed. Other tasks may run in *parallel*, that is, at the same time. The more tasks that are undertaken at once, the sooner the project will be done. Therefore, task sequence must be established before you can estimate a project's total duration.

Words at Work

Parallel tasks are those that take place in the same time period as another task. In essence, more work is being done and more resources are required in that timeframe. Running tasks in parallel tends to produce shorter schedules.

Similarly, resources are important in the determination of total project duration. Consider the following: If several tasks require the same resource, only one task could be done at a time, the others would be forced to wait until the resource was available. In general, doing more tasks in any given time period requires more resources. Conversely, the fewer resources you have, the longer the duration will be.

Obviously all four elements—tasks, task duration, workflow sequence, and resources—work together in determining overall project duration. With Project 2003, creating a schedule is easy—we put in the data and a schedule instantly appears. But is it a good schedule? Will the stakeholders support it?

A Strategy for Better Schedules

Working with a project's complex set of variables might be easy for Einstein, but for me, and probably for your stakeholders, it has to be simplified to be understood. Trying to optimize time and resources against the confines of tasks and workflow, while meeting everyone's optimistic expectations, reminds me of the circular logic in the chicken and egg conundrum. What should drive the schedule: Time? Resources?

Tasks? Workflow? Which should come first? Often the priority is set by a stakeholder's loudness, not by logic. One thing is certain, no matter which point of view you advocate, it never makes complete sense with everyone.

Here's a better approach. For the moment, assume there will be enough resources and plenty of time. Of course, that's not likely, but it serves the purpose of simplifying things. Then create a safe, simple, efficient, likely to succeed plan—the way you'd do things if you had all (reasonable) options open. This is what I call a *normal* plan—a safe simple approach under average conditions (average resources, average vendors, average problems, etc.).

The normal plan does two things: It helps you understand what an optimal plan could look like and it exposes issues, options, and implications. The normal plan serves as a basis for thinking, teaching, and negotiating your way to the best plan that the constraints will allow. With a normal plan for reference, it's easier to make quantified recommendations and it's easier to negotiate better options. The resultant plan, presumably the one with the best mix of options, becomes the *baseline* plan for execution, monitoring, and control.

By the way, don't expect anyone to know what a *normal* plan is until you teach them—it's not in the Project Management Institute's (PMI's) Project Management Body of Knowledge (PMBOK) glossary. Normal is my way of describing a first draft plan focused on simplicity, safety, and effectiveness, within the confines of average conditions. The normal plan's purpose is to help us create a good baseline plan.

Words at Work

The **baseline** plan is the scheduled dates, durations, resources, and costs, that the project will use as a guide to implementation, monitoring, and control.

Secrets of Success

Your ability to estimate durations improves with experience and feedback. Here's an easy way to get better at it: Estimate the durations for the items on your to-do list. Keep track of the results as best you can—you don't have to use a stopwatch—just jot down the tasks, estimated durations, and actual durations. In the art of estimating, practice never makes perfect, but you do get better!

Scheduling One Step at a Time

By now you've probably completed the first step in scheduling, identifying all the essential tasks. In this chapter you'll accomplish the next step, estimating task durations. Next, move to Chapter 7 and create a normal schedule. At that point you'll have a good understanding of the project's issues, options, and likelihood of success.

If the plan is satisfactory, stop planning! Jump to Part 4, set a baseline, and start executing. If the plan reveals problems or issues, plan more! I recommend moving sequentially from Chapter 8 through Chapter 12 when dealing with challenging projects.

Accurate Schedules Are Helpful Schedules

The whole process of building effective schedules depends on good duration estimates. The better you can estimate individual task durations, the more accurately you can answer these important questions:

- How long will the project take?

- When can we be finished?

- When must we begin?

- Is there any flexibility in the schedule?

An accurate schedule helps keep you in control. As problems arise and situations change, you need to know where your plan is flexible and where it isn't. For example, what if specially skilled people needed on your project were busy elsewhere? Should you get alternative resources, delay starting the work, or perhaps change your approach altogether? With an accurate schedule, you can confidently adapt to meet current needs and conditions.

Getting people started on time is one of the project manager's most important roles. With an accurate schedule, you can communicate and enforce scheduled start dates far more effectively. As every project manager knows, if they don't get started on time, they won't get finished on time!

> **Secrets of Success**
>
> Project managers only take corrective action when they have confidence in their baseline plan. With good data they *may* act; with confidence in the data, they *will* act. To enable action, make your schedules as accurate as possible.

Estimating Task Durations

There are six fundamental ways to estimate task durations and, needless to say, none of them are perfect! (That's why they're called estimates.) By using the most appropriate method for your situation, you can dramatically improve your accuracy. And with a little experience, people will begin to wonder where you're hiding your crystal ball!

Using Historical Data

The most accurate and trustworthy data you can use is your own. Experience really is the best teacher. How long did your team take to accomplish a task like this last time? Although no two projects are identical, the similarities in tasks, skill levels, tools, and approaches form a solid base for better estimates. Whenever possible, rely on your own historic data as much as possible.

Secrets of Success

If you are not already collecting historic information, start now. Even if you can't formulate a perfect system, collect what data you can. Capture it even if you don't have time to organize or analyze it now. The next time you face a similar project, you'll be glad you did!

Using References

If you can't use your own history, use someone else's!

In almost every industry you'll find estimating reference works. With a little research, you can find everything from how long it takes to pour a yard of concrete to how many lines of code a programmer can write in a year.

It is important to understand how the reference data was collected and what assumptions were made for its use. Don't assume someone else's methods are representative of your team or situation. Be sure to adjust the data for your team's skill level, working conditions, equipment, and any other factors you can identify.

References are rarely as good as your own data, but they can be helpful.

WAGing It

If you've been around estimating for long, you've probably heard the term *WAG* used in jest—the wildly aimed guess. (You may have heard another explanation for the acronym, as well.) But it goes beyond jest. With no experience, no reference materials, and no clue where to start, a WAG may be all you have! WAG describes any estimate that has little or no grounding in fact. Consequently, our confidence in a WAG is low.

With that said, WAGs may be adequate. Consider a long series of tasks. If you WAGed the duration for each, it stands to reason that

Secrets of Success

Improve duration estimates by breaking large tasks into smaller tasks. For example, break Design Software into several smaller tasks—Interview Users, Review System, Create Schema, Write Specifications, Prototype, and so on. On some projects, you may improve results by using the next smaller unit of measure—minutes rather than hours, hours rather than days, days rather than weeks, or weeks rather than months.

you would rarely hit any one duration exactly right (although you occasionally might get lucky). However, if you added up the total independent estimates, the high estimates are balanced out by the low estimates. The accuracy of the total is therefore much better than the accuracy of any one estimate.

Why not just flip a coin? Well, essentially you are. Pick heads or tails, flip the coin, and see what happens. On any one toss, your call is going to be 100 percent right or 100 percent wrong. The more you flip the coin and WAG the result, the more your actual results will approach the expected 50-50 point.

If you are estimating many individual tasks (20 or more), taken as a group accuracy is typically quite good. Accuracy tends to improve as the number of individual estimates goes up. Statisticians call this the law of large numbers. Nonstatisticians call it the law of averages. In project management, we call it the WAG.

SWAGing It

Add to a WAG one reference point, one similar experience, or one piece of data, and your estimate greatly improves. We describe such an estimate as a SWAG, a scientific wildly aimed guess.

SWAGs are often quite good. You not only have the law of averages working for you, there is also at least one bit of information guiding the estimate. Consequently, SWAGs are generally far better than WAGs.

The moral of the story is simple. Slight improvements in information can make large improvements in accuracy. If you can't use history, use references. If you can't SWAG it, then WAG it.

The last two estimating methods use history, references, WAGs, or SWAGs as their data basis. Let's take a look at how they work.

The Delphi Approach

In Greek mythology, the Delphi oracle was able to see into the future, answering all questions with ease. My guess is that it relied on abilities of query and observation to glean answers from the same people who were asking the questions. Don't all good team leaders? Today adept project managers use the approach when faced with a difficult estimating task.

Start by bringing together an appropriate collection of experts (called a cross-functional team). Ask each expert to independently estimate the duration in question.

Then have each reveal their estimate and reasoning to the group. Then with the benefit of one another's rationale, make another round of estimates.

More Good Stuff

A team member's willingness to accurately estimate task durations dramatically decreases in climates of fear or distrust. New teams are typically less trusting of one another than are mature teams. Therefore, they can't estimate as accurately as mature teams. For better estimates, build a climate of trust and respect. Let your team know that you expect an equal number of high and low estimates. Too many high estimates makes it look like they're padding. Too many low estimates makes it look like they're in over their heads. The goal is to minimize the estimate's variance to actuals. Posting estimates and actuals in the conference room sends a strong message that accuracy counts.

By the second or third round a pattern or consensus is typically revealed. The Delphi approach is part myth, part science, and part statistics. Although it is somewhat time-consuming, a skilled team can provide surprisingly accurate estimates even in complex situations.

Okay, that pretty well covers the superstition and skill methods. I've saved the best for last. Here comes the science and fourth-grade math.

PERT Analysis

PERT analysis uses the power of statistics and probability theory to improve the accuracy of your estimates. But don't be alarmed, it all boils down to fourth-grade math. And better yet, Microsoft Project 2003 does all the math!

Program Evaluation and Review Technique (PERT) was created to help the Navy manage the design and building of its nuclear submarine fleet. At that time, no one had ever powered a submarine with a nuclear reactor. Nor had anyone ever built the submarine's internal systems and then built a hull around it all.

Before this project, submarine hulls were completely assembled, and then all the equipment was squeezed in through small hatches. Reversing this procedure was a radical

Secrets of Success

Accurate task durations enable you to create accurate project schedules. Accurate project schedules reveal hidden resources such as slack (flexibility of starting or finishing a task). Remember, the better you plan, the easier it is to manage the project.

approach. It created a high degree of uncertainty with individual task duration estimates. A better way of dealing with this uncertainty was needed.

To solve this dilemma, the Navy created a cross-functional team. Scientists, shipbuilders, engineers, statisticians, project managers, and others perfected this widely used estimating method we call PERT.

Although it sounds complicated, it really isn't. All you have to do is make three duration estimates for each task: an optimistic, a pessimistic, and a most likely. (Microsoft Project calls this the expected duration.) The optimistic estimate approximates the shortest expected duration over a theoretical 100 trials. It answers the question, what is the fastest this task would be accomplished if it were undertaken 100 times? In a like manner, the pessimistic and most likely durations are estimated.

Notice that the most likely duration is not necessarily a midpoint between the optimistic and pessimistic values. It can and frequently does tend toward either extreme. PERT's weighted average methodology allows for this and returns the duration estimate where the value is midway in likelihood.

For example, consider a task with 12 hours, 32 hours, and 100 hours as the optimistic, most likely, and pessimistic values. PERT weighs the most likely value with four times the probability of either extreme. The PERT estimate = ([Pessimistic + Optimistic + {4•Most likely}])/6. In this case, PERT returns an estimated duration of 40 hours. The PERT estimate is midway in probability (40 hours), not midway in distance (44 hours), between the two extremes (12 and 100 hours). Because of this central tendency and the ability to take into consideration the extreme (although unlikely) possibilities, PERT is your most accurate method of estimating durations. Projects with as few as 20 tasks can benefit from this approach. Overall durations for projects with only a few tasks have too few data points to benefit from the law of averages and can be greatly affected by one or two key tasks. You may still use PERT, just be alert for tasks that wield heavy influence on the schedule.

> **More Good Stuff**
>
> PERT was created to manage high-risk projects with a heavy research and development content. Now that computers manage the probability calculations so easily, PERT duration estimating is favored by many astute project managers even on smaller projects.

The more you're dealing with uncertainties in your project, the more you should consider using PERT. Microsoft Project 2003 makes it fast and easy, as you will soon see.

Entering Task Time Estimates

Before you enter task durations, you should have already decided which tasks are necessary to complete the project. If you haven't done so, enter these tasks now. Make sure that your work breakdown structure is at or near its final format, with indentations clearly showing the work hierarchy. Because indented task durations roll up into the summary tasks, it's best to enter durations after the arrangement of summary phases, tasks, and milestones have been finalized.

More specifically, Project calculates summary task durations as the difference between the earliest start date and the latest finish date of any task within the summary's subsection. Because you have not yet sequenced task workflow, the summary task durations are equal to the longest tasks in their subsections. Notice in Figure 6.1 that the duration for New Product Launch is equal to the longest subordinate element, "Screening Phase" (in this case a summary task), whose duration is set in turn by the longest subordinate task, "Secure Seed Capital." After you've established workflow sequences, the longest sequence of tasks determines summary duration. For complete work breakdown structure instructions, refer to Chapter 5. You'll find complete information on sequencing tasks in Chapter 7.

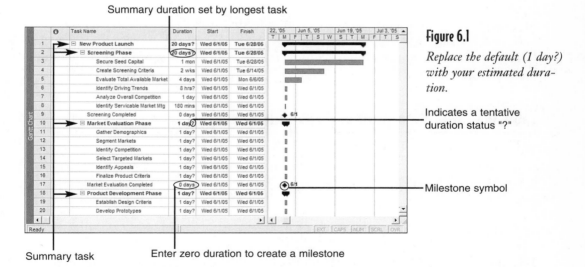

Summary duration set by longest task

Figure 6.1

Replace the default (1 day?) with your estimated duration.

Indicates a tentative duration status "?"

Milestone symbol

Summary task

Enter zero duration to create a milestone

As each task is entered, the duration defaults to "1 day?". The question mark (?) associated with each default duration is Microsoft Project's estimated duration indicator. Its purpose is to facilitate team communications. When seeing this indicator, a team member is supposed to assume that the duration value is tentative—that a final estimate has not yet been established. This can be confusing. Because all durations are "estimated" durations, a better name for this indicator would be the "tentative" estimate. If you choose to use the estimated symbol, avoid confusion with your team members and take the time to describe it as the tentative indicator. The indicator automatically disappears when entering durations.

Setting Milestones

As described in Chapter 5, milestones are managerial points of control that have no duration. These points in time represent completion points. When all the tasks they rely on have been completed, a milestone is reached. In Microsoft Project, a milestone is indicated as a 0 duration event. Placing a 0 in the duration column tells the scheduling engine to treat this as a point in time and to display the default milestone diamond symbol. I find it useful to scan the task list for milestones and place a 0 in their durations before I estimate each task's duration. This helps ensure that there are adequate control points within the plan. It also gets this piece of work out of the way. Review your tasks and enter 0 durations for each milestone before continuing.

Entering a Duration for Each Task

Whether your duration estimates are based on a historical, reference, WAG, SWAG, or Delphi approach, it's easy to enter them into Microsoft Project. From the default Gantt Chart view (and Entry table)as shown in Figure 6.1, replace the default (1 day?) with your estimate. You may use minutes, hours, weeks, or months. Duration units may be indicated as shown in Table 6.1.

Table 6.1   Duration Units and Their Abbreviations

Unit	Abbreviation
minute	m, min, minute, or minutes
hour	h, hr, hrs, hour, or hours
day	d, dy, day, or days
week	w, wk, wks, week, or weeks
month	mo, mon, mons, month, or months

When using day, week, and month as the duration unit, Microsoft assumes each day consists of 8 hours of productive time, each week consists of a 40 hours, and each month has 160 hours. If your organization's normal workdays deviate from this, you can modify working hours by editing the project or resource's calendars. For information on modifying calendars times, see Chapter 8.

After entering the durations, you might realize that additional input would be helpful from a team member. This is an excellent time to use the estimated duration symbol. Place your best guess in the task's duration, double-click along the task, and the Task Information dialog box appears as in Figure 6.2. Select the **General** tab if it isn't already visible, then check **Estimated** in the top-right field. Notice that the duration also displays and the question mark (?) toggles on or off with the check mark (!). After a consensus has been reached on the estimated duration, just enter the final number into the Gantt Chart view and the indicator toggles off.

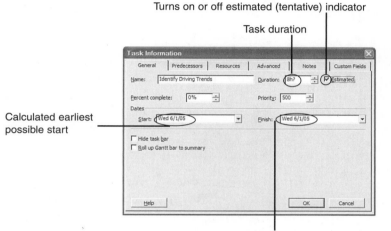

Turns on or off estimated (tentative) indicator

Task duration

Calculated earliest possible start

Calculated earliest possible finish

Figure 6.2

Double-clicking a task reveals the Task Information dialog and everything you need to know about a task.

Using PERT Analysis to Estimate Time

PERT estimates are equally simple to enter into the program. But before you proceed, it is always a good idea to save a copy of your project file. Then, from the **View** menu, point to **Toolbars** and click **PERT Analysis,** as shown in Figure 6.3. Alternatively, you can right-click the toolbar space and check **PERT Analysis** in the pop-up menu.

When the Pert Analysis toolbar appears, click the **PERT Entry Sheet** button on it, as shown in Figure 6.4. For each task, enter an Optimistic, Expected (the most likely), and Pessimistic value. Do not leave any of these three fields blank. The **Tab** key quickly moves you between fields when entering data in the PERT Entry Sheet view. After entering all estimates, save your file again, but with a sequential name. You may want to be able to recover to this point, and Project's undo command won't help here. When you're backed up, click the **Calculate PERT** icon. A warning dialog box appears, reminding you that these calculations will replace all entries in the duration column. If you wanted to use PERT on all but a few durations, you'll have to reenter them after PERT calculations have been made. Click **Yes** to proceed, and the weighted average estimate is calculated and placed into the Duration field.

Figure 6.3

To use PERT calculations, select the **PERT Analysis** *toolbar from the* **View, Toolbars** *menu.*

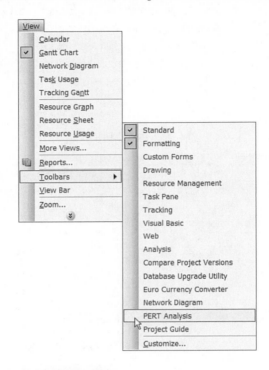

Figure 6.4

The PERT Analysis toolbar has all the functions you need and some that you should avoid.

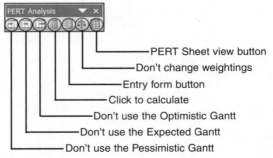

Completed PERT estimates are shown on the PERT Sheet view in Figure 6.5. You'll notice some odd-looking durations. We humans like our estimates rounded off to the nearest full unit; PERT calculations display durations with up to two decimal places. Care to meet me in .01 days (5 minutes) to discuss this further? To deal with possible team communication issues, it's a good idea to edit these durations to a familiar unit before publishing the plan.

A few cautionary tips are appropriate here. Don't use the Optimistic Gantt, Expected Gantt, or Pessimistic Gantt views. Being able to estimate the probability of schedule durations is a powerful tool, but Project doesn't allow for probability factors. These tempting buttons on the PERT Analysis toolbar are grossly misleading. Here's why:

Microsoft Project calculates these three schedules by simply adding up either the pessimistic, or expected, or optimistic durations along the paths (workflow sequences), with no regard to probabilities. On any one task, the likelihood of it actually requiring the pessimistic duration is approximately 1 in 100. In other words, do that same task 100 times and only once would it actually require the pessimistic duration. That's true for every task in your project. Now take three tasks in a workflow sequence (all on the same path). The likelihood that all three tasks will require their pessimistic durations is incredibly low. In round numbers, that's 1 in 100 for each task alone, or taken together, about one in a million—with just a three-task path! Most projects have more than three consecutive tasks. You're more likely to win the lottery than have one of your projects land on any of Microsoft's Optimistic Gantt, Expected Gantt, or Pessimistic Gantt project durations.

If you want to calculate the expected or pessimistic project durations correctly, you must allow for probabilities. The way PERT does this is with the notion of standard deviation. For additional information, download the PERT Analysis Excel spreadsheet from my website listed in Appendix B. You can export the Project data into it and calculate the likelihood of any schedule duration.

There's one item to warn you about on the PERT Analysis toolbar: Don't change anything with the Set PERT Weights button. The PERT formula weightings should not be adjusted unless you are well versed in statistical theory and have a scholarly reason to change them. Personally, I've never seen one! Simply put, these weightings model PERT's basic theory of 1 in 100 probabilities, a well-grounded statistical principle.

Don't let me scare you off. It's not only safe, it's smart to use PERT analysis, just don't touch those buttons! So right now while I have your attention, get rid of them and you'll never have to worry about it. To remove buttons from a toolbar, see Figure 4.11 in Chapter 4.

Alternatively, you may enter the estimates one at a time, using a form, as shown in Figure 6.6. When you click the icon on the PERT Analysis toolbar, the PERT Entry form pops up with the current task's optimistic, expected, and pessimistic values displayed.

Figure 6.5

The PERT Entry Sheet allows you to enter the Optimistic, Pessimistic, and Expected (most likely) durations estimates as in a spreadsheet.

Duration will be calculated

Enter data in these fields

	Task Name	Duration	Optimistic Dur.	Expected Dur.	Pessimistic Dur.
1	⊟ New Product Launch	31.67 days?	25 days	30 days	45 days
2	⊟ Screening Phase	31.67 days?	25 days	30 days	45 days
3	Secure Seed Capital	31.67 days?	25 days	30 days	45 days
4	Create Screening Criteria	13.5 days?	10 days	14 days	15 days
5	Evaluate Total Available Market	5.5 days?	3 days	5 days	10 days
6	Identify Driving Trends	5.5 days?	24 hrs	40 hrs	80 hrs
7	Analyze Overall Competition	1 day?	4 hrs	8 hrs	12 hrs
8	Identify Servicable Market Mtg	1.33 days?	8 hrs	10 hrs	16 hrs
9	Screening Completed	0 days	0 days	0 days	0 days
10	⊟ Market Evaluation Phase	10.33 days?	7 days	10 days	15 days
11	Gather Demographics	9.33 days?	2 days	10 days	14 days
12	Segment Markets	5 days?	3 days	5 days	7 days
13	Identify Competition	10.33 days?	7 days	10 days	15 days
14	Select Targeted Markets	1.33 days?	3 days	0 days	5 days
15	Identify Appeals	0.67 days?	1 day	4 hrs	8 hrs
16	Finalize Product Criteria	0.94 days?	3 hrs	8 hrs	10 hrs
17	Market Evaluation Completed	0 days	0 days	0 days	0 days
18	⊟ Product Development Phase	18 days?	12 days	18 days	24 days
19	Establish Design Criteria	11.83 days?	2 days	12 days	21 days
20	Develop Prototypes	15 days?	2 wks	3 wks	4 wks
21	Select Design Concept	10 days?	5 days	10 days	15 days

Ready

Figure 6.6

The PERT Entry form provides an alternative method of entering duration estimates.

PERT Entry

Name: Create Detailed

Duration: 18 days

Durations

Optimistic: 12 days

Expected: 18 days

Pessimistic: 24 days

OK   Cancel

Understanding Project's View of the Work Week

Before the days of Microsoft Project, project managers would laboriously calculate task and project durations as if every day were a working day. Then as the project was kicked off and a baseline plan was established, the project days were transferred onto the organization's annual calendar. In this way, holidays, workdays, and shifts factored into the schedule. Because the process was so time-consuming and difficult, it was almost impossible to keep a plan up-to-date. Microsoft Project handles all this for you. By default, each day consists of 8 hours, each week is 40 hours, and each month is 20 working days in length. Workdays are Monday through Friday, from 8:00 A.M. to 5:00 P.M. If you need to change these settings to match yours (or if you want to start working 20 hours a week instead of 40), from the **Tools** menu select **Options** and then click the **Calendar** tab (see Figure 6.7). In Chapter 8, I show you how to adjust working calendars for projects, resources, and even tasks.

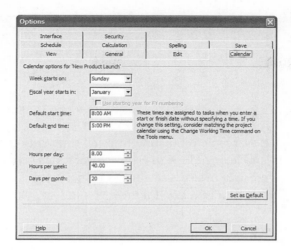

Figure 6.7

Change these default work-day settings to match your standard working days and hours.

Some task durations occur during nonworking time. For example, consider a concrete retaining wall that must cure five days before being backfilled. If it was poured at 3:00 P.M. on a Wednesday, it would be ready for backfilling in five days, Sunday at 3:00 P.M. It's completion is not dependent on the organization's normal work hours. To allow for situations like this, place an **e** at the beginning of the duration unit, for elapsed duration. These notations are shown in Table 6.2.

Table 6.2   Elapsed Duration Units

Unit	Description
emin	elapsed minute
ehr	elapsed hour
eday	elapsed day
ewk	elapsed week

When you enter an elapsed duration, Microsoft Project ignores work calendars, workday settings, weekends, and holidays. Duration is continuous, based on a 24-hour, 7-day week. This is illustrated in Figure 6.8. Notice how the first task requires 3 working days to complete a 24-hour duration. The second task completes the 24-hour elapsed duration in 1 day, from 8 A.M. (the default task start time) to 8 A.M. the next day.

Figure 6.8

Elapsed durations schedule a task to occur on a 24-hour, 7-day week, ignoring standard working hours and holidays.

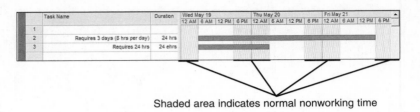

Shaded area indicates normal nonworking time

Congratulations! You've overcome estimating fear and superstition with science, skill, and fourth-grade math and learned how to estimate durations with Microsoft Project! You're almost ready to create a project schedule. The next step is to establish the sequence of work. So when you're ready, I'll meet you in Chapter 7.

The Least You Need to Know

◆ Accurate durations are essential to establish how long the project will take and when it must be started to finish on time.

◆ Accurate durations reveal where your project's schedule is flexible and where it isn't.

◆ Your ability to manage a project successfully increases with the accuracy of your duration estimates.

◆ In projects of 20 or more tasks, PERT estimating is generally the most accurate method.

Chapter 7

Sequencing Tasks to Fit Your Needs

In This Chapter

- ◆ Create a project schedule, with start and finish times for every task, using Microsoft Project 2003

- ◆ Find out how long your project will take to complete

- ◆ Choose the best scheduling strategy to make sure your project is completed on time

- ◆ How to restrict task scheduling with constraining dates

You're plan is about to really take shape. As soon as you sequence the workflow, you'll have a project schedule! You'll know how long the project will take, where the schedule is flexible, and where it isn't. Your understanding of the project is about to go into warp drive!

A Good and Simple Scheduling Approach

As you begin to sequence the tasks, remember that a simple plan that your team can understand will likely be more useful than a complex plan that only you can understand. Scheduling is much like building a model of the project. The more detail you use, the more realistic it becomes. However, detail brings complexity that can prevent users from seeing what's really important.

If you're ever in doubt whether to go for accuracy or readability, remember who will be using your plan. You can always resort to greater levels of detail if you must. For now, to make your plan good, keep it simple.

Project Work Strategies (Your Mother Was Right!)

The project manager's obsession with speed is well founded. If you need to create better, cheaper, or safer project results; or deal with extremely limited resources; the workflow strategies are clear:

Workflow Strategy 1: Faster Is Better

For most organizations, reducing total project duration is always important. We're always in a hurry to get projects started and to get them done. There are some good reasons for this focus with speed: It reduces the time to market with new products and offerings; it improves our competitive posture; it allows faster adaptation when dealing with change; and it creates new revenue streams sooner.

Workflow Strategy 2: Faster Is Cheaper

An improvement in project speed also helps your organization reduce expenses and increase profitability. I'll stay away from the financial talk here, but consider a project team that could complete three projects per year. Each of these projects created revenues for their organization. Each of these projects incurred certain costs. If project duration was reduced by one third on each project, the same team and supporting infrastructure could accomplish four projects a year. They would not only produce one more project's profits, they would also spread the overhead costs of the project team over four projects instead of three. Costs go down, and profits shoot up. (Nonprofits, could deliver more goods or services on the same budget.) Reducing duration by one third frequently increases profitability by two or three times. Faster is not only sooner, it's more profitable!

Workflow Strategy 3: Faster Is Safer

This strategy I attribute to mothers everywhere. With your forbearance, I'll try to explain: Did your mother ever tell you, "Never put off until tomorrow that which can be done today?" I remember the conversation with my Mom, "What's the difference if I clean the garage today or tomorrow? It takes an hour today or an hour tomorrow, it won't save any time." I thought I had her with that logic. Mom didn't hesitate, "Today, you know you have time, tomorrow, something might come up." As usual, Mom was right. It didn't save time, it saved flexibility.

On projects, you never know what might come up. Do everything as soon as you can.

Workflow Strategy 4: Faster Mediates Scarcity

Along the same line of thinking, when adequate resources are available, the determinants of project duration are workflow logic and task durations. When there are resource shortages, project duration can be greatly impacted, even by a singular shortage. For example, if you needed one week for a task and you only had half the required labor resource, streamlining the schedule everywhere else might produce the additional week required to compensate for the scarcity. When you shorten the schedule, you can deal more effectively with the effects of resource scarcities.

Scheduling for Speed

These strategies generate two primary tactics that shorten overall project durations. First, move everything as far forward in the schedule as is possible—that is, as soon as possible (*ASAP*). Second, run as many tasks in parallel as possible (*concurrently*).

For example, consider the project of preparing a pasta dinner. While you wait for the water to a boil, you can prepare the salad (two concurrent tasks). While the pasta cooks in one pan and the sauce simmers in another, and the bread warms in the oven, you can set the table (four concurrent tasks). On the other hand, some tasks need to be done individually, such as chopping the garlic—multitasking can be dangerous!

> **Words at Work**
>
> **ASAP** is the least restrictive of eight date constraints project managers use. It means to literally do the work "as soon as possible." In some organizations usage implies an interruptive urgency. For project teams it is not interruptive, however; it is supportive of legitimate priorities, meaning more like "as soon as priorities permit." All eight constraints are described in Table 7.1 later in this chapter.

Words at Work

Slack, or **float,** is the amount of time a task can move out without causing the project's finish date to be extended. Slack is an indication of flexibility within the schedule, and thereby provides scheduling options. You can think of slack as the project manager's resource, as long as it's hidden—when people know you have slack, they'll likely use it for their own purposes.

Words at Work

The **ES,** or early start, date is the earliest possible date a task or project can begin, as determined by the completion of preceding tasks, deliverables, or authorizations. The **LS,** or late start, date is the latest possible time a task can start and still be completed without forcing the project to finish late. It is, in effect, the true, but hidden deadline on a task or project. Manage late dates starts carefully.

Generally speaking, the more tasks you run concurrently, the more scheduling flexibility (*slack*) you have. Schedule flexibility is a hidden resource. What if the pasta isn't ready when you are? The astute project manager could throw a load of clothes into the washer, help the oldest with his math, and stop the twins from fighting.

Most of the benefits of well-crafted schedules have been covered, but there's one more that deserves your attention because people procrastinate. We think in terms of deadlines, and while we're juggling dozens of responsibilities and tasks, we're constantly prioritizing our work based on when we have to have it done—the later the deadline, the lower we set the priority.

Obviously, scheduling tasks earlier tends to raise the priority listing, but there's a more important concept: You can't manage the finish without managing the start.

Perhaps the single best reason to understand your project's workflow is to identify and assertively manage the earliest possible start (*ES*) and the latest possible start (*LS*) for every task in the project. When early start dates are honored and late start dates are not violated, your project is on a successful track. To keep your project in a normal state of forwardness, manage start dates assertively.

Project management techniques aren't just for the large projects anymore. Now even on small projects, crafting finely tuned schedules makes sense. Your Mom was right.

The Vocabulary of Modeling Workflow

With just five terms and four relationships, project managers can quickly and effectively model the workflow of any project, no matter how complex it may be. Moreover, they easily communicate workflow to anyone who shares this vocabulary. The key to the system is a common reference point. Let me explain.

Think of yourself as standing on a task, call it the *dependent task*, and from that vantage point describing what comes before and what comes after. It's intuitive and effective. From that vantage point, there are only two workflow sequence possibilities: those tasks that immediately precede (the *predecessor* tasks), and those tasks that immediately follow (the *successor* tasks). Figure 7.1 displays their relationships in a block diagram.

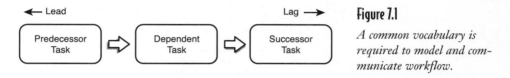

Figure 7.1

A common vocabulary is required to model and communicate workflow.

The other two terms are used to describe the integral of time between tasks. Again, from the dependent task's point of view, predecessors given a head start (moved forward in time) are described as having *lead time*. Conversely, the amount of time a successor waits before starting is known as *lag time*. Lead and lag are often confused. So in Microsoft Project, if you ever want to move a task left or right on the timeline in relation to the dependent task, and it moves the wrong way, just put a minus sign in front of the integer and try again.

To have a full set of workflow modeling tools, all that's left are the four types of relationships: *FS, SS, FF,* and *SF.* I know you've already got this project management abbreviation thing down, but here are the deciphered versions: finish to start, start to start, finish to finish, and start to finish. Each of these is a description of how the dependent task is related to its predecessor task. Hopefully, this is intuitive by now; the question every in-a-hurry-to-get-it-done project manager constantly asks is: "Can I start this now? If not, what must precede it? What has to finish before this task can start?" That question brings us to the most common and intuitive workflow relationship model, the FS.

Finish-to-Start Dependencies

When a task can't begin until another task ends, the workflow has a finish-to-start (FS) dependency. Recalling the earlier example, you can't start the pasta sauce until you've chopped the garlic. The task that affects the dependent task, the *predecessor,* must finish before the dependent task can begin.

Even simple dependencies are restrictive. The fewer dependencies you have in your schedule, the fewer chances you'll have of encountering work stoppages and bottlenecks; more tasks can run in parallel; your project will finish sooner. The last two tasks in Figure 7.2 have finish-to-start dependencies with their predecessor tasks. The sequence of work and the amount of time required to complete the project is largely determined by task-dependency relationships.

Figure 7.2

Project duration and schedule flexibility depends on task durations and dependencies.

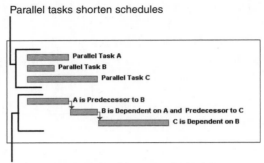

Parallel tasks shorten schedules

Finish-to-start relationships extend schedules

Modeling Workflow with Project 2003

Just as we'd prefer, Microsoft Project schedules everything as soon as possible unless you tell it otherwise. With that in mind, let's use it to build a simple workflow model.

Start Project 2003 and make sure the default Gantt Chart view is showing. Drag the vertical divider to the right until the Duration, Predecessor, Start, and Finish columns are visible. Type in a few tasks to work with and enter their durations. Don't get too fancy here; you just need something to work with.

A quick and easy way to enter workflow relationships is to type the predecessor's identification number (ID) into the dependent task's Predecessor column.

Begin at the top of your task list and consider what task must immediately precede the current task. If there are none, leave the column blank. Place the predecessor's ID number into the Predecessor field. If more than one predecessor must *immediately* precede this task, separate their ID numbers with a comma.

In a flash, Project's scheduling engine recalculates the ES and EF (which appear in this table as the Start and Finish), as well as the LS and LF (which are available in other views), and redraws the Gantt chart (see Figures 7.3 and 7.4).

Early Start date   Early Finish date

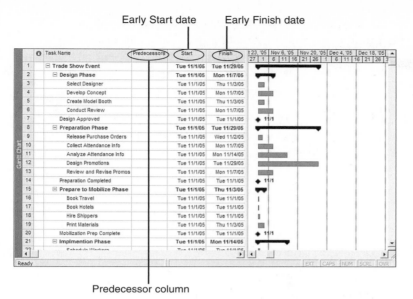

Predecessor column

Figure 7.3

Enter each task's predecessor ID into the Predecessor column to model workflow dependencies. The Duration column is not shown in the illustration to conserve workspace.

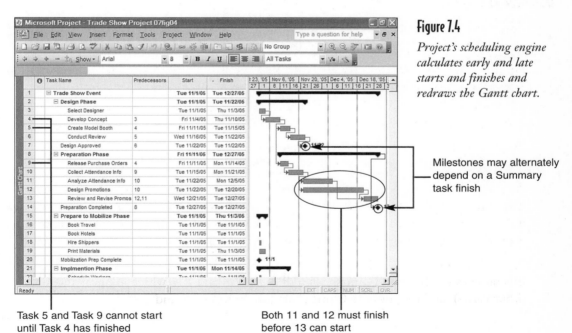

Task 5 and Task 9 cannot start until Task 4 has finished

Both 11 and 12 must finish before 13 can start

Milestones may alternately depend on a Summary task finish

Figure 7.4

Project's scheduling engine calculates early and late starts and finishes and redraws the Gantt chart.

As the Gantt chart begins to take shape, relationships that weren't obvious become easier to see and understand. It's simple to modify the relationships if you need to. This makes it easy to investigate how different approaches can reduce project duration or create more slack (flexibility). We'll talk more about that in Chapter 11.

If you used to create schedules with an eraser in one hand and a pencil in the other, you'll love Project! What used to take days to analyze, calculate, and draw now takes seconds. The net result, besides keeping guys like me entertained, is that it's easy to apply the benefits of scheduling, even to small projects.

Now's the time to go with the (work) flow! Let's check out other ways to enter dependencies into Project 2003.

Dependencies on the Gantt chart are shown with an arrow between each task by default. If your chart doesn't show the dependency links, choose **Format** and then **Layout** from the menu bar. Select from the options as shown in Figure 7.5.

Figure 7.5

Modify the format of dependency links in the Layout dialog box.

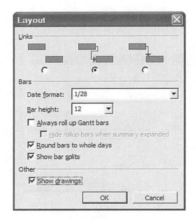

You may also link tasks by clicking the predecessor taskbar and dragging a link to the dependent task. An easy way to remember which direction to click and drag is with these first letters: link *F*rom the *F*inish to the start. A window pops up to ensure the results are what you want, as shown in Figure 7.6. When you release the mouse button, the dependent task jumps to its new location. This process can be somewhat confusing. It's easy to accidentally click a taskbar and move it left or right in time. This changes the start and finish dates and prevents the scheduling engine from calculating them. In other words, it really messes up your schedule! Just make sure the link curser appears before dragging and you'll be alright.

If you see a calendar-like icon appear in the Information column of a task, you've accidentally set a constraint and it should be removed before proceeding. You can learn more about setting constraints and removing them later in this chapter.

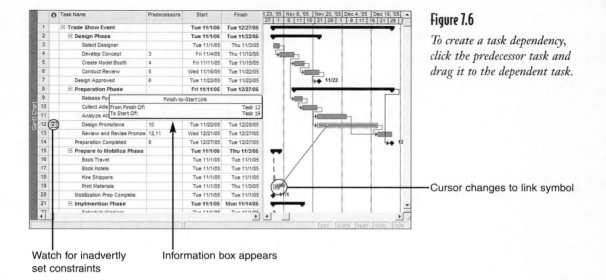

Figure 7.6

To create a task dependency, click the predecessor task and drag it to the dependent task.

Watch for inadvertly set constraints

Information box appears

Cursor changes to link symbol

There's another way to enter task dependencies when working with large projects, where the dependent or predecessor tasks may be out of view. In this situation, double-click anywhere on the task in the Entry table to access the Task Information dialog box. Then open the **Predecessor** tab, click the right edge of an empty field in the **Task Name** column, click the pull-down list, and choose the predecessor from the list of task names. Click **OK** and check the results in the Gantt chart.

Dependent task

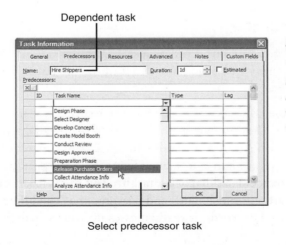

Figure 7.7

The Task Information dialog box is an easy way to set dependencies on large projects when the predecessor is out of view.

Select predecessor task

As soon as you have entered all necessary task dependencies, your schedule is complete. Be sure to review it for workflow, overall project duration, and possible work bottlenecks. As you examine the schedule, pause the cursor over any link, task, milestone, or summary task and an information box similar to the one in Figure 7.8 appears.

Figure 7.8

Hovering over any chart feature pops open an information box.

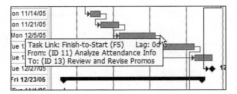

The person who coined the phrase "A picture is worth a thousand words" must have been a project manager! Our understanding of the project dramatically increases as the work sequence is shown in a time-phased diagram—in this case, a Gantt chart. Chances are you'll want to make a few adjustments in your schedule. If you must, you can tune it up with the following tactics.

When Simple Scheduling Isn't Good Enough

Not all relationships can be adequately represented with FS dependencies. You may need to use other relationships to get the schedule you want. These include the SS, SF, and FF task relationships. All of these describe special kinds of parallel task relationships, as you shall see.

Start-to-Start Dependencies

Consider the project of building a high-speed commuter rail line between two cities. Using an FS dependency, you would have to wait for the entire roadbed to be finished before placing the first tie!

It would obviously be better to give the crew preparing the roadbed a head start on the tie-placing crew. Then as soon as the tie crew had a head start, the rail placing crew could begin. Roadbed, ties, and rails should all run concurrently, with a slight staggering of the starts. This type of dependency is a SS dependency with a time lag. The start of the dependent task lags behind the start of the predecessor task, as shown in Figure 7.9.

To speed the completion even more, you might decide to build the line from both ends at once. The east and west construction teams could then work in parallel on the converging lines. (Okay, so I had to sneak a geometry pun in there. You still get the point, right?)

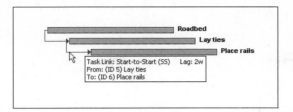

Figure 7.9

When using an SS dependency, adjust when the dependent task will begin with lag time.

Finish-to-Finish Dependencies

In the FF relationship, the dependent task can't finish until the predecessor task finishes. This sounds like a classic case of, "Which came first, the chicken or the egg?" It's easier to understand using the example of scrambling a dozen eggs. You can't finish scrambling the eggs until you have finished cracking them and putting them in the pan. If you used a standard FS and cracked all the eggs before you began scrambling, you'd risk burning the first few eggs. Okay, so you don't like to cook. Consider the project tasks in Figure 7.10. A new fiber-optic cable has been installed in a building. The project manager knew they could begin testing two weeks after the installation begins. However, the finish of testing is dependent on when installation finishes.

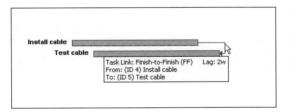

Figure 7.10

Finish-to-finish dependencies are useful in some situations. Use lag to offset the scheduled finish.

Start-to-Finish Dependencies

Another occasionally helpful dependency is the SF dependency. This is when the dependent task can't finish until its predecessor has at least started.

Consider the project of installing new equipment on several assembly lines. Training the operators could not be completed until the predecessor task—install new equipment—has at least been started. The operators need at least one machine to train on. This is illustrated in Figure 7.11.

Figure 7.11

Start-to-finish tasks are rare, but great when you need them. Use lag time to vary task overlap.

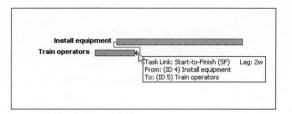

Entering SS, FF, and SF Dependencies

To use any of the dependencies except the FS, you must specify the type of dependency and any lead or lag required. Project 2003 keeps it simple and intuitive. In the Predecessor column of the Gantt chart Entry table (or in the Task Information dialog box in the Predecessor tab), type in **SS, SF,** or **FF.** You could type in an **FS,** but Project assumes all relationships are finish to start unless otherwise indicated. To add lead or lag time, simply enter a positive or negative number next to the dependency type. Lag time can be entered in duration time units or as a percentage. Watch the Gantt chart to make sure you get the effect you want. Figure 7.12 shows a few of the endless modeling combinations you can create.

Figure 7.12

When entering SS, FS, or SF dependencies, watch the Gantt chart carefully to ensure the results are what you want.

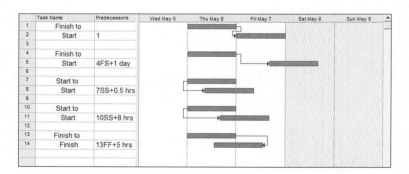

In addition to setting task dependencies, Microsoft Project handles all eight date-constraint types with ease. These are described next.

Restricting Workflow Logic with Constraining Dates

Suppose you don't want to allow Project to schedule work based strictly on workflow logic. You can also force the scheduling engine to restrict options according to the eight standard project management date types.

These eight constraints are shown in Table 7.1. All of these, except As Soon As Possible (ASAP) and As Late As Possible (ALAP), severely restrict the schedule's flexibility.

Table 7.1   Using Constraints to Restrict the Schedule

Constraint	Description
ASAP (As Soon As Possible)	This is the default constraint for projects scheduled from a start date. The schedule remains as flexible as possible.
ALAP (As Late As Possible)	This is the default constraint for projects scheduled from a finish date. The schedule remains as flexible as possible.
FNLT (Finish No Later Than)	Use for tasks that must finish on or before a date. Useful for including contractual obligations into a schedule. Automatically used when a finish date is typed in for a task in projects scheduled from a finish date.
SNLT (Start No Later Than)	Used to schedule tasks around a latest possible start date. Automatically used when a start date is typed in for a task in projects scheduled from a finish date.
FNET (Finish No Earlier Than)	Used for tasks that must not be finished any earlier than a certain date. Automatically applied on projects scheduled from a starting date when a finish date is typed in.
SNET (Start No Earlier Than)	Prevents a task from beginning before a certain date. Automatically set when a task start date is entered on projects scheduled from a project start date.
MSO (Must Start On)	Restricts the task to a single starting date regardless of dependencies.
MFO (Must Finish On)	Restricts a task to being completed on a specific date.

Don't anchor tasks with constraints unless you must. Carefully consider which is most appropriate. Then, as shown in Figure 7.13, double-click any task in the Task Information dialog box and choose the **Advanced** tab. Select the constraint from the pull-down menu. Enter the date in the Constraint date box. A small calendar icon in the Indicator column shows that a constraint is set.

Figure 7.13

Always use task constraints carefully and sparingly. Keep your schedule as flexible as possible.

Hover cursor over icon for detail   Enter the anchoring date

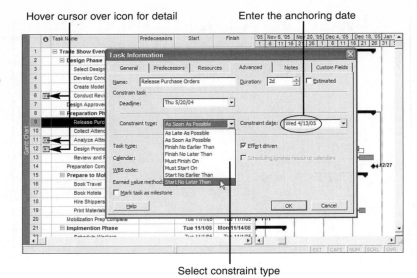

Select constraint type

To make the project easier to manage and more likely to be successful, follow your mother's and my advice:

- Start everything as soon as you can.
- Keep workflow logic as simple as possible.
- Use constraints carefully, and only if you must.
- Create flexible plans.
- To make a good schedule, make it good and simple!

The Least You Need to Know

- Shorter schedules can improve profitability, competitiveness, and reduce problems of resource scarcity.
- Good schedules allow managers to focus on managing start dates rather than deadlines.
- Parallel tasks help to shorten project duration.
- Creating schedules helps project managers understand the nuances and intricacies of projects and improves their ability to communicate, coordinate, and control.
- Experienced project managers try to maintain as much schedule flexibility as possible.

Chapter 8

Setting Up Resources, Costs, and Calendars

In This Chapter

- ◆ Create a resource list of people, equipment, facilities, and material
- ◆ Customize calendars for your project and resources
- ◆ Create resource groups to speed reporting and tracking
- ◆ Set pay rates, costs, and availability for each resource

You can't do it alone! It takes people, equipment, and material to accomplish any significant project. And the larger the project, the harder it is to effectively coordinate and control all these resources. Microsoft Project 2003 offers many powerful features that can help.

Before you can manage resources with Microsoft Project 2003, it needs to know what resources are available, when they work, and how much they cost. You'll set up your resources in this chapter. Later, in Chapter 9, you'll assign resources to the project tasks.

The Benefits of Tracking Resources

Setting and tracking resources in your project enables you to accomplish several important things:

◆ You can schedule according to resource availability, in addition to work sequence and task duration.

◆ You can identify work bottlenecks caused by resource limitations.

◆ You can budget and track costs of the entire project, each task, and each resource.

◆ You can distribute workloads fairly throughout a team.

Don't try to control too many cost details in Microsoft Project 2003. It's primarily a scheduling system, not an estimating, bill-of-material, or cost-control program. For these tasks, you will discover that attaching spreadsheets is frequently more convenient and effective. For additional information, see Chapter 21.

There's one other precaution Project 2003 users need to be aware of regarding resource costs. Make sure that you're operating within the guidelines set forth by your organization's financial policies and procedures. No matter what your official job title might be, as a project manager you may have a fiduciary responsibility concerning the funding for your project. Project 2003 is great at creating a schedule and managing resource interrelations, but it isn't an accounting system and it doesn't adhere to generally accepted accounting principles.

Defining Resources and Costs

The first step in setting up your resource list is to decide how much detail is best for your project. You may want to enter each member of your team by his or her name. You could alternately enter each of the job titles, such as Programmer I, Senior Analyst, Electrician, or Apprentice Electrician. Whenever possible, opt for the least-restrictive choice. Remember that unneeded precision places a heavy burden on you and doesn't necessarily improve your control.

There are four types of project resources: people, facilities, equipment, and materials. People, facilities, and equipment have similar parameters, so Microsoft Project combines them into a category called *work resources*. Here you would find such items as scientists, carpenters, laboratories, air compressors, and electron microscopes. In the *material resources* category, you would find all the consumable goods. These might include concrete, nails, chip sets, and gallium arsenide wafers (or in my case, iced mochas and pistachios).

Creating a Basic Resource List

To create a resource list, select **Resource Sheet** from the **View** menu. Then point to **Table** (also in the View menu) and click **Entry,** as shown in Figure 8.1. Alternately, you can access the Resource Sheet view from the **View** bar by clicking **Resource Sheet.** The table that appears will be the last one accessed, so select the Entry table if necessary. Figure 8.2 shows an example resource sheet. Notice that many fields have pull-down menus to make data entry fast and easy. Each of the columns of the resource sheet is described in Table 8.1.

Words at Work

In Microsoft Project, **work resources** are sometimes confused with **material resources.** Work resources include people, machinery, tools, meeting rooms, and production facilities. The value work resources provide is time based, such as an hour of labor or use of the meeting room for an hour. Material resources include raw materials, subassemblies, paper clips, and blank CDs. The value material resources provide is consumption based.

Figure 8.1

To set up or modify resource information, check Resource Sheet and select the Entry table from the View menu.

Figure 8.2

The resource sheet provides a spreadsheet-like table for easy data entry.

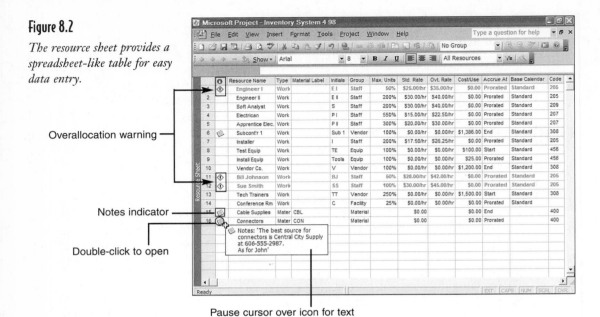

Overallocation warning

Notes indicator

Double-click to open

Pause cursor over icon for text

Words at Work

When a resource does not have sufficient capacity to do the scheduled work within the duration allowed, the resource is described as **overallocated**.

Watch the indicator column for additional information. For example, a warning icon appears when a resource is *overallocated*. This one is hard to miss: A yellow diamond with a red exclamation mark appears in the indicator column and the entire line of text turns red. (It can be embarrassing when you realize that you've scheduled 27 hours of work for one person in one day). For more information on dealing with resource overallocations, see Chapter 12.

Another useful icon looks like a notepad. Hovering over it with the cursor displays the first few lines contained in the note section of the Resource Information dialog box. You can even link or embed spreadsheets, documents, pictures, and other items there, and the icon keeps you aware that the note section has contents. This is a great place to link quotes, bill-of-material listings, contracts, and any other resource specifics you'll want easy access to. For more information about linking or embedding information into Microsoft Project, see Chapter 21.

Table 8.1—Resource Sheet Columns

Column	Description
Indicator	Column used to alert you to special information. A note icon indicates additional comments are available in the resource dialog box. These may include spreadsheets, pictures, documents, or other items associated with this resource. Resource overallocations are indicated here with a caution sign icon.
Resource Name	Text or numbers used to identify the resource. The name should be distinct from all other resource names. For example, the name may be an individual (such as Bill Smith), a type of resource (electrician), a job title (senior analyst), a department (accounting), or a vendor (Good and Fast Company).
Type	Select either work or material as the type of resource to allow Microsoft Project to correctly calculate costs and usage. (For example, if the type of resource is material, Project ignores calendar restrictions because material items are theoretically always available.)
Material Label	For material items, enter the unit of measure for costing, such as each, foot, meter, ton, cubic yard, kilogram, and so on.
Initials	Add or edit the initials to provide a space-saving name for use on Gantt charts.
Group	Enter a group name to allow filtering and reporting by groups. The resource may be added to more than one group by separating each group name with a comma.
Max. Units	Enter a percentage to indicate how much of this resource is available for the project. The default is 100 percent, but it may range from 0 percent to 6,000,000,000 percent. One full-time programmer would be indicated with 100 percent. If the programmer is only available for this project one quarter of her time, enter 25 percent. Five full-time available programmers are shown as 500 percent.
Std. rate	This is the cost per unit of the resource. The default work unit is per hour (h), but year (y), week (w), day (d), or minute (m) may also be used. Simply type in the rate, a forward slash, and then the unit abbreviation. For example, 45,000/y ($45,000 per year) or 1,500/d ($1500 per day).

continues

Table 8.1–Resource Sheet Columns (continued)

Column	Description
	Microsoft Project converts all amounts to an hourly rate for calculations, using a 52-week year and 40-hour week. These defaults may be changed in the Options dialog box.
Ovt. Rate	Enter the overtime rate for the resource in this column. If left zero, no charges will accrue for overtime work. Be careful! This may (or may not) be appropriate for salaried employees who are not paid overtime.
Cost/Use	This is a one-time charge for the resource. It may be used in addition to the standard rate and overtime rate. It accrues each time a work resource is used and only once when assigned to material resources.
Accrue At	This selection enables you to change when the program charges the resource to the task. The default is prorated, so the cost is accrued on a percentage of completion basis. You may also select **Start** if, for example, a vendor must be paid upon arrival. Select **End** if the vendor will be paid upon completion.
Base Calendar	There are three default base calendars in Microsoft Project: Standard, Night, and 24 hours. You may set up other base calendars if your project uses other work shifts.
Code	You may place any text or numbers in this column. A frequent use is to enter accounting codes for integration with other applications.

Another way to add new resources is to add them from the Gantt Chart Entry Table view. This trick is especially useful when you are assigning resources to tasks (see Chapter 9) and you realize the resource you need is not yet listed on the resource sheet. Simply enter the new resource in the task's Resource Name column, as shown in Figure 8.3. Be sure to go back to the resource sheet to enter complete resource costs and availability information.

If you have more than one project that uses the same resources, they don't have to be entered all over again. Instead, you can share them with a resource pool. To learn more about resource pools, go to Chapter 18.

		Task Name	Duration	Start	Finish	Pred	Resource Names
1		⊟ Transpod Project	1 day?	Fri 5/21/04	Fri 5/21/04		
2		Gather Research	1 day?	Fri 5/21/04	Fri 5/21/04		Ian Weaver
3		Compile Data	1 day?	Fri 5/21/04	Fri 5/21/04		Naomi Singh
4		Analyze Results	1 day?	Fri 5/21/04	Fri 5/21/04		Parker
5		Evalute Options	1 day?	Fri 5/21/04	Fri 5/21/04		

Figure 8.3

Resource names can be entered into the project from the Gantt Chart Entry Table view by typing them into the Resource column.

Add Tailoring Detail to Your Resources

Resources may be customized in several ways in the Resource Information box. To open the dialog box from the Resource Sheet view, you may either double-click a resource row or right-click and select **Resource Information** from a pop-up menu. Figure 8.4 shows the Notes section, Figure 8.5 is the General section, Figure 8.6 is Costs. The Working Time tab is shown later in this chapter in Figure 8.11.

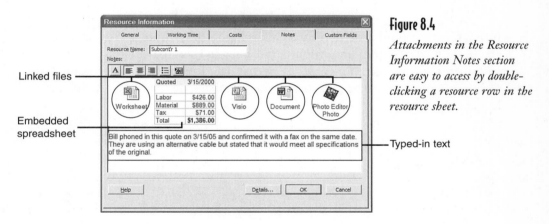

Figure 8.4

Attachments in the Resource Information Notes section are easy to access by double-clicking a resource row in the resource sheet.

In the General section, you can enter an e-mail address for the resource, or you can select one from your e-mail address book by clicking **Details.** (Your e-mail client must be compliant with Microsoft standards.) When the contact exists in your address book, all detailed contact information no more than a few clicks away! To learn how to send e-mail messages from within Microsoft Project, see Chapter 20.

To modify when and to what extent a resource is available for scheduling, edit the Resource Availability table. If, for example, a part time employee were going to work full time at a certain date, you could enter the appropriate dates and percentage of availability in this table. All other fields on the General form are accessible in the Sheet view.

Enter e-mail information

Figure 8.5

The General section of the Resource Information box is where you'll find or modify e-mail and resource availability information.

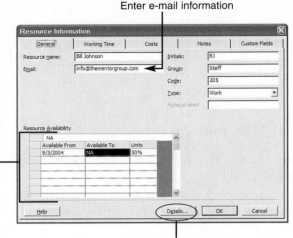

Limit dates and percentage of availability

Access contact information in address book

In the Costs section of the Resource Information box, future rates can be set for resources. For example, an upcoming rate change could be entered and Project would automatically begin accruing costs from that date forward at the new rates. Tabs B through E allow for other rate structures and are applied from the Assignment Information box.

Figure 8.6

Future costs changes may be entered under the Costs tab in the Resource Information dialog box.

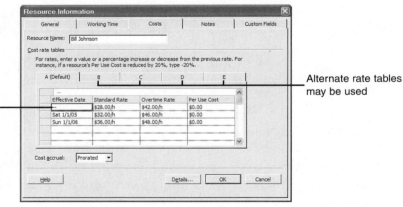

Enter the date the new rate takes effect

Alternate rate tables may be used

Adding Fixed Costs to Tasks

Another method of adding costs to your project is by adding a fixed cost directly to a task. These costs are one-time charges, and are not dependent on changes in work durations. Fixed costs may be used in addition to the resource costs. The two types of costs are added together to calculate the total cost for each task.

As shown in Figure 8.7, to enter a fixed cost, on the **View** menu click **Gantt Chart.** Again on the **View** menu, point to **Table** and click **Cost.** Select the task for which you want to set a fixed cost, and type a cost value in the Fixed Cost field. Use the Fixed Cost Accrual field to control whether costs will be realized at the beginning or end of the task, or prorated throughout its duration.

Enter one-time cost   Select accrual method

	Task Name	Fixed Cost	Fixed Cost Accrual	Total Cost	Baseline	Variance	Actual	Remaining	May 2005
1	⊟ Inventory System	$0.00	Prorated	$38,290.00	$0.00	$38,290.00	$0.00	$38,290.00	
2	⊟ Design Phase	$0.00	Prorated	$22,950.00	$0.00	$22,950.00	$0.00	$22,950.00	
3	Do needs assessment	$12,500.00	End	$12,980.00	$0.00	$12,980.00	$0.00	$12,980.00	Sue Smith
4	Write specifications	$0.00	Prorated	$1,280.00	$0.00	$1,280.00	$0.00	$1,280.00	Bill Jo
5	Create prototype	$5,000.00	Prorated	$6,880.00	$0.00	$6,880.00	$0.00	$6,880.00	
6	Conduct user's review	$1,500.00	Start	$1,810.00	$0.00	$1,810.00	$0.00	$1,810.00	
7	Design approved	$0.00	Prorated	$0.00	$0.00	$0.00	$0.00	$0.00	
8	⊟ Writing Phase	$0.00	Prorated	$15,340.00	$0.00	$15,340.00	$0.00	$15,340.00	
9	Purchase software	$2,700.00	Start	$2,700.00	$0.00	$2,700.00	$0.00	$2,700.00	
10	Create database	$0.00	Prorated	$1,000.00	$0.00	$1,000.00	$0.00	$1,000.00	
11	Write reports	$0.00	Prorated	$2,400.00	$0.00	$2,400.00	$0.00	$2,400.00	
12	Write programs	$0.00	Prorated	$9,240.00	$0.00	$9,240.00	$0.00	$9,240.00	
13	Test and debug	$0.00	Prorated	$0.00	$0.00	$0.00	$0.00	$0.00	
14	Writing complete	$0.00	Prorated	$0.00	$0.00	$0.00	$0.00	$0.00	
15	⊟ Document Phase	$0.00	Prorated	$0.00	$0.00	$0.00	$0.00	$0.00	
16	List code	$0.00	Prorated	$0.00	$0.00	$0.00	$0.00	$0.00	
17	Write help files	$0.00	Prorated	$0.00	$0.00	$0.00	$0.00	$0.00	
18	Get screen shots	$0.00	Prorated	$0.00	$0.00	$0.00	$0.00	$0.00	
19	Print documentation	$0.00	Prorated	$0.00	$0.00	$0.00	$0.00	$0.00	
20	Documentation comple	$0.00	Prorated	$0.00	$0.00	$0.00	$0.00	$0.00	
21	⊟ Training Phase	$0.00	Prorated	$0.00	$0.00	$0.00	$0.00	$0.00	
22	Identify audience	$0.00	Prorated	$0.00	$0.00	$0.00	$0.00	$0.00	

Figure 8.7

Enter one-time charges, sub-contracts, or any other fixed cost for a task in the Cost Table view of the Gantt chart.

Creating Calendars for Your Project (or a Vacation)

Creating a project plan and scheduling tasks, resources, and costs requires a robust understanding of when each item is needed and available. Microsoft Project solves this problem by building several calendars into the program. These include standard calendars, base calendars, project calendars, resource calendars, and task calendars. Fortunately, you don't have to find space on your office walls for all these calendars! They're really simple after you get the hang of it. Just think of them in terms of a work calendar hierarchy. The resource calendar is based on a project calendar, which is based on a base calendar, which is based on a standard calendar. Got it? Let's take a closer look.

The standard calendar is just that, a standard annual calendar without holidays. It includes all the days of the year and all the working hours set up in three different work schedules: a standard day shift, a night shift, and a 24-hour continuous schedule.

Of the three calendars that come with Microsoft Project, the standard day shift calendar is most frequently used. It consists of an eight-hour day (8 A.M. to 5 P.M.),

Monday through Friday work schedule. The night shift calendar is an eight-hour (11 P.M. to 8 A.M.), Monday through Friday work schedule. And the last one is a 24 hours a day, 365 days a year calendar. (This one is typically used for equipment, machines, robots, and people who need to learn how to negotiate better with their boss.)

No holidays are preset in any of these three calendars. You may add holidays or other nonworking times (such as plant shutdown periods) to each of these. If none of these calendars describes your normal working hours, create a new one by copying the most similar, as shown in Figure 8.8, and editing it as shown in Figure 8.9. From the **Tools** menu, select **Change Working Time,** and then click **New** on the Change Working Time dialog box.

Select each day you want to modify (such as national holidays or your birthday). Then click either **Nonworking time** or **Nondefault working time** to edit the day. To revert back to the original, click **Use Default.** To edit all days of the week, click each weekday column heading while pressing **Control.**

Figure 8.8

Create a new calendar by copying and editing any calendar.

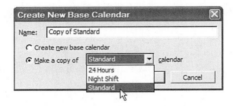

Figure 8.9

Edit the new calendar's working days and hours to match your requirements.

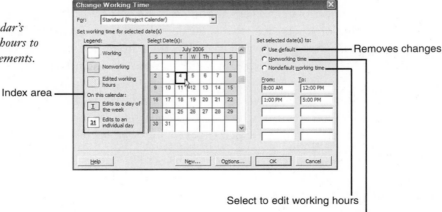

It's easy to use any calendar as your project's base calendar (to make sure the company doesn't work on your birthday). First, select **Project Information** from the **Project** menu. Then click the **Calendar** option in the Project Information dialog box, as shown in Figure 8.10, and select a base calendar for your project.

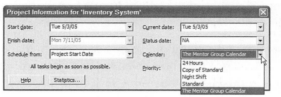

Figure 8.10

Select a base calendar for your project.

Controlling Resource Availability with Calendars

Good job! Now that your project is running on your company's base calendar, you're ready to look at each of your resource's availability. In the Resource Sheet table, select the appropriate calendar from the pull-down menu in each resource's Base Calendar field. Figure 8.11 shows an example.

If the selected base calendar doesn't perfectly match the resource's availability, customize each resource's calendar. For example, if resource Sue Smith is going on vacation during the project, modify her calendar to prevent Microsoft Project from scheduling her during that time. To keep Sue happy, open the Resource Information box, click the **Working Time** tab, and make your adjustments as shown in Figure 8.11.

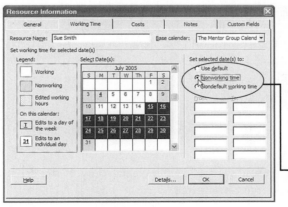

Figure 8.11

To change a resource's availability, select the closest fitting calendar from the Working Time tab in the Resource Information dialog box, and then edit as required.

A resource's vacation period has been set as nonworking time.

Controlling Work on Task Calendars

Although it is not frequently used, there is one other calendar you should be aware of: the task calendar. Occasionally you may need to limit when a task can be undertaken. For example, if you are upgrading equipment on an assembly line, it's important not to impact normal operations. You can limit when Microsoft Project 2003 schedules work on these machines.

You can assign any base calendar to a task. In this case, the night shift calendar is appropriate. Otherwise, create a new base calendar, and then from the Gantt Chart view select the task and right-click to open the Task Information dialog box. As shown in Figure 8.12, select the **Advanced** tab and choose a calendar from the pulldown list. Checking the **Scheduling ignores resource calendars** box will override any resource availability restrictions.

Figure 8.12

Assigning a calendar to a task restricts when work may take place.

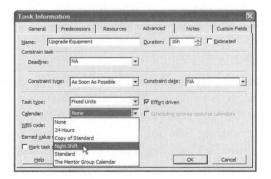

Congratulations! You've just given Microsoft Project 2003 all the cost and calendar information it needs to schedule resources and track costs. And if you were clever about it, you won't have to work on your next birthday! (There has to be some benefit in being a project manager, doesn't there?)

The Least You Need to Know

- ◆ The project's base calendar sets working and nonworking times for the entire project.

- ◆ Individual work resources are available according to the calendar selected for them in the Resource Sheet table.

- ◆ Calendars are easily adjusted to match working and nonworking times of the organization, project, or individual resource.

- ◆ Costs for people, equipment, facilities, materials, and supplies may be entered and tracked in Microsoft Project 2003.

The Resourceful Use of Resources

In This Chapter

- ◆ Assign one or more resources, full or part time, to each task

- ◆ Balance workloads and responsibilities throughout the team

- ◆ Identify where resources are over- and underallocated

- ◆ Make the best use of your limited resources

How long a project takes to complete and the results it ultimately achieves are largely dependent on the quality and quantity of the resources used on the project. Better trained, more experienced people turn out better work. Better materials, equipment, and supplies facilitate better results.

But as you well know, project managers don't always get the quantity or quality of resources they want. The good news is, you're not the first one to face this dilemma. Project managers who came before you developed sound principles of resource usage and control. We call this process *resource loading* (assigning resources to tasks) and *leveling* (optimizing resource utilization).

Words at Work

Resource loading is the activity of applying resources to the project tasks. The term is also used to describe the quantity and type of resources required to meet the project's schedule requirements. **Resource leveling** describes the process of redistributing resources or work to maximize the efficient use of resources committed to the project.

In this chapter, you'll learn how Microsoft Project 2003 brings the power of loading and leveling to your project.

Resource Allocation: Loading

Whereas creating the work schedule is relatively straightforward—tasks, dependencies, and durations are identified and integrated—loading the project with human resources is anything but straightforward. Varying skill levels, personalities, attitudes, and motivations can turn a theoretically simple process into a project management conundrum. Would you choose the skilled worker with a poor attitude or the motivated rookie, an overworked single parent or an overworked single, an untested newcomer or a slow but steady performer? The art and science of project management becomes more art than science when dealing with human resources. Before assigning resources, consider the tasks from these points of view:

- How important is quality in this task? How good is good enough? At what point should it be considered fit for purpose?

- How critical is time in this task? Is there slack in its scheduled completion or will a delay impact the project's finish?

- Does overall project workflow depend on this task's timely completion?

- What levels of skill are needed to accomplish this task? Are they available or relatively scarce?

- Can the task be accomplished faster with more resources? Would a different approach provide the same outcomes?

- Can this task be accomplished slower, later, or incrementally without adverse effects?

Keep an open and inquisitive mind to optimize the use of available resources. Although there are no clear-cut rules to success when dealing with people, the following principles have proven helpful:

- Place your most trusted resources on the tasks with the most risk (schedule or technical risk).

- Place untested resources where they can cause the least damage (tasks with slack, or where failure has fewer repercussions).

- When possible, mix rather than separate differences. Pair rookies with veterans, linear thinkers with intuitive thinkers, organized with disorganized, the creative with the traditional. The strength of a team is in its ability to assimilate differences and embrace one another's strengths, for the good of the project.

- Champion all people. Assume that everyone on the project can contribute, and take on the responsibility of ensuring everyone succeeds. Their success is project success.

In Chapter 7, you created a schedule for your project and in Chapter 8 you set up its resource list. With the above principles in mind, now is a good time to judge whether there are plenty of resources or whether they'll be marginal. For even the smallest of projects, it can be difficult to tell. But don't worry. By the time you've completed loading your project with resources, you'll have a clear understanding of how things really stack up.

Secrets of Success

If you'd like to attract the best people to your project, make sure your projects' schedules are consistently accurate, well communicated, and demanding. Those who are motivated by teamwork and high performance will be attracted to your project. Those who prefer to lurk in the shadows, hiding their inadequacies in projects with inaccurate schedules, weak performance measures, and anemic control, will do you a favor and remain hidden.

Effort-Driven Scheduling

Project's *effort-driven* (its default method) scheduling assumes that your tasks take less time to complete if more resources are applied to them. That is, overall task duration extends or shortens as the required work is completed faster or slower. This is true for tasks that have either fixed units (also the default) or fixed work task types.

Words at Work

An **effort-driven** task's duration is responsive to resource loading levels. Theoretically, the application of more or better resources will reduce the task's duration and fewer or poorer resources would lengthen the task's duration.

For example, you're putting a new sprinkler system into your yard. Digging the ditches (ugh!) will take one person (you) 40 hours of pick and shovel work (ouch!). You could look at this as *fixed units* (so many feet of ditch or yards of dirt to move) or *fixed work* (40 hours of digging). When you add resources (a teenager with shovel and work gloves) to a fixed unit or fixed work task type, you'll complete the total work in half of the original duration (now 20 hours). With eight equipped teenagers, you can reduce the task duration to five hours. In both cases, the units and work remained fixed as the duration changed.

More Good Stuff

When calculating effort and durations, just because the math works doesn't mean the resources will! Be careful to allow for the law of diminishing returns when loading a task. For example, if it takes one person four days to knit a pair of socks, you might assume that two equally talented knitters could accomplish the job in two days. In reality, they may be slower. If neither knitter is familiar with the pattern, both have to overcome the same learning curve, thereby increasing the actual work performed! In addition to learning curves, another problem plagues the effort to shorten task durations. Every task has an optimal work force. Four knitters, no matter how qualified, can't shorten this task's duration.

Effort-driven scheduling works great for most tasks because in most tasks a certain amount of work (fixed) or a certain number of units (fixed) must be completed.

On the other hand, some tasks do not respond to the addition of resources. These task types are called *fixed duration*. For example, hiring that same energetic teenager to help you watch new grass grow will not speed the greening of your yard. Growing grass, drying paint, and waiting for the Food and Drug Administration to approve a new formulation are all examples of fixed-duration tasks.

Words at Work

A **fixed-duration** task is not responsive to resource loading levels. For example, application of more or better resources wouldn't shorten the task "wait for delivery."

Microsoft's default effort-driven scheduling doesn't model fixed-duration tasks accurately—their durations don't respond to the addition or removal of resources. To correctly model the project's workflow, be alert for fixed-duration tasks and mark them as such when assigning resources. (See Figure 9.3 and the accompanying text for changing task types.)

More Good Stuff

When the resources you need don't report directly to you, it's easy to come up short. Help prevent shortfalls by establishing open and frank communications with the resource holder early on. Provide an accurate schedule of when you'll need resources and when you'll return them. When you've gained access to the needed resources, publicly acknowledge it. A genuine thank you and positive public exposure builds bridges. Good planning, professional courtesy, and political awareness are prerequisites to successfully borrowing resources.

Taming the Duration, Units, and Work Formula

As the sprinkler system example demonstrated (a fixed unit or fixed work example), a task's duration is equal to the amount of work that must be done and the number of resources doing that work. Project 2003 uses the following formulas (and a little algebra) to describe this relationship:

Duration = Work / Units	(Used when first assigning a resource)
Work = Duration / Units	(Used when reassigning a resource)
Units = Work / Duration	(Used when reassigning a resource)

There is a problem, however. When you change any of these numbers, Project has to choose which of the other two should be balanced. Although it does a pretty good job of staying in sync with the typical project manager's thought process, you can't expect it to always make the right adjustment. Be alert and make sure your changes are having the desired effect.

Most of the tasks in a typical project are effort-driven with fixed units. That is, a certain amount of work needs to be done; and the more resources assigned to the work, the shorter the task duration. In a typical situation, you enter a task into Project, enter an estimated duration, and then assign one or more resources. Project assumes the resources you first assign were those you had in mind when you set the duration, so it calculates the hours of work and leaves duration as originally entered. If you go back and change the original resource loading, Project then assumes you're trying to adjust the schedule by reallocating resources, so it recalculates duration. Similarly, if you add resource units, the duration gets shorter; if you remove resources, the duration gets longer. Table 9.1 lists Project's recalculation behaviors by task type and field modified.

Table 9.1   The Duration, Work, Unit Recalculations

In the default situation with fixed-unit tasks:

Modify	Project Recalculates
Units	Duration
Duration	Work
Work	Duration

For fixed-work tasks:

Units	Duration
Duration	Units
Work	Duration

For fixed-duration tasks:

Units	Work
Duration	Work
Work	Units

It's best to see for yourself how this works. Open a project you can experiment with, and let's assign some resources to your tasks.

Assigning Resources with Full Control

The best way to ensure Project 2003 responds appropriately to your resource assignments is with the task form in combination with the Gantt chart. This combined view is shown in Figure 9.1. First, select the **Gantt Chart** from the **View** menu. Now split the window by selecting **Split** from the **Window** menu. Click anywhere in the bottom pane to activate it, choose **Details** from the **Format** menu, and then click **Resources Work.** You're ready to put your team to work!

At first glance this view may look intimidating, but closer inspection should reveal that you're familiar with most of the selections from use in other views. The top and bottom panes are synchronized by task. Regardless of which columns are hidden in the top pane, notice that Duration, Work, and Units are always in view in the bottom pane, right where you can keep an eye on them!

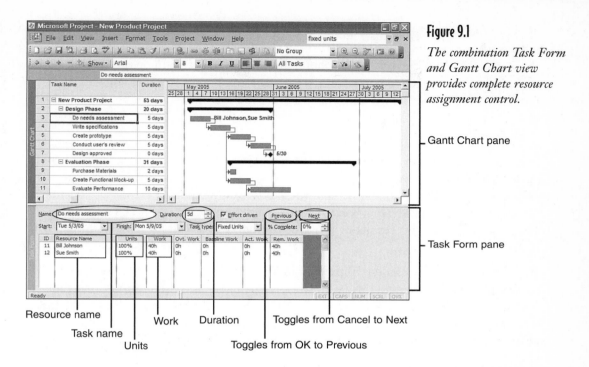

Gantt Chart pane

Task Form pane

Resource name

Task name

Units

Work

Duration

Toggles from OK to Previous

Toggles from Cancel to Next

When the program is set to automatically calculate (the default), the Gantt chart instantly responds as you assign resources and make changes. (When working in the bottom pane, you'll have to click OK to calculate after modifications are made.) It's a good idea to use the Automatic calculation option until project size makes it unwieldy. Check this setting before you continue. From the **Tools** menu, select **Options.** When the dialog box appears, select the **Calculation** tab and make sure **Automatic** is selected under the Calculation options for Microsoft Project area, as shown in Figure 9.2.

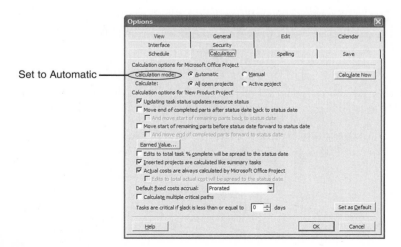

Set to Automatic

Figure 9.2

To stay in control of your resource assignment changes, set the program to automatically calculate.

To assign resources, select the task in the top pane. You may scroll through the tasks with the Next and Previous buttons on the task form. Now, in the task form, click in the Resource Name field. If you've defined resources, they'll all pop up in a list. If you haven't, or if the resource you want is not listed, simply type it in. (If you add new resources here, go back to the Resource Sheet view and finish inputting rate and availability information.) It's usually best to select from the menu. This way you won't inadvertently enter the same resource with two different spellings.

Select a task and begin assigning a resource to it. Choose the resource name. Then click the **OK** button on the task form as you saw back in Figure 9.1. Notice that resource Units defaults to 100 percent (as Scotty would say, "I'm givin' her all she's got, Captain!"), and the work is calculated as the Duration times the Units. With a Duration of 2 days, this results in Work of 16 hours. That's all pretty straightforward, so far ….

In a like manner, if you enter 50 percent in Units (perhaps the resource only needs to work half time to complete this task), work is calculated as the Duration times the Units. So the result might surprise you—it produces eight hours of work for the task. The math is the same, but we've revealed what may be a surprising effect of the effort-driven scheduling approach.

It turns out to be a good way of handling many situations. If you want to share the task responsibilities, add each resource, enter each Unit of resource percentage, and click **OK.** In our example of a 2-day Duration, with 2 resources at 50 percent Units each, work for each is 8 hours. And the total work for the task is 16 hours. In a like manner, if you want multiple resources to work 100 percent of their time on a task and have the duration remain as it is, just add all your resources before clicking **OK.**

The program's behavior really isn't as weird as it first sounds. Just remember that Project 2003 makes it easy on us (most of the time) by making assumptions. The more it assumes, the less we have to enter! The missing elements of the Duration, Work, Units formula is calculated based on which items are entered before you click the **OK** button.

You'll get the results you want most of the time. When you don't, it will be instantly apparent with automatic calculation turned on. In that case, adjust your entries and click away until you're happy!

As shown in Figure 9.3, other important scheduling elements are accessible in the combination Gantt Chart and Task Form view.

More Good Stuff

Most organizations are overly optimistic regarding resource availability. In reality, it is the rare worker who can remain on task 100 percent of his or her time! Other obligations and responsibilities—and, of course, many interruptions—all conspire to reduce their actual effective working time. In addition, there is always someone at less-than-full capacity. Babies, bereavement, appendices, root canals, and soccer games can and will show up on most projects. The only insurance you have is in adding bench strength. If you don't need the "extra" resources, why not complete the project a ahead of schedule? Don't cut staffing too closely. If you do, any small aberration in resource availability can endanger the project's success.

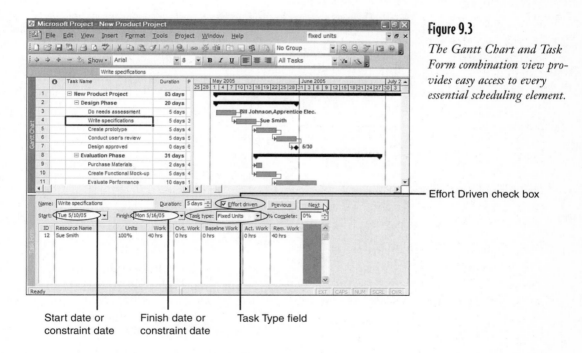

Figure 9.3

The Gantt Chart and Task Form combination view provides easy access to every essential scheduling element.

— Effort Driven check box

Start date or constraint date   Finish date or constraint date   Task Type field

Notice that the Task type field is readily accessible in this view. From time to time you'll need to change Fixed Units to Fixed Duration or Fixed Work. And if you must rethink workflow based on resource availability, work sequence is easily modified from this view. A word of warning: Don't modify the start or finish dates unless you want to set a scheduling constraint. (Workflow and constraints are covered in detail in Chapter 7.)

Assigning Resources with Speed and Perspective

After you're grown accustomed to how Project handles duration, work, and resources, you may find this next method for assigning and reassigning resources is more convenient. In the **Tools** menu, select **Assign Resources.** (This box also has a button on the Standard toolbar.) Drag the Assign Resources dialog box shown in Figure 9.4 to a convenient screen location.

Click the first task in the Gantt Chart Entry Table view that you want to assign a resource to, and then in the dialog box highlight the resource, change (the percentage of units if desired) and click **Assign.** Repeat this process to add multiple resources.

Figure 9.4

Use the Assignment Resource box to assign, remove, or change resources and access helpful workload charts.

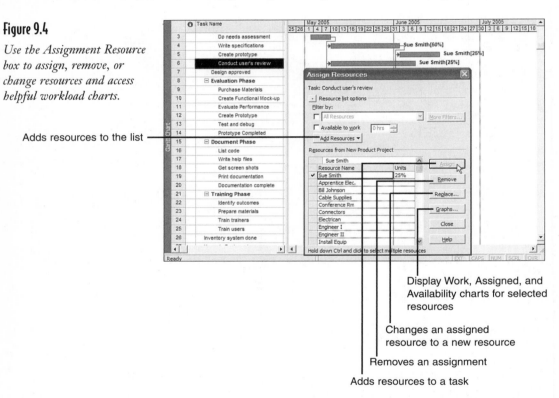

Adds resources to the list

Display Work, Assigned, and Availability charts for selected resources

Changes an assigned resource to a new resource

Removes an assignment

Adds resources to a task

To remove a resource, just highlight and click **Remove.** And to change from a resource already assigned to another one, highlight the new resource and click **Replace.** In the Gantt Chart view, select the next task you want to add or change resources on and repeat the process.

This method is especially convenient when resources are assigned to multiple tasks. In Figure 9.4, Sue Smith has been assigned on a part-time basis on three tasks, with at least two always running in parallel. Her availability is tabulated and can be viewed in a resource chart by clicking **Graphs** and selecting the **Assignment Work** graph as shown in Figure 9.5. Zooming in or out changes the timescale, providing a clear understanding of Sue's workload. The project planner can readily identify over allocations as assignments are made. Multiple resources can be selected and viewed by pressing and holding the Control key while clicking the resources.

> **More Good Stuff**
>
> Users of Project 2000 will notice that they cannot access Resource charts or additional resources from the Resource Assignment dialog box. However, creating a combination view with the Gantt chart in the upper pane and a Resource chart in the lower pane provides a similar perspective.

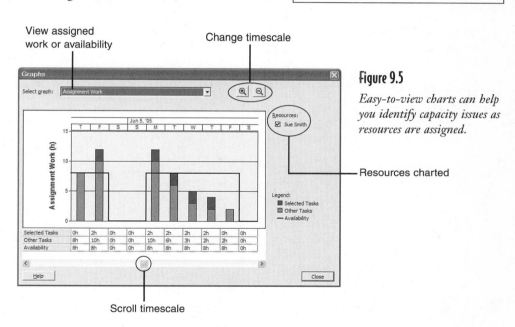

View assigned work or availability

Change timescale

Resources charted

Scroll timescale

Figure 9.5

Easy-to-view charts can help you identify capacity issues as resources are assigned.

Assigning Responsibilities in a Hurry

One other method of assigning resources merits consideration. In both of the foregoing methods, resource units are easily controlled. If you do not need precise control when loading resources, adding them directly in the Gantt chart Entry table may be the best option. In many situations detailed resource information and control isn't needed. The project manager just wants to ensure that responsibility for every task is clearly owned by someone. This concept is known as single-point responsibility.

Every task needs to be owned by someone, not a group, not a department, and certainly not a "to be determined." Work only gets done when someone takes ownership of it.

An easy way to denote assigned responsibility is to type in the name of the resource in the Gantt chart Entry table Resource column as shown in Figure 9.6. You can also pull down the menu and select from any resource available in the resource sheet. You can add more than one resource to a task by inserting a comma between the names. You can change available units by typing a percentage in brackets (no spaces are required). However, for purposes of communicating responsibility, the fewer resources assigned to a task the better, and a single resource is best.

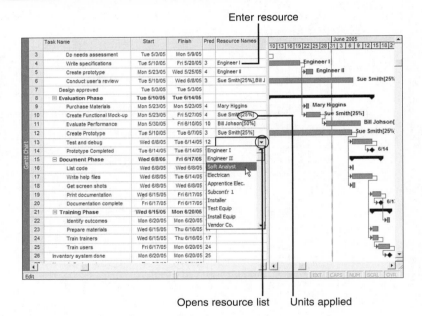

Figure 9.6

Add resources directly into the Gantt chart Entry table at any time.

Resource Reallocation: Leveling

When you don't have enough resources to accommodate the required work and duration of a task, you've got a problem! Somehow you need to get the project done. Generally, you can do three things:

◆ Get more resources.

◆ Reduce the scope of the project.

◆ Work longer with the resources you have.

Assuming that the project sponsor (your boss?) and the project end user (your customer?) are the last people you want to negatively impact, Project 2003 tries to do the right thing. It automatically slides the work out in time based on your resource assignments, task dependencies, and durations. This is usually a pretty good solution. But if the project pushes out too long, you may not get everything done in time. In that case, you'll need some fancy project management footwork. Table 9.2 shows a checklist of solutions to consider. In Chapter 12 you'll learn how to use Project's resource-leveling capabilities to make the most out of difficult schedule-resource situations.

Table 9.2　When the Schedule Isn't Working

If You're Short on ...	Try This ...
People	Schedule tasks later.
	Ask for more project time.
	Balance skills with tasks more accurately.
	Break tasks into simpler activities and then give senior people helpers.
	Add part-time, temporary, or full-time staff.
	Use outside services.
	Purchase rather than make.
	Limit project scope.
Time	Assign more resources.
	Work overtime.
	Rethink workflow sequence to schedule tasks sooner and parallel more tasks.
	Use outside services.
	Purchase rather than make.
	Limit project scope.
	Provide assistance by adding junior people to work with senior people.
Materials	Rethink workflow sequence to schedule tasks later and parallel less frequently.
	Use alternative vendors.
	Reconsider make or buy options.
	Ask for a time extension.

continues

Table 9.2 When the Schedule Isn't Working (continued)

If You're Short on ...	Try This ...
Facilities	Rethink workflow sequence to schedule tasks later and to avoid parallel workflow.
	Work additional shifts.
Short on everything	Stop project planning and revisit the project initiation phase to choose a more realistic strategy.

The Least You Need to Know

◆ Microsoft Project 2003 uses an effort-driven scheduling method to compute the amount of work based on task duration and resources assigned.

◆ The schedule adjusts automatically to workflow sequence, constraints, durations, effort, and resource availability when automatic calculate is on.

◆ Project can schedule around individual resource issues such as vacations, downtime, and full- or part-time commitments.

◆ The combination Gantt Chart and Task Work view provides excellent control when assigning resources.

Part 3

Optimizing Your Plan

When you have too much to do and too little to do it with, you need some project management magic. And that's what this part is all about—pulling rabbits (in this case people, materials, machines, and money) out of the hat.

Part 3 shows you how to put your resources to work where they'll do you the most good. You'll discover how to put the critical path to work, why slack is your hidden resource, and what your options are when there just isn't enough time or resources to go around. You'll learn to create resource pools, allocate work, smooth workloads, and the ins and outs of shortening your schedule. Making do with what you have has never been easier. And that's the kind of magic that makes a project manager successful!

How to Get the Schedule You Want with Project 2003

In This Chapter

◆ Understand how Microsoft Project 2003 schedules so you can make the best choices for your project

◆ Plan your project from a start or finish date perspective

◆ Use constraints effectively to control key events

If you're new to projects you may have expected software to take care of all the messy scheduling details. For the most part, it does. However, because no two projects are alike, and no two project managers want a schedule exactly alike, Microsoft Project has many features that allow you to alter its basic results. These options provide flexibility, but in turn, they produce a potentially confusing array of choices. When you learn how Microsoft Project schedules, you'll know when to trust, and when to adjust, Project's output.

This chapter shows you how Microsoft Project schedules and how you can adjust it to suit your project's needs. After all, your judgment is the project's most important asset; don't let Project replace it.

How Microsoft Project Schedules

Don't let Microsoft Project's scheduling engine intimidate you. Creating a schedule is actually quite rudimentary; there's just a lot of calculations to make, blending many simple interrelationships together. You probably knew most of the important scheduling theory before you learned what to call it! It's intuitive. To prove this statement, consider why you even bother to schedule. It boils down to knowing *what* needs to be done, *when* it can (or must) be done, and *who's* going to do it. The information needs to be easy to read, share, and use. That way everyone on the project team can do his or her share and stay out of each other's way. You see, this isn't rocket science (although many rockets have been built with it).

Here's an example done by hand to demonstrate what goes on inside Microsoft project. Assume you're in charge of creating a schedule for the boss's pet project (nothing new, right?). This one has five tasks: A, B, C, D, and E. Several minutes after you've received the assignment (by e-mail), the boss pops in and asks, "How long will it take to complete that project?" Of course, you don't know yet—you still have to estimate how long each task will take and what the order of work can be. "Come back in 15 minutes," you plead, "and I can tell you." You dig out a piece of graph paper and get to work. On it you create a table with a column for the tasks, one for durations and one for the order of workflow, as shown in Figure 10.1.

After some consideration of the skills required and the work involved, you estimate that tasks A, B, and C will each take a week to complete. Task C will require three weeks and task D one week. You list each task's predecessor as you think through the best order of work. After reviewing the list, you see that the project will take a minimum of four weeks, assuming the boss provides enough resources.

Figure 10.1

Microsoft Project 2003 replicates the natural thought process project managers undertake when analyzing a project's required tasks.

Tasks	Dur.	Pred.
A	1w	-
B	1w	A
C	1w	B
D	3w	A
E	2w	-

All too soon the boss pops back in and asks, "I want this done in three weeks, can you do it?"

"Probably not," you say, knowing it's a sensitive subject and that it will take some persuasive communications to convince the boss. "Give me another 10 minutes and I'll do a Gantt chart so you can see what I'm talking about." The boss acquiesces and you sharpen your pencil. Next to the task table you create a timeline. Beginning with the first task you ask yourself, "How soon can I start this task?" Because there are no predecessors, task A can start right away, so you note its earliest possible start date with an ES at the beginning of the timeline, time zero. Then you check the duration column and see the estimated duration at one week. Adding the duration to the ES, you calculate the earliest possible finish date and note it with an EF on the chart. In a like manner, you continue down the list, identifying the ES, adding the duration, and noting your chart with the resultant EF. The result of your work is shown in Figure 10.2.

Knowing that the boss wants this project done in a hurry, you locate the earliest finish date, of the last task, on the longest series of tasks. You mark it as the project's scheduled finish and draw a diamond to denote its importance. This is the theoretical earliest date the project can be completed. No extra time is allowed for problems, slowdowns, or resource shortages—the boss is in a hurry. You identify the longest series of tasks that created this finish date and mark it with a bold color. You don't want any slowdowns on this path because they would force the project to finish later. Of course, this longest path has a special name to help us manage it. We call it the *critical path*.

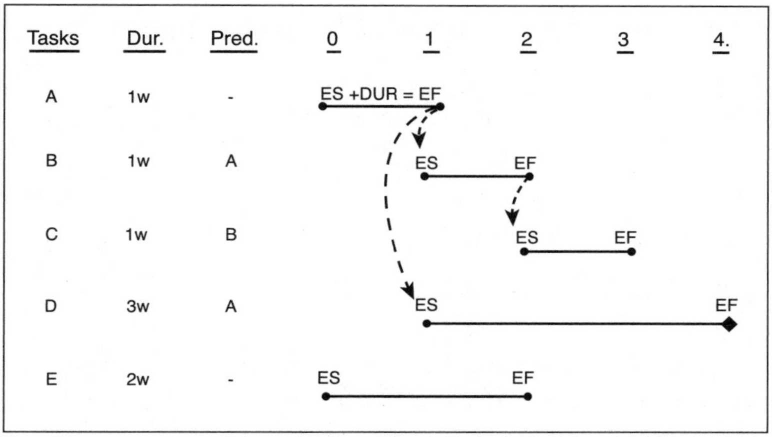

Figure 10.2

Adding durations to early starts yields the early finish date. The longest path determines the shortest possible project duration.

Reviewing the chart, you can see that task E could start two weeks after project go ahead and still have enough time to get done before the critical path is completed.

Words at Work

The **critical path** is the longest series of tasks that runs from the beginning to the end of the project, as determined by duration and workflow sequence. This longest path sets the managerial standard for how quickly a project can be completed, given appropriate resources. The tasks that make up this longest path are known as **critical tasks**. If a critical task is not completed on time, the project's completion will be delayed unless corrective action is taken.

Wanting to identify any other flexibility *(slack)* in the schedule, you calculate the latest possible finish and latest start dates for each task by working back in time from the critical path's finish. LF minus duration equals the LS, and you note each tasks accordingly. As always, the *early* and *late starts* (or *early* and late *finishes*) are the same date whenever a task is on the critical path.

You're ready and waiting for the boss, with the chart shown in Figure 10.3. If she has a finish date in mind, you can subtract four weeks and determine the latest possible start date. If she wants to begin immediately and complete the project as soon as possible, you can show that it will be four weeks after the start before it can be finished. By applying simple forward-pass and backward-pass math, and a few drafting skills, you've created a compelling communication document.

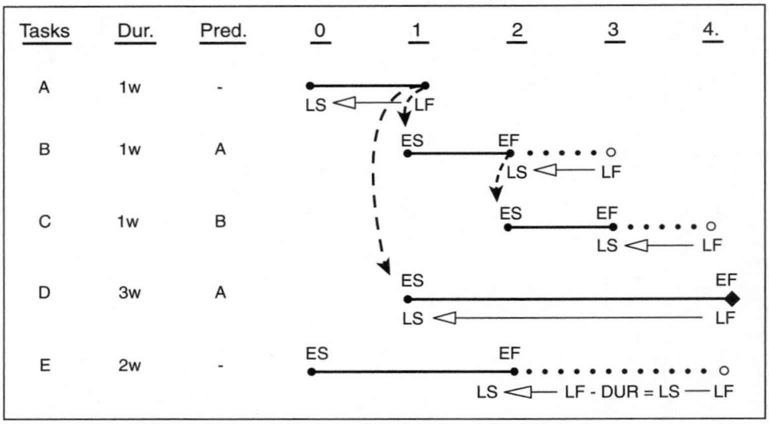

Figure 10.3

LS dates are determined with a backward pass, subtracting the duration from the late finish date of each task. The schedule flexibility between a task's ES and LS is slack.

Tasks	Dur.	Pred.	0	1	2	3	4.
A	1w	-					
B	1w	A					
C	1w	B					
D	3w	A					
E	2w	-					

In project management, it's not enough to have the answers. To be successful you must be able to relate information to others in a credible and convincing manner. You know what they say: To get some people to understand, you have to draw them a picture!

Scheduling Factors at the Project Level

Some of the adjustments you can make to Project influence the entire schedule. Others options influence a single task. We'll begin with the options that have the broadest effect.

Start Date or Finish Date Scheduling

One of the first things you want to decide when creating a project schedule is whether the project should be scheduled based on a completion deadline or on a start date. If you use the default, Schedule from Project Start Date, Project attempts to start each task as soon as possible, depending on each task's duration and predecessor dependencies. Working from the start date forward (the forward pass), each duration in the longest sequence of tasks (the critical path) is added together. This determines when the project may be completed (the *early finish* date).

When scheduling from a project finish date, tasks on the longest sequence of tasks (the critical path) are started as late as possible. To use this scheduling method, select **Project Information** from the **Project** menu to open the Project Information dialog box (see Figure 10.4).

Adjust dates at any time before execution

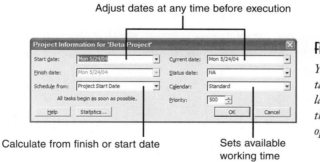

Figure 10.4

You may choose to schedule tasks as soon as possible or as late as possible depending on the start or finish date option.

Calculate from finish or start date

Sets available working time

When scheduling from a finish date, Project 2003 adds the duration of each predecessor task, working from the project deadline (late finish date) back to the first task. This calculation (a backward pass) determines when the first task must begin (late start date) to finish the project on the date entered. Tasks that do not fall on the longest sequence of tasks (the critical path) are scheduled to begin as soon as possible without beginning before the first task's start date. The results of scheduling from a finish date are shown in the bottom example in Figure 10.5.

Figure 10.5

For schedules planned from start date, all tasks begin ASAP. When planning from finish date, critical path tasks are scheduled ALAP, and all others are scheduled ASAP.

Tasks A, B, and C are on the critical path

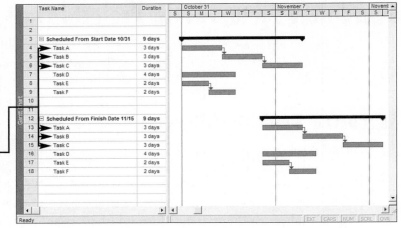

Notice that Project uses as late as possible starts, and finishes for all *critical tasks*; and all other tasks are scheduled as soon as possible. The net result is to maintain all available slack. Therefore, when scheduling to a finish date is used for the purpose of seeing whether there is enough time to do a project or determining what the latest start could be set as, Project does a good job modeling your intended strategy. However, what if your intention is to slow down work as much as possible without missing the finish date (perhaps to slow expenditures or wait for improving weather conditions)? In this case, you would want to remove all slack from the project, and Project would not appropriately model your intended strategy without some adjustments. To get the schedule you want, each noncritical task needs to be constrained to start as late as possible.

Words at Work

An accurate schedule is your most important project control tool. It shows when every task must start and finish to complete the project as intended. The four key control dates are **early start, late start, early finish,** and **late finish.** The early start specifies how soon a task may begin according to its predecessor's finish. The late start specifies how late a task may begin according to its successor's start. In a like manner, the early and late finish dates specify when a task may or must be completed. The difference in the early and late start dates (or finish dates) is called **slack.** Slack (also known as *float*) is flexibility in your schedule. When a task has no slack, it is called a **critical task**—it has no flexibility in time. Manage critical tasks carefully.

For more information on the critical path and its effect on the project's schedule, see Chapter 11.

Project Calendar Effects

Tasks are scheduled according to the workdays, holidays, shifts, and hours of work described in the project's base calendar. Select your project's base calendar in the Project Information dialog box, as shown previously in Figure 10.4. Resources may also have calendars that restrict their availability. For more information on using resource calendars, see Chapter 8.

Scheduling Factors at the Task Level

When only one or a few tasks schedules need to be adjusted, Project provides several useful methods. The most restrictive of these are task constraints. Even when applied to only one task, they can dramatically affect the entire schedule. One of subtlest is task placement. We begin with it.

Task List Placement

Project 2003 begins all scheduling calculations with the first task in the Task Name field and proceeds down the list, as shown in Figure 10.6. With all other things being equal, the higher on the list the task resides, the sooner it will be considered for scheduling and resource assignments. Try to place tasks that will be performed early in the project high on the list. This also makes the schedule easier for others to understand. Chapter 5 describes in detail how to create and enter the task list.

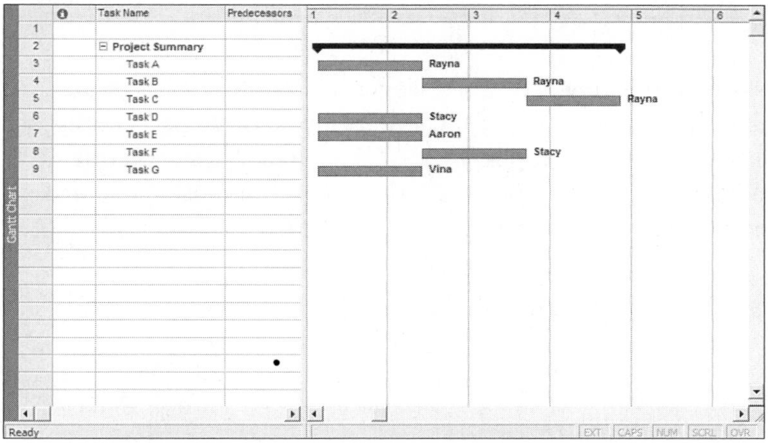

Figure 10.6

Project begins scheduling from the top of the task list and then applies dependencies, resource assignments, and other constraints.

Task Duration

Duration is handled in a straightforward manner when resources are not assigned. The longer the duration, the longer a task will take to finish. However, as soon as you assign a resource to the task (assuming it is not a fixed-duration task), the duration/work/units formula kicks in with what sometimes can be unexpected results. Depending on task type (fixed units, fixed work, or fixed duration) and the resources assigned (work or material), duration can be dramatically changed. Project 2003 checks each of these elements when it calculates the schedule.

Establishing accurate durations is essential to creating effective project schedules. Chapter 6 provides all the tools you need to get the job done.

Task Dependencies

The sequence of workflow is set with task dependencies. Much depends on the task-to-task relationships within a project schedule. Workflow sequence becomes the backbone of all scheduling activities. Frequently the greatest decisions the project manager can make lie within the realm of workflow sequencing.

Alternative approaches may speed completion, reduce resource requirements, minimize project risk, reduce project costs, or increase schedule flexibility. Generally speaking, the fewer dependencies in a project, the more options you have.

Chapter 7 shows you how to use task dependencies most effectively.

Task Lag Time

When two or more tasks with the same workflow sequence are undertaken in the same time frame, lag time is the amount of the head start given to the predecessor. Lag time adds to the project's overall duration when it is applied to a task on the longest (the critical) path. It forces the dependent task to start and finish later than it would without lag time. To keep your schedule as short as possible, use lag time sparingly.

More information on lag time can be found in Chapter 7.

Task Constraints

Constraints confine the scheduling of a task in some way. The more restrictive constraints anchor tasks to specific dates, thereby restricting scheduling flexibility or its ability to respond to changes in resource loadings. There are eight constraint types in

Project 2003 (see Figure 10.7). ASAP (As Soon As Possible) is the default constraint used by Project for all scheduling tasks unless overridden.

For comparison all dates are the same

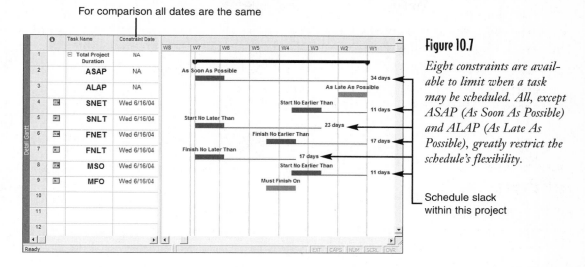

Figure 10.7

Eight constraints are available to limit when a task may be scheduled. All, except ASAP (As Soon As Possible) and ALAP (As Late As Possible), greatly restrict the schedule's flexibility.

Schedule slack within this project

When scheduling from the finish date, the ALAP constraint is used on the critical path only. The ALAP and ASAP constraints allow flexibility and are the least restrictive. All others greatly confine the capability of Project to schedule tasks. For example, these restrictive constraints include the FNLT (Finish No Later Than), which can be used to ensure a contract requirement is met. Use the six restrictive constraints when you must, but use them sparingly. See Table 7.1 in Chapter 7 for more information on using constraints to restrict the schedule.

More Good Stuff

Project 2003 sets a constraint when you type a start or finish date into the schedule or drag a taskbar from the Gantt chart to a new location. To avoid inadvertently reducing your scheduling options, allow Project to calculate all start and finish dates. A small calendar icon appears in the indicator column when restrictive constraints are set. Double-click the icon and select the **Advanced** tab in the Task Information dialog box to review or modify the constraint.

Scheduling Factors at the Resource Level

When it comes to loading and leveling resources, Project 2003 has many features and options. The most frequently used are described here.

Resource Availability

As mentioned previously in the "Task Duration" section, when resources are assigned duration shortens or extends according to the duration/work/units formula. The task type and scheduling method are also taken into consideration as the schedule is calculated. Generally, adding more resources to the project helps reduce overall project duration, as shown in Figure 10.8.

Better use of resources on critical tasks (the longest sequence of work) may help shorten the project duration. See Chapter 12 for more information.

Figure 10.8

Assigning additional work resources to effort-driven tasks shortens the path's duration.

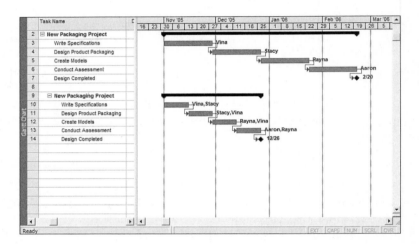

Task Work

The amount of work on a task is calculated with the duration/work/units formula. The formula is called into play to determine a task's duration when resources are assigned to an effort-driven, fixed-units, or fixed-work task.

Effort-Driven Scheduling Options

This is the default scheduling method for Project 2003. It affects the schedule calculations as soon as a work resource is assigned to a task. Task duration is calculated based on the initial loading of resources to the task. The version of the formula used (where Duration = Work / Units), depends on which factor is entered and which of the remaining factors Project assumes it should calculate. When additional resources are assigned, you usually prefer work to remain constant and task duration to shorten. When effort-driven scheduling is turned off, total duration remains constant even as you assign more resources.

Task Type Options

There are three task types in Project 2003. Both the fixed-work and fixed-units type are affected by the assignment of work resources. When more work resource units are applied, task duration shortens. On fixed-duration tasks, adding or removing resource units does not affect the duration.

Well, there's the big picture of how Project 2003 schedules. You might want to keep a bookmarker in this section. Then if you get unexpected results, just double-click the task and check out the settings as listed above. Think of it as your not-the-last-one-at-work-again insurance policy.

The Least You Need to Know

- ◆ The schedule is your single most important management and control tool.

- ◆ Microsoft Project 2003 calculates schedules based on the project's start or finish date, task durations, task dependencies, resource assignments, and constraining dates.

- ◆ Project uses the critical path method in all schedule calculations, where the longest sequence of tasks determines the overall duration of the project.

- ◆ Minor changes in any planning element can ripple significant changes throughout the schedule.

Shortening the Schedule

In This Chapter

◆ Making the most of your project's time

◆ Finding the hidden resource slack and putting it to work

◆ Understanding the critical path and why its management is essential to project success

◆ Techniques to speed up a slow project

Successful project managers are known for their ability to get things done on time, even with limited resources. They understand the significance of "never put off until tomorrow anything that you can do today." They've learned through experience, training, good parenting, or the school of hard knocks, that time is a precious commodity.

In this chapter you'll find the strategies, techniques, and instructions on how to maximize the use of your project's available time, using Microsoft Project 2003.

Understanding the Critical and Noncritical Paths to Success

If there is one word that is misunderstood in project management, it is the word *critical*. People tend to use it as a way of describing tasks that are important. However, as you may recall from Chapter 5, every task we include in the project is important. In fact, we should only include tasks in our project that are essential. Nonessentials are luxuries most projects can't afford—they drive up project complexity, costs, and risks; and depending on where they fall in the workflow, they can create longer project durations. If a task is important enough to be included in a project, it must be accomplished. The difference between critical tasks and noncritical tasks is all about time, not importance.

Identifying Critical Tasks

You'll recall from Chapter 10, that a sequence of tasks within the project is known as a path. Some of these paths are shorter in total duration then others. It is the longest path—the *critical* path—that describes the shortest possible project duration. Because short project completion times are usually desirable, identifying the critical path provides a sound time perspective from which to manage the project.

> **Secrets of Success** _____
>
> To improve communications on the project team, be careful how you use the words *critical, essential,* and *important*. Use *critical* only to describe those tasks that, if not completed on time, will cause the project to finish late. *Essential* tasks are those required to achieve the intended results of the project. Use *essential* to remind your team that even tasks that are not glamorous or interesting are still essential to the project's success. Finally, when using *important* to describe a task, always include your reasoning so others don't have to guess why. For example, a task may be important because its completion opens several paths of work or because it has high visibility to stakeholders.

To find the critical path, all paths are identified and then their durations are compared. Microsoft Project calculates both early and late starts and finishes, finds the longest path, and identifies those tasks not on the critical path. If a task is critical (a part of the critical path), it has no schedule flexibility. Critical tasks must start and finish on or before the earliest possible start and finish dates, or else project duration will be longer than necessary. Tasks that aren't on the critical path have slack (schedule flexibility). By identifying critical tasks and those with slack, project managers can better understand the options and the implications of accelerations or delays.

Figure 11.1 illustrates these concepts using Microsoft Project and the data from Figure 10.3 in the previous chapter. Notice that tasks A and D make up the longest path and, therefore determine the shortest possible project duration. Tasks B and C may start and finish up to one full week later than their early starts, and Task E may start up to two weeks later than its early start, without impacting the project's earliest finish.

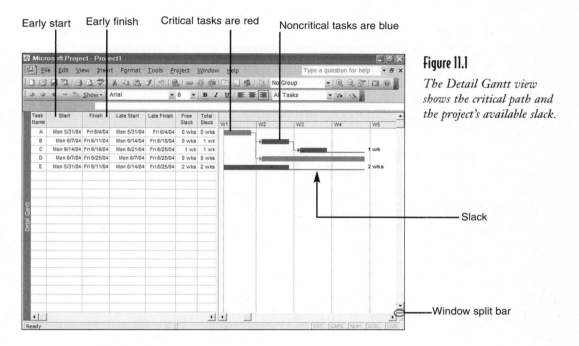

Figure 11.1

The Detail Gantt view shows the critical path and the project's available slack.

Slack Is Your Hidden Resource

When you stop and think about it, project managers don't have much authority. They seldom set project goals, objectives, or deadlines. Often they don't pick their own teams, set their own budgets, or even participate in the selection of vendors. However, project managers do have power—they control the schedule and any slack they can build in to it.

Slack works like a resource because it increases your options when dealing with problems or issues. For example, it can be used to reduce a spike in resource requirements by allowing work with slack to be delayed until resources are available. Similarly it can help smooth varying resource requirements, or to release resources for work on more problematic tasks. In some cases slack can be used to slow expenditures or purposefully reduce progress without endangering the final completion date. Not only is slack useful to the astute project manager, it may be the only resource you actually control.

Build as much slack as possible into your schedule. Slack is your friend, and you can never have too many friends on a project. How much slack you can create depends on your creativity and your scheduling skill. Don't however, publicize your slack—don't let it be commandeered. As soon as others find your schedule's slack, it can be used for their purposes and the one resource you control will vanish.

Microsoft Project 2003 makes it easy to identify critical tasks and those with slack. From the **View** menu, click **More Views,** and then select **Detail Gantt** (see Figure 11.1). Slack is revealed as a small line in the Detail Gantt view. You can visualize how much flexibility is in the path by mentally sliding the tasks down the slack line. If it looks like you may be able to make some improvements, save a copy of your current plan and explore your options. This view is useful when modifying the work breakdown structure or viewing alternative workflow strategies.

When you're satisfied with the schedule, don't publish it as a Detail Gantt. Too much is revealed. Rather publish the plan as a Network Diagram, as shown in Figure 11.2. While a trained eye can find the slack in a network diagram, it is not instantly recognizable to most, and therefore, isn't as likely to be commandeered. To create a network diagram, select **More Views** from the **View** menu and apply the **Network Diagram** option from the dialog box. Chapter 14 provides additional information on using the Network Diagram.

Figure 11.2

The network diagram communicates workflow responsibilities and the critical path to your team but doesn't call attention to available slack.

Hover cursor over
box for details

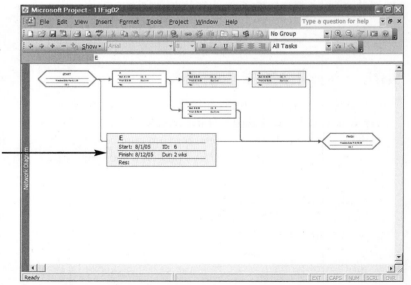

Those who understand how to create and use slack to their best advantage have found Project Management Nirvana!

Hustling While You Wait

Some of the techniques project managers use to get more done in less time are almost magical. Thomas Edison was one of the most prolific project managers of our century. He summed up those techniques nicely when he said that all things come to those who hustle while they wait. Hmmm ... as the mental whiplash subsides, consider your project's schedule and these questions:

 ◆ Can I the shorten the project's duration by arranging workflow and creating more concurrent work?

 ◆ Can any tasks or workflow sequences be broken into smaller segments and then run concurrently?

 ◆ Can I delay any tasks and apply their resources on more time-important or unexpectedly difficult tasks?

 ◆ If work is prone to delay, do I have alternative uses for these resources?

 ◆ Can I move difficult or risky tasks forward in the schedule and reduce overall schedule risk?

Viewing project workflow from a perspective of critical and noncritical paths is a prerequisite to shortening the schedule. Whether you're intent on getting done sooner, coping with problems, or trying to reduce schedule risk, there is much power in the concepts of *critical path* and *slack*.

Not only does hustling while you wait have it's own language, it also has several effective strategies we'll cover next.

A Need for Speed? Load Up on Resources

One of the most frequently used tactics to speed up a project is to add resources. Theoretically, as long as the tasks are effort driven (duration shortens as effort is applied to required work), and the tasks are critical, project duration will decrease. Of course, the critical path changes as task durations change, but the first area to hustle on is always the critical path.

There are a few caveats, however.

Diminishing Returns

For many tasks, there are limits to the number of resources that may be effectively engaged. It is no surprise to project managers that too many cooks can spoil the broth. Every task has an optimal number and type of resources that if not met, or if exceeded, will likely result in lower efficiencies and a reduction in the return on effort. To speed up the preparation of a meal, adding resources (cooks, stoves, utensils, ingredients, etc.) beyond those normally required for the size and type of meal being prepared may shorten the duration, but it might also increase overall cost, lower quality, and slow the task. A scientific research team, group of financial analysts, or crew of pipe fitters all have an optimal configuration. Unless you thoroughly understand the intricacies of a task, don't assume that adding resources beyond the norm will markedly improve duration, quality, or the cook's attitude!

Productivity Reductions

Other subtle decisions can hamper efforts of shortening project durations. A common strategy is to work available resources for longer hours or more days. This may work well for machinery and equipment (assuming care and maintenance is adequate), but human resources have their limits. Beyond the North American traditional 40-hour work week, productivity drops for most workers after sustained periods of long hours.

In a study I observed, knowledge workers tracked hours and ranked their productivity and quality of decisions. Separately, peers, supervisors, and subordinates judged their performance. Despite the glowing self-assessment for those working 50 hours or more, peer review ranked their performance in the lowest quartile on all counts. One can only speculate about the consequences of their sub-par decisions. (Beware of workaholics—they can do a lot of damage in a short time!)

Construction work is also effected by longer-than-normal hours. One study shows that 10-hour days can reduce productivity by as much as 30 percent. To this I can only ask: would you rather have 100 percent of an 8-hour day, or 70 percent of a 10-hour day?

You can't count on longer hours to speed up your project, but you can count on longer hours to speed up expenditures!

Brook's Law

In the mid-1970s, Fredrick Brooks, a project manager for IBM, concluded that adding resources to a late software project to speed it up had the opposite effect, and slowed it down. Others have noticed a similar effect in any task that has a large learning or team communication component. Visualize yourself knitting a pair of booties for your newborn nephew. (Yes, guys can visualize this, too.) Here's the scenario:

You know how to knit, but the baby arrives ahead of schedule. In an attempt to speed up production, you enlist the aid of a talented knitter. Only too late will you realize that by the time you've collected yarn, knitting needles, and discussed the finer points of the pattern, you might as well have continued alone. Further, if neither you nor your assistant knew how to knit, the learning curve would cause even more delay. Theoretically, adding additional resources to this project would eventually result in bootie delivery just in time for your nephew's retirement.

Resource Allocation in a Critical World

When a task can be delayed without affecting the start of another task, the slack is called *free slack*. And it really is free. Free slack doesn't cost the project any time, anywhere. *Total slack* is the total amount of time a task can be delayed without affecting the project's completion date. Using total slack probably won't hurt anything, but you may have additional schedule juggling to do and team members to notify.

> **Words at Work**
>
> **Total slack** (also known as total float) is the amount of time a task or path can be delayed and not extend the completion of the project. **Free slack** (free float) is the amount of time a task can be delayed out without delaying the start of any immediately following tasks.

Free slack isn't shown in Project 2003, but it is relatively easy to spot in the Detail Gantt view. For example, in Figure 11.1 task B has no free slack but it does have one week of total slack. If B is delayed, it will force the start of C to be delayed; as long as the delay is one week or less, the project finish won't be delayed.

There is a lot to watch when you juggle resources and tasks. The critical path can change rapidly. Project 2003 makes it easy to stay in control. First, select the Detail Gantt view by opening the **View** menu, clicking **More Views,** and selecting it from the dialog box. Then from the **View** menu, make sure that the **Schedule** table is selected. And for even more information, open a pane in the bottom of the window and display the Resource Usage Sheet, the Resource Graph view, or the Resources & Predecessors Form. These provide a great perspective when moving resources around the project.

You need lots of room to view a complex project's paths, so be ready to switch back and forth between views frequently. Here's the best trick for this: To open a lower pane quickly, click the **Window** split bar and drag open a lower pane. The split bar is identified in Figure 11.1. It appears just below the vertical scrollbar. Then right-click in the lower pane and select the **Resources & Predecessors Form** view (see Figure 11.3). To open the Resource Usage view in the lower pane, point at the View bar indicator and right-click. Select **Resource Usage** (Figure 11.4) for a tabular view and **Resource Graph** (Figure 11.5) for an informative chart. To quickly close the pane, drag it out of sight to the bottom of the window.

Detail Gantt view

Figure 11.3

The Detail Gantt with the Schedule table in the upper pane and the Resources and Predecessors form view in the lower pane provides excellent access when changing resources or workflow.

Schedule Table view

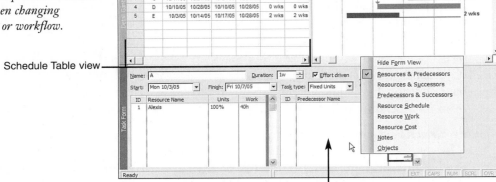

Right-click for form options

Figure 11.4

For a tabular accounting of resource usage and availability, select the Resource Usage sheet for the lower pane.

Right-click bar for optional views

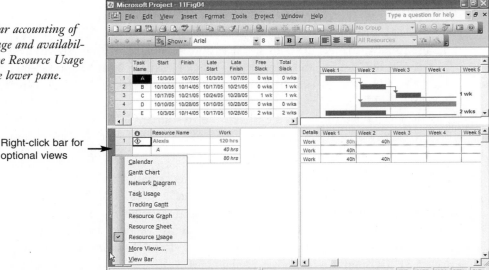

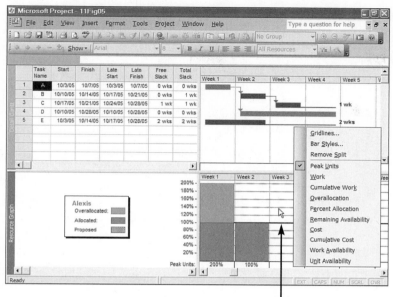

Right-click the chart for options

Adding Resources

The problem with adding resources to speed up a project is that you may not have any to add! When was the last time you heard someone complaining they didn't have enough to do? One option is to hire additional people. However, if that's not in the budget, what's a project manager to do? Well, it's time to steal (oops, sorry Mom!) er, borrow, some resources from your own project.

A good place to find extra resources is on tasks that have slack. Certainly, reducing a task's resources may slow it down, but that's okay, as long as there is enough slack so nothing goes critical. To find all tasks with slack, make sure the Schedule table is showing, and then click **AutoFilter** on the Formatting toolbar. A pull-down arrow will appear on each field heading in the Schedule table Sheet view. Click the **Total Slack** heading arrow, and then select **Custom.** In the Custom AutoFilter dialog box, choose **is greater than** from the selections in the top-left pull-down field and enter a duration in the top-right field. Click **OK** and only tasks with greater total slack than the duration you entered will be shown (see Figure 11.6). Click **AutoFilter** again to remove the filtering effect.

Pull-down arrow on Total Slack column   AutoFilter button

Figure 11.6

To find all tasks with total slack, use the AutoFilter with the Schedule table showing.

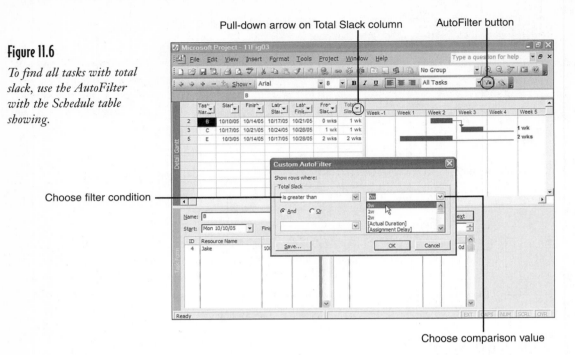

Choose filter condition

Choose comparison value

Increasing a Resource's Available Time on Task

Another way of applying more effort to a task is by increasing the resource units. For example, in lieu of having people work a quarter of their time on a task and taking four weeks to complete it, schedule them for half of their time and complete the task in two weeks. Better yet, convince the resource person that it's easier to do a good job when they're focused on a single task. Then schedule them full time and reduce the task to a week! As you might guess, when you need to shorten a project, persuasion skills are as important as scheduling skills.

Project Pitfalls

Although you can use Project's resource calendar to increase the number of hours a resource is available, you might notice I don't recommend that approach. Specific resources, such as mainframe computers, might be available 24 hours a day, but in most cases this approach is a good way to make the schedule work and the project fail. Changing a resource's calendar beyond the 40 or 50 "standard" hours will likely reduce productivity, increase costs, and sooner or later cause burnout. Avoid extending the work calendar in all except the most desperate of situations.

Assigning Overtime Work

Overtime usually costs more, so it isn't always in the budget. However, sometimes the financial cost is actually lower with overtime. For example, consider the salaried employee who is paid the same for 40 hours as for 50 hours of work. If the person's productivity, quality, and judgment (not to mention health, family, relationships, and so on) isn't adversely affected by the long hours, the more she works, the less it costs the project. (And the more it costs the resource!)

Sometimes it makes sense to use overtime. Consider a time-sensitive project where the completion of a single task opens several other paths of work, such as "Design approved" in the project shown in Figure 11.7. We call a situation like this a *work burst*. These points in the workflow sequence are important to identify and carefully manage. When negotiated sooner than planned, work bursts can create slack time on all subsequent paths—in effect multiplying the benefit of a single duration-shortening cost. Work bursts can also be a dangerous bottleneck. If not successfully negotiated, all subsequent work will be delayed and the project's progress may be severely hindered. In these cases, paying a little more to open the workflow may be smart.

To identify work bursts, use the Network Diagram view from the View menu and zoom out for a broad perspective. To increase the number of tasks in view on one screen or printed page, open the **Network Diagram** toolbar from the **View** menu, select **Toolbars**, and click **Hide Fields**.

Secrets of Success

Champion every team member's success: effective team leaders assume that everyone is capable of making a positive contribution. Projects are successful only when the team is successful. Teams are successful only when team members are successful. What's good for the team, is good for the project, and that's good for you!

Words at Work

The terms **work burst** and **work merge** describe points within the workflow where multiple paths intersect. Works bursts open into several new paths. At work merges several paths form into a single path. Both are strategically important to manage since any impact on their timeliness has a broad effect.

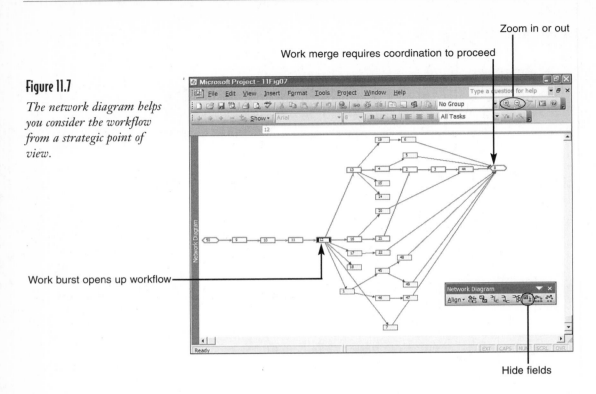

Figure 11.7

The network diagram helps you consider the workflow from a strategic point of view.

Zoom in or out

Work merge requires coordination to proceed

Work burst opens up workflow

Hide fields

Other Speedy Tricks

In addition to shortening tasks with the thoughtful use of slack time and resources, another key strategy is to compress the schedule: Move as many tasks as far forward in time as possible. This takes on two basic forms, as discussed in the following sections.

Breaking Down Critical Tasks into Subtasks

The first of these tactics is to break critical tasks into smaller work units. It is often possible to move some of these smaller tasks off the critical path. To demonstrate this approach, the Advertising and Promotions Phase of a new product launch project is re-created in Figure 11.8. Design Campaign originally included a subtask, Determine Media Mix. When broken out, it could run concurrently in a finish-to-finish relationship with the Design Campaign. Two days of lag were applied to Determine Media Mix under the assumption that the media mix could not be finalized until shortly after the overall campaign had been laid out. Besides shortening the critical path by three days it also allowed Set Up Web Site to begin two days into Determine Media Mix (assuming by then it would be clear if an Internet effort was included in the campaign). This resulted in a five-week improvement for the finish of the website. Continuing the subtask approach, each media type was broken down into its own subtask, which allows many more resource and workflow options, described more fully in the next section.

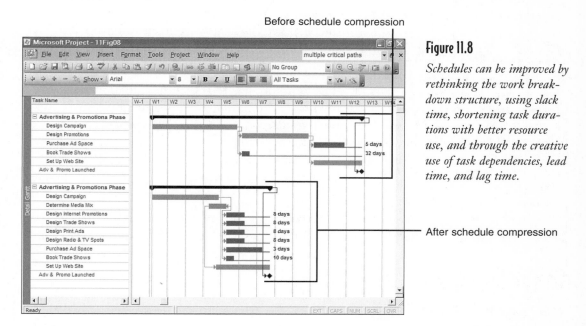

Before schedule compression

After schedule compression

Figure 11.8

Schedules can be improved by rethinking the work breakdown structure, using slack time, shortening task durations with better resource use, and through the creative use of task dependencies, lead time, and lag time.

The Parallel Approach

Another fruitful tactic is to parallel more tasks; that is, run more tasks concurrently. This usually takes more resources, but if they are available, the parallel approach can be productive.

In our product launch example, when each subtask was broken out of the Design Promotions task, skill sets and resource consideration were easier to consider. It was then clear that Designing the Internet, trade show, print, and radio or TV ads could easily run in parallel, given adequate resources; as could purchasing these venues and reserving trade show space. Some of these activities could be resourced by the vendor, and with the improvement in slack time on all tasks, overall schedule risk was markedly improved.

Now that's what I call hustling while you wait!

If Nothing Else Works

What if it you've tried every trick, stretched every resource, and negotiated for more time and the project is still too long? Two options remain:

The first is to go ahead and hope something changes. It always does, and sometimes it's for the better! In tough situations, courage and conviction may be all that separates those who survive from those who fail. Your insight to the situation is probably the best there is, so trust yourself and make the decision. If you move forward, hedge your bets and stay positive! All is not lost until your attitude is lost.

The best option is to revisit the initiation phase of the project. Rethinking the project's objectives, narrowing the scope, or setting a portion of the project aside for a later project may improve the odds of success. You may be able to break the project into smaller phases and engage only what can be accomplished.

In the end, the most important determinates in shortening the schedule, reducing schedule risk, and maximizing the effective use of scarce resources is your creativity.

> **CAUTION**
>
> **Project Pitfalls**
>
> Contrary to the popular saying that all things are possible given enough time and money, some projects are impossible. Beware of pet projects, projects with overly optimistic goals or fuzzy assumptions, projects without slack time, and especially those that someone has already failed on. It takes only one impossible project to destroy your reputation.

The Least You Need to Know

◆ Understanding the critical path is the key to unlocking a project's hidden resource: slack.

◆ Project durations may be decreased by applying three primary strategies: reducing task duration, removing tasks from the critical path, and running more tasks in parallel.

◆ The Detail Gantt view in combination with the Resource & Predecessors view provides a powerful method of applying each of the project shortening strategies.

◆ Not all projects can be accomplished in the desired time with the available resources. Be alert for impossible projects and be willing to revisit the initiation phase.

Leveling Workloads

In This Chapter

◆ Locating resource overallocations

◆ Using manual leveling techniques to solve resource allocation problems

◆ Using contours to model workloads within tasks

◆ Using Microsoft Project 2003's automatic leveling features to solve resource-overallocation problems

The process of leveling resources has one primary purpose: to create the most appropriate schedule within time and resource constraints. Given the complexities of even a simple project, this can be an awesome task. However, once your resource information has been entered (Chapter 8), and you've assigned resources to tasks (Chapter 9), *leveling resources* and optimizing their use is amazingly easy in Microsoft Project 2003. This chapter shows you how.

Fine Tuning Your Use of Resources

Having the right number of people on a project is always a challenge. When assigning resources to tasks, problems will slip into the schedule.

You may find that you've overallocated a resource—trying to accomplish too much, too soon, over taxing it. Or you may find you've underallocated a resource—someone is standing around without their full capacity being used. (Wouldn't that be a nice change?) In most projects, there are just too many interrelated variables to get it right the first time.

Words at Work

Loading resources describes the process of assigning resources to tasks: matching skills and availability, with the required work. **Leveling** is the process of adjusting resource loadings: optimizing their use within cost and time constraints.

In addition, changes from the original plan are virtually inevitable. People come or go. Some tasks finish early and others late. Labor strikes, faulty materials, and global warming might not have been anticipated. At some point in most projects, you'll have to adjust the project's *resource loading*.

Having too many resources is seldom viewed as a problem—it's usually easy to use (or release) extra resources. It's having too few resources that is difficult to deal with. We'll take a close look at these. This adjustment process is called leveling. Two basic strategies are used. One way is to change the number of resources available on a project. Worker shortages, budget considerations, or the demand for resources on other projects may foil this approach. The second strategy is to move work around to fit resource availability. This method is usually the best approach, assuming that the project's finish no later than date won't impacted. To make the best leveling decisions, project managers must have an understanding of the project's drivers, an accurate schedule, and a thorough understanding of the project.

Secrets of Success

Planning is an iterative learning process. Don't try to make a schedule perfect on your first pass. Start with a safe, simple, workable schedule. But don't stop there. Continue to adjust tasks, resource usage, and work sequence until you minimize risk, maximize slack time, finish on time, and most effectively use your resources. The schedule is often the only thing a project manager truly controls. Master it.

Solving Resource-Overallocation Problems

As resources are assigned to tasks, Microsoft Project 2003 checks the resource's calendar to make sure it is a working resource. However, it doesn't check to see whether the resource is being used anywhere else in this same timeframe. It lets you overassign resources all you want. In other words, you can assign more work to one resource than that resource can possibly accomplish in a given time. (I'm not talking about your supervisor, honest!)

Allowing resources to be overassigned may sound a little mean-spirited at first. However, some projects are scheduled from a different point of view. For example, you may want to schedule a project in the shortest possible timeframe, and then go back and add extra resources where a shortage becomes apparent. Allowing over-allocations gives you more creative freedom as you build an optimal schedule.

To avoid trying to execute with overloaded resources, you'll probably want to fix them before saving a baseline plan and beginning project execution. However, to fix them, you must first find them. Project 2003 makes this quick and easy.

Finding Resource Overallocations

Overallocations are easy to find. Indeed, they almost jump off the page to get your attention. To scan for overallocations, open the Resource Sheet view by selecting **Resource Sheet** from the **View** menu. The Resource Usage view provides task detail sorted by resource and it can be opened alone or in a combination view with the Resource Sheet view. For a combination view with both of these sheets, click **Split** from the **Window** menu, click the lower pane to make it current, and then from the **View** menu select **Resource Usage**. Figure 12.1 displays this informative combination view. In the upper pane, the resource sheet provides a status overview of all resources and in the lower pane tasks details are sorted by each resource. The lower pane is synchronized with the fields highlighted in the upper pane. To select multiple resources, just hold the Control key while clicking each resource.

Overallocated resources are indicated with a yellow warning icon and the listing appears in red. Wouldn't it be nice if the name on your cubicle entry did the same thing when your boss overallocates you?

The Resource Sheet View

The Resource Sheet view shown in the upper pane in Figure 12.1 is a good first look at resource loading status. If you planned your project with less than a resource's full capacity being allocated, this is a handy view. Before digging into the detail, the easiest thing to do is to change a resource's maximum available units here. Raising a person's half-time availability (50 percent) to three-quarter-time availability (75 percent) might be all you need. In any case, increasing the units available until the resource overallocation disappears provides a cursory understanding of how large the overallocation really is. After all, 5 percent or 10 percent out of balance is one issue, 50 percent to 150 percent is quite another!

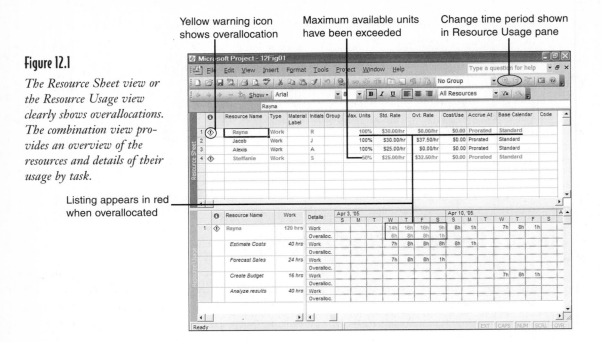

Figure 12.1

The Resource Sheet view or the Resource Usage view clearly shows overallocations. The combination view provides an overview of the resources and details of their usage by task.

Resource Usage View

The Resource Usage view shown in the bottom pane of Figure 12.1 shows how many hours of overallocation exist for a given resource, sorted by task, and displayed by time period. To change to hourly, daily, weekly, monthly, quarterly, or biannual time periods, just click the **Zoom** buttons on the Standard toolbar Resource Usage view. It may be opened from the View bar or from the View menu. Add the Overallocation field to the view by selecting **Details** from the **Format** menu. The view appears in Figure 12.1.

Resource Graph and Detail Gantt Combination View

The Resource Graph view shows where a single resource is over- or underallocated. You can zoom in or out to see as much of the schedule as needed. This view, shown in combination with a Detail Gantt chart in the upper pane, provides a clear understanding of a single resource's allocation. To create the combination view, first select the **Detailed Gantt** view from the **View, More Views** dialog box. Open a lower pane in with **Window, Split.** Then click in the lower pane to make it current and from the **View** menu and click **Resource Chart.**

The Gantt Chart has been sorted in Figure 12.2 to show only the resource in question. To perform the sort, click the upper pane to make it current, click the **Filter** pull-down menu on the Formatting toolbar, select **Using Resource,** and in the pop-up dialog box choose the resource to sort by. In the timescale chosen, the Resource Graph will indicate an over- or underallocation for the entire time period when any fraction of the time period has an over- or underallocation. For example, if the time scale shows one-week intervals, if any day has an overallocation the entire week is shown as overallocated. After a problem has been found, zoom in for more precision.

This combination helps you understand the resource's effect on the critical path, the availability of slack, and resource loading levels.

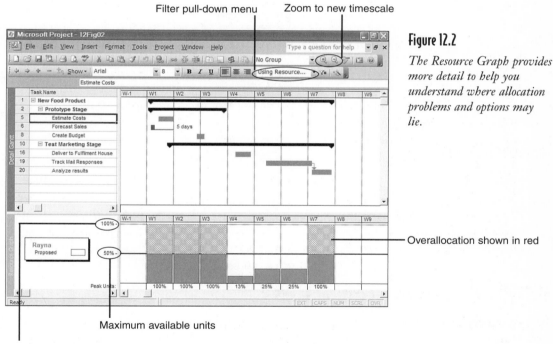

Figure 12.2

The Resource Graph provides more detail to help you understand where allocation problems and options may lie.

Manual Resource Leveling

Before proceeding, be sure that Project's automatic leveling feature is off. Until you're more experienced with Project 2003, the automatic option can make it more difficult to see what's going on. Later in this chapter, I show you how to use the automatic leveling features. From the **Tools** menu, select **Resource Leveling,** click the **Manual** option, and then click **OK,** as shown in Figure 12.3.

Check the Manual option

Figure 12.3

When the Manual leveling option is checked, it is easier to get the results you want when leveling by hand.

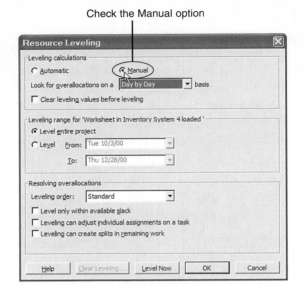

On smaller projects, those with perhaps 6 to 12 resources and up to 30 tasks, the fastest way to level your resources is to do it manually. There are no settings to select or choices to think through. You simply make changes until you get the results you want. There are several good ways to manually level resources.

You could use the combination views in Figures 12.1 and 12.2 to locate the trouble spots and adjust resources using the Resource tab in the Task Information dialog box or the Assign Resources dialog box as described in Chapter 9. This approach assumes that you have resource flexibility when and where it is needed. Alternatively, you may be able to move work out by delaying tasks, as described in the next section.

Delaying the Start of Noncritical Tasks

If you can't get more resources, or if their acquisition would add to the project's cost, the next best strategy to preserving the schedule is to move tasks around within their available slack time. Using a task's slack doesn't require additional resources or costs, nor does it impact the critical path. Using slack usually has the least adverse impact and is the easiest to accommodate within the confines of the schedule.

The best way to manually level resources within available slack is from the Resource Allocation combination view. To quickly access this view, select **Resource Allocation** from the **View, More Views** dialog box, as shown in Figure 12.4.

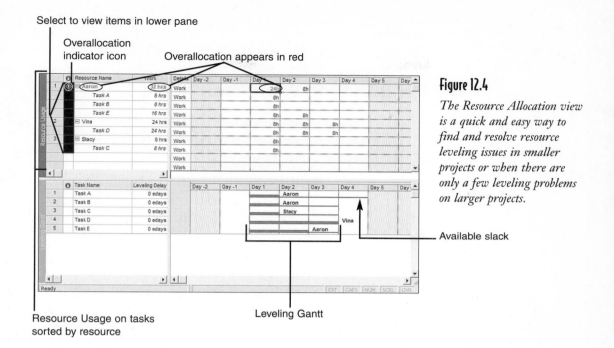

Select to view items in lower pane

Overallocation indicator icon

Overallocation appears in red

Resource Usage on tasks sorted by resource

Leveling Gantt

Available slack

Figure 12.4

The Resource Allocation view is a quick and easy way to find and resolve resource leveling issues in smaller projects or when there are only a few leveling problems on larger projects.

The Resource Usage sheet is in the upper pane of this combination view. It shows the daily hours of work on each task sorted by resource. Overallocations are flagged with a warning icon in the indicator column. Selecting a resource or multiple resources in this pane brings up a Leveling Gantt chart for them in the lower pane. The narrow blue-green bar trailing from the task shows slack, a narrow light-brown bar shows task delay, and the blue bar shows the task's duration. If a green bar the same diameter as the blue bar appears, it is the preleveling location of the task. By increasing the leveling delay manually in the lower pane, work can be moved out in time until overallocations are removed, as shown in Figure 12.5.

To level tasks without extending the critical path, select the first task needing to be leveled that has available slack. Place your cursor in the task's Leveling Delay field and add or subtract delay. Click outside of the field. Check the Detail Gantt view for the results and observe the allocation changes in the Resource Usage view in the top pane. If the effects are acceptable, go to the next overallocated task. If they are not acceptable, reverse the procedure and try again until through trial and error, you've optimized the results. Remember, this process is learning how to level and for projects with only a few required adjustments. After you've worked through this process once or twice, you'll definitely appreciate Microsoft Project's automatic level features!

Figure 12.5

Adjust the amount of Leveling Delay to reduce overallocations manually.

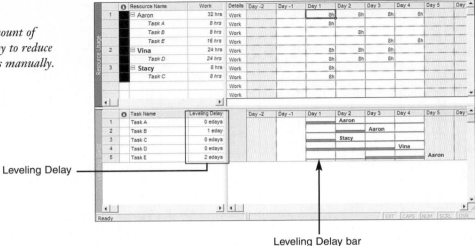

Leveling Delay

Leveling Delay bar

The Resource Allocation view is a good way to see your adjustments and their impact on each task's related resources. However, it also shows leveling that has already been accomplished. This can cause some information overload! To avoid this problem, you can replace the Leveling Gantt chart with the Detail Gantt chart in this combination view. The other benefit of using your own combination view is that you can see how your adjustments affect both the critical path and tasks with slack.

Select **Detail Gantt** from the **More Views** choice in the **View** menu. Split the window by dragging the split bar up or selecting **Split** from the **Window** menu. Click in the lower pane to make it active. Then select **Resource Usage** from the **View** menu. You'll see something similar to the screen shown in Figure 12.6.

Slack

Figure 12.6

The combination Detail Gantt and Resource Usage view is a good way to adjust leveling issues manually.

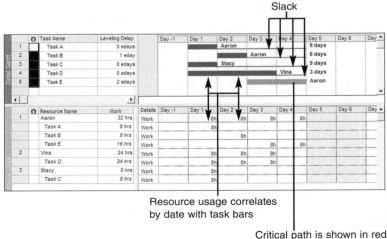

Resource usage correlates by date with task bars

Critical path is shown in red

The Nonparallel Approach

Another strategy to reduce overallocations is to remove parallel tasks. This requires some careful consideration of workflow logic. Running tasks in sequence that were originally in parallel has the effect of lengthening the time it takes to accomplish that path. Typically, lengthening a noncritical path is not a problem. The project can still be accomplished according to the original schedule.

If tasks on the critical path are changed from parallel to sequential, overall project duration increases. This may or may not be acceptable, depending on your situation.

To change workflow sequence, right-click the task in Detail Gantt view or its row in the Entry table. Select **Task Information** from the pop-up menu. Go to the **Predecessor** tab and change the **Predecessor, Type,** or **Lag** that describes the parallel relationship, as shown in Figure 12.7. You'll recall that negative lag on a task with a standard finish-to-start relationship produces a parallel relationship. (See Chapter 7 for more information.)

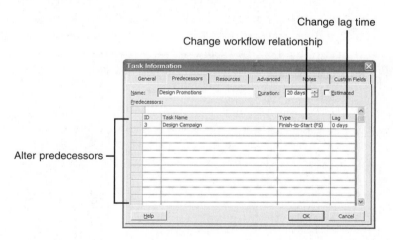

Figure 12.7

The Resource Information box and the Predecessor tab allows quick changes in workflow dependencies.

Adding Overtime

When all else fails, you may decide to work resources overtime. In most situations, this is an expensive option. Overtime work usually comes at a premium price. Contrary to popular beliefs, even salaried employees' overtime work is likely to cost extra due to productivity losses and increased errors. Nonetheless, there will be situations when adding overtime is the best option.

> **Project Pitfalls**
>
> Many project contracts don't state how much total time will be allowed by the prime contractor for the subcontracted work. In this case, subcontractors (through no fault of their own) might be forced to pay overtime rates to keep the project on schedule. Rightly or wrongly the prime contractor would be sheltered.

To add overtime, create a combination view with the Detail Gantt in the top pane. Open a lower pane by selecting **Split** from the **Windows** menu. Click in the lower pane to make it active. Now select **Resource Form** from **More Views** in the **View** menu. Then right-click in the lower pane and select **Work details.** Adjust the overtime hours as needed, as shown in Figure 12.8, and then click **OK.**

Figure 12.8

To add overtime to a task, open the combination view Resource Form with Work Details showing.

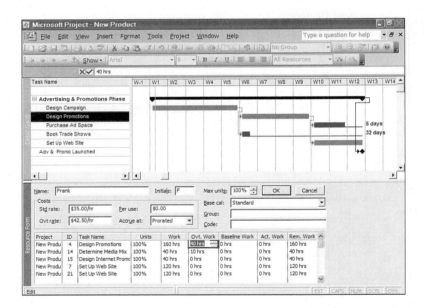

Splitting Tasks

In the real world, one of the options a project manager has is to partially complete a task, finish a more important one, and then return to the original task. It's called *task splitting.* And even though Project 2003 makes it easy, the same may not be true in the real world. Splitting a task can add to the overall duration if the task requires mobilizing, setup time, or getting back up to speed. So be careful how you use it.

To use this feature, right-click a task bar in the Gantt Chart view and select **Split Task** from the pop-up menu. Place the mouse at the split point, as shown in Figure 12.9, and drag the remainder of the task to the right. To remove this adjustment, drag the split bars back together.

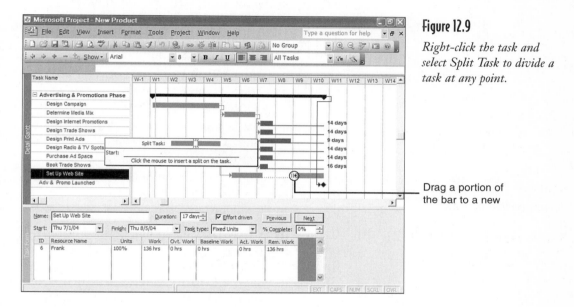

Figure 12.9

Right-click the task and select Split Task to divide a task at any point.

Drag a portion of the bar to a new

Automatic Resource Leveling

After all the hard work you've just completed leveling a project by hand, automatic resource leveling probably sounds like a wonderful thing. When the time available for your project isn't too tight, it is wonderful. However, care must be taken to get the results you want.

Project 2003 takes into account a resource's working capacity, its assigned units, the resource's calendar, the task's duration, and any constraints that may be in place. It pushes tasks out in time until resources are no longer overallocated. It does this by using available slack, splitting tasks, and adding start delay time. Your project's duration can easily be extended, so be careful.

To begin leveling your project automatically, select the **Leveling Gantt** view. Then from the **Tools** menu, choose **Resource Leveling.** A dialog box appears (the one you saw earlier in Figure 12.3). To level, save your current schedule. Then select the options you want, as described in Table 12.1. Click **Level Now** and presto! Be sure to carefully check the results.

Table 12.1   Resource Leveling Dialog Box Options

Option	Description
Automatic	Automatic leveling constantly levels all resources when a task or resource is entered or adjusted. This option is not normally selected.
Manual	This default leveling option requires you to click the **Level Now** button to induce automatic leveling.
Look for overallocations on a	Day by Day is the default and works best for projects scheduled in hours or day units. Sets the point at which a basis for leveling is induced.
Clear leveling values before leveling	When automatic leveling is selected, clear this box to speed up leveling. The default for manual leveling is to enable this option.
Level entire project	Selected is default. When cleared you may choose a date range to level.
Level from	Enter a date range of tasks to level.
Leveling order	Choose **ID** to level tasks in ID number order. Choose **Standard** (usually the best choice) to level based on dependencies, slack, dates, priorities, and constraints. Choose **Priority, Standard** to first check task priorities and then undertake the standard leveling order.
Level within available slack	When Selected prevents the project finish date from being extended. Depending on the schedule's slack, there may little or no leveling performed.
Leveling can adjust individual assignments on a task	This selection allows leveling to adjust all resources on any task. To set this feature on an assignment-by-assignment basis, add a Level Assignments field to the task sheet and set it to Yes or No.
Leveling can create splits in remaining work	This selection allows leveling to split all tasks. To set this feature on a task-by-task basis, add a Leveling Can Split field in the task sheet and set it to Yes or No.
Clear Leveling	This button clears all leveling on all tasks.
Level Now	Click this button to level when Manual Leveling calculations has been selected.

Contouring Work Assignments

Project 2003 provides one other important method to distribute resource loading over the task's duration: a work contour. The default is a flat contour, where work is equally distributed throughout the task's duration. The Back Loaded, Front Loaded, Double Peak, Early Peak, Late Peak, Bell, and Turtle contours all distribute work on a preset percentage. The duration of the task is broken into 10 equal divisions and the resource's work is distributed over the task according to the table in Figure 12.10.

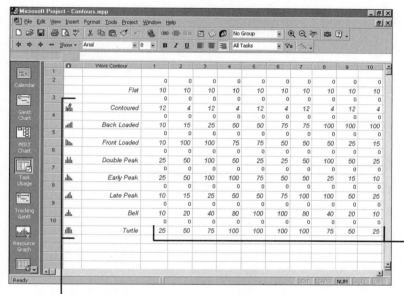

Figure 12.10

Tasks with 100 hours of work over a 10-day duration and 10-hour workday were created to demonstrate the available work contours.

The resource's effort is distributed over the task as a percentage of the daily total assignment.

Icons indicate contour type

To use this feature, go to the sheet portion of the Task Usage or Resource Usage views. Right-click a task assigned to a resource and open the Assignment Information dialog box. This is shown in Figure 12.11. Select the contour you want and click **OK.** The Indicator column displays a Work Contour icon. If you manually adjust the work contour, the icon changes to an Edited Contour icon.

Figure 12.11

*Change a resource's Work
Contour in the Assignment
Information dialog box.*

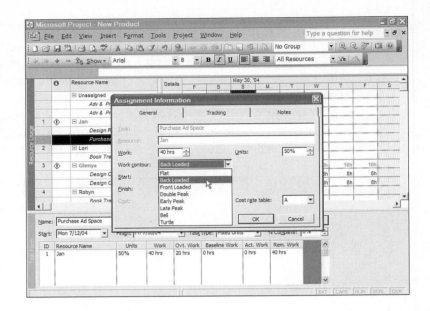

The Least You Need to Know

◆ Resource overallocation can be leveled manually or automatically with
Microsoft Project 2003.

◆ Leveling resources on the critical path may extend the duration of the project.

◆ Resource overallocations should first be reduced by using available slack time.

◆ Resource contours can be used to fine-tune resource usage within a task.

Part 4

Managing for Success

Unfortunately, you can't do everything alone. It takes a lot of other people, resources, and information to bring in a successful project. And it doesn't take a very big project to create a large problem controlling all this. Microsoft Project 2003 really comes to the rescue in the control department.

In Part 4, you'll learn how to use your project plan and Microsoft Project 2003 to monitor and control every important aspect of your project. A good plan helps you get and stay in control. It helps you understand where the project is flexible and where it isn't. You'll learn how to identify potential problems, plan alternative courses of action, and use your resources most effectively. You'll learn how to use reports, views, and charts to aid in decision making. You'll learn how to gather and use all the information you need to take early and effective corrective action with confidence—managing for success. And when the project concludes, you'll be ready to wrap it up like a pro, archiving information, gaining signoffs, and gracefully transitioning to the next project.

Chapter 3

Monitoring Progress

In This Chapter

- ◆ How to collect and update the plan with starts and finishes, durations, and costs
- ◆ Why tracking progress doesn't always reveal achievement
- ◆ Establishing a baseline to monitor performance
- ◆ Uncover hidden problems before they sidetrack your project

Creating a project plan provides three major benefits, the first of which is that planning is a learning process. The more you plan, the more you learn about the project, the possible problems, and the most effective implementation strategy. Second, the plan provides the basis of all communications to the project team and the project's stakeholders, both before and during implementation. Finally, the plan provides a scale to gauge project progress. And at that point, the race is on!

When the Plan Is Complete and You're Ready to Go

Now comes the process of moving the project forward until you've achieved success. Staying in control of a project requires information—a lot of it! However, the last thing you need is busy work. You already have enough to do, don't you? So the information needs to be in a format that's easy to collect, easy to enter, and easy to understand.

In this chapter, you'll gather the information you need to measure project progress. You'll learn how to use the hard data on completion status, resource use, and budget compliance. However, projects are about more than just data. Projects are about people. It takes high levels of communication, cooperation, and motivation to bring a difficult project in successfully. With Microsoft Project 2003, you'll be able to stay in touch with the data and still have time to stay in touch with your most important resource—the people.

Project 2003 facilitates your ability to understand what's happening quickly. And with better information, you're able to act more decisively and with greater confidence. Better, faster information means better, faster decisions. And that means better, faster project results!

What could be better?

More Good Stuff

If you're a rookie project planner, there's a common mistake you'll want to avoid. In fact, it's a perfectly common mistake to make. It's the belief that with foresight and skill, a plan can be created that, if closely followed, will ensure project success. Alas, the myth of the perfect plan! Need I remind you that Murphy, uninvited guest though he may be, is on your project team?

When your plan is complete and you're ready to go, remember, the plan is never actually finished. You're dealing with the unknown, so be ready and willing to change the plan as you must. The perfect plan is only as perfect as your willingness to adapt it to changing conditions. Adjust, amend, and improve it as you proceed.

There is no such thing as a perfect plan. The closest thing you can get is a perfectly adaptable plan.

Chaos Control for Project Managers

To maintain control of a project, the project manager must have an understanding of the project's state of forwardness. As the phrase *state of forwardness* implies, the true status of a project goes beyond the percentage of completion, units achieved, or budget compliance. Although all these measures of project progress are important, none of them, whether considered alone or together, tells the whole story.

Measuring Progress

Collecting and measuring progress data, as set forth in typical project plans, may ignore essential indicators of achievement:

- ◆ Is the implementation strategy producing the expected results?

- ◆ Are problems being effectively dealt with as the project unfolds? Or are problems being avoided, perhaps piling up, only to block progress at some point in the future?

- ◆ Is the project team staying focused, positive, and productive?

- ◆ Is stakeholder interest remaining at satisfactory levels or is their interest waning?

- ◆ If the project is a success, will it achieve the desired results?

Measuring progress solely against a plan has other problems as well. Even the best plans are only estimates of how the future will unfold. No one gets the future right all the time. Even the best planners occasionally overlook essential elements or critical phases, or fail to realize the significance of unexpected difficulties.

For example, consider a major health-care company's project of developing a revolutionary new medical device. For over a year, the project was on budget, on time, and according to the project plan, progressing well.

There was, however, one flaw in the project's progress. The results of this device, as predicted in the initial laboratory research, couldn't be replicated in the prototype stage. Literally millions of dollars had been spent. The project team was under pressure to show results. They pressed on, hoping this stumbling block could be resolved. All the while, the project was on track and on budget, according to the plan. But rather than picking up speed on the way to success, the project was picking up speed on the way to disaster!

In retrospect, the plan had overlooked one small, but essential element. In this case, a milestone that should have signaled go or no-go hadn't been noted in the plan. As the project manager related this oversight to me, I couldn't

> **Project Pitfalls**
>
> Even ill-fated projects can (and usually do) show progress. What ill-fated projects are missing is accomplishment. Remember, project management software can't separate progress from achievement. Only knowledgeable project managers with good judgment skills can do that. Judging a project's progress solely against the plan is folly.

help but recall a sign I once saw while driving across a desolate part of the western United States. It read, "You might be lost, but you're making good time."

Minutiae to Milestones, What Should You Monitor?

Determining how much detail to track can be a difficult choice. Greater amounts of detail don't automatically increase your control. More detail does, however, increase your workload and the workload of your team.

When deciding how much detail to track, keep it as simple as possible. Consider the experience level of your team, the difficulty of the project, and the priority of the triple constraints. Also check to see whether the contract documents require any specific progress reporting. Many organizations have a set policy for reporting progress. You'll want to keep your project in compliance with all contractual and organizational procedures.

In all cases, monitor everything that you decided was important enough to include in your plan. This usually includes workflow progress, task durations, and milestone accomplishments. In addition, you may want to include resources, equipment, material usage, and expenditures.

Don't, however, get trapped in the detail. Successful project managers monitor achievement and attitude as well as budgets and durations. The best way to do that is to make sure your project plan identifies all key achievement milestones. For additional information on setting milestones, see Chapter 5.

Manage your milestones with an obsession! They are the key to achieving success.

> **Secrets of Success**
>
> In the dynamic world of projects, you may be forced to veer from the original plan frequently. Teams, durations, equipment, and resources may be in constant flux. In this environment, keeping the plan perfectly up-to-date may prove impossible. Nonetheless, by selecting the right milestones and focusing on this achievement, you can complete even the most chaotic project successfully.

> **Secrets of Success**
>
> Seasoned project managers realize that progress reported by hours of work or percentage of completion can be grossly misleading. Difficulties may arise, or worse yet, the person responsible for the task may not accurately report his progress. To avoid these problems, rely on observed achievement rather than reported progress. With this approach, the project manager gauges three checkpoints for each task or milestone—not started, in progress, or completed. This progress information should be weighted heavily in all management decisions.

Collecting the Information

The fastest way to collect project information is to have the person in charge of each task provide status updates. With a little work, this can be input directly into the project plan via e-mail or the web. These methods are described in Chapters 19 and 20.

These methods work great in some situations, but for most projects, progress reporting is still done the old-fashioned way—people talking to people.

Whether it's done electronically or person to person, remember that until a task is completed, progress is always a judgment call. Furthermore, when asked to evaluate progress, some team members are naturally optimistic (perhaps overly so), and others may be pessimistic. Always consider the source and quality of the progress information you're relying on. Whenever possible, get out of your office. Go see for yourself!

> **Secrets of Success**
>
> There was a time when MBWA (managing by walking around) was in vogue. Managers were encouraged to get out of their offices and see what was going on. That's still good advice. The game is won or lost on the field of play, not in the bleachers. The closer you get to the work and the people doing the work, the better your perspective will be.

Finding the Bad News Is Good News

Effectively managing a project requires the ability to find out what's not going well, and then fix it. Moreover, spotting the problem early is important—that's when you have more options available to solve the problem. (For problem-solving techniques, see Chapter 15.)

Unfortunately, the natural tendency in most project teams is to delay announcing problems or to minimize a problem's significance. In fact, good news travels faster than bad news in the project environment! Because bad news won't come to you, you've got to go to it! Seek it out. When you find bad news, that's good! Now you can fix the problem.

The best way to uncover problems is to ask open-ended questions. Don't wait for trouble; ask your team probing questions on an ongoing basis. You'll get best results with a polite and gracious demeanor, so keep rapport levels high. The following list of questions is effective:

What problems have you encountered thus far?

What problems do your foresee?

> What is your biggest concern right now?
>
> How might this change in the future?
>
> How is the project going?

If you receive a one-word answer such as "fine," continue probing with this, my all-time favorite probing technique:

> Tell me about it.

You needn't stop after using it once. In fact, it becomes increasingly useful as you continue:

> Tell me about that!

Open-ended questions uncover essential information that your plan does not directly address. When using these probing questions, remain emotionally neutral. Don't send messages of mistrust, fear, or condemnation with your tone or demeanor. Make sure they see you as a project manager who seeks the good and the bad news with equal candor and professionalism.

Collecting Progress Information

You need a steady stream of information to monitor project progress. As a rule, collect data on everything included in your plan (tasks, durations, resources, equipment, budgets, and milestones). This may include the actual start and finish dates of tasks, the percentage of work completed, and the actual costs incurred. We refer to these experienced values as *actuals*.

You'll get the best results if the actuals are collected at set intervals of time. On projects a year or more in duration, collecting data monthly is probably sufficient. For projects two or three months in duration, you may want to collect data weekly. In fast-moving projects with a duration of a few days to a month or two, you may need daily updates. Collect actuals often enough to identify problems early.

Establishing a Baseline

To provide an easy reference point for comparing actuals against the plan, Project 2003 enables you to set baselines. Key information about tasks, resources, and assignments is captured and stored for comparisons.

Seasoned project managers understand the need to manage expectations and performance in different ways for different stakeholder groups. Consider using a separate set of baselines for each major stakeholder group. You may want a more aggressive baseline to manage vendors than for your core project team. A third, more conservative baseline, could be used for reporting to owners and sponsors.

> **More Good Stuff**
>
> In Microsoft Project 2003, if the Planning Wizard is active, it prompts you to set a baseline when you save the project file. (You can turn the wizard on or off by selecting **Options** from the **Tools** menu and going to the **General** tab in the dialog box. Then check or uncheck **Advice from Planning Wizard.**)

To set a baseline, open the **Tools** menu, select **Tracking,** and then choose **Save baseline** and **Entire project.** The dialog box appears as shown in Figure 13.1. Select **Entire project** to establish the initial baseline. Baseline information is stored for nearly 20 fields including durations, resources, costs, start and finish dates. Now actuals are entered, Project can keep you up to date on progress and variances. You may store up to 11 baselines in Project 2003.

Select to save initial baseline

Select to amend baseline changes

Figure 13.1

Setting a baseline after the plan has been completed and just before execution begins allows you to compare actuals against the plan.

If you add or change a task after you've set the initial baseline, don't worry. You can always set new baseline information for them. First, select the tasks for which you want to set a baseline. If the tasks are next to one another, click the first one, and then press **Shift** and click the last one. If the tasks are not adjacent, click the first one, and then press **Ctrl** while you click each additional task. After they are all highlighted, select the **Select tasks** option in the Save Baseline dialog box and click **OK.**

Now that your baseline is set, you can begin recording the project's actual performance.

Updating Your Project Plan

Entering actuals can be as complex or as simple as you want to make it. At a minimal level, you can track the start and finish dates of each task. If you need to track more, there are many options available. Project 2003 enables you to track durations, work, resources used, and costs incurred.

Entering Task Start and Finish Actuals

Tracking the start and finish dates of tasks helps you keep the project on schedule. As we have seen, if tasks on the critical path finish late, the entire project will finish later than planned. Always keep a close watch on all critical tasks' start and finish dates.

One of the easiest ways to enter the actual start and finish dates is in a combination view. Open the **Tracking Gantt** view by selecting it from the **View** menu. Now open a lower pane by clicking **Split** from the **Window** menu. Click the lower pane to make it active, and then right-click the lower pane's indicator bar and select **More Views** from the dialog box. Find the **Task Details Form** view and apply it. Your screen should now look like the one in Figure 13.2.

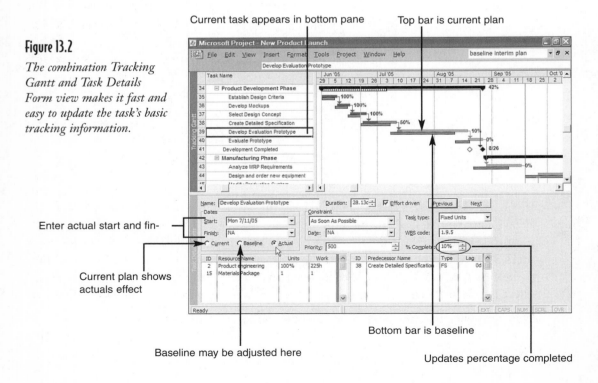

Figure 13.2

The combination Tracking Gantt and Task Details Form view makes it fast and easy to update the task's basic tracking information.

Entering Actual Work or Duration

Every once in a while, Project 2003 does so much that it can become a little tricky. Remember how Project calculated work, duration, and units in Chapter 9? When you update work or duration actuals, these relationships are at it again. It's easiest to understand how duration and work affect one another by reviewing their definitions:

Actual duration is the amount of time the task has been in progress.

Actual work is the amount of work that has been accomplished.

Obviously, work may proceed better or worse than planned. Therefore, Actual Duration and Actual Work may not always be in direct proportion to one another. For example, if resources were assigned to an effort-driven task (the default), you should ignore Actual Duration and enter Actual Work completed. Project 2003 then calculates Remaining Work as Work (planned) minus Actual Work. It also calculates Percent Work Complete as Actual Work divided by Remaining Work.

When you update a task's Actual Duration, Project 2003 calculates the Percentage of Completion as Actual Duration divided by Duration. Remaining Duration is calculated as Duration minus Actual Duration.

The easiest way to enter updates for Actual Duration or Actual Work is to use the Tracking table in the Task Sheet view. Open the **View** menu and select **More Views.** Then find **Task Sheet** in the More Views dialog box and apply it. To make the Tracking table active, open the **View** menu, select **Table,** and then choose **Tracking.** Figure 13.3 shows this view.

Enter Actual Duration

Calculated or when entered calculates Work and Duration

Enter Actual Work

	Task Name	Act. Start	Act. Finish	% Comp.	Phys. % Comp.	Act. Dur.	Rem. Dur.	Act. Cost	Act. Work
1	⊟ **New Product Launch**	Wed 6/1/05	NA	12%	0%	26.87 days	190.25 days	$114,742.50	926.5 hrs
2	⊟ **Screening Phase**	Wed 6/1/05	Fri 6/24/05	100%	0%	18 days	0 days	$43,460.00	316 hrs
3	Secure Seed Capital	Wed 6/1/05	Tue 6/14/05	100%	0%	0.5 mons	0 mons	$10,000.00	160 hrs
4	Create Screening Criteria	Wed 6/1/05	Tue 6/14/05	100%	0%	2 wks	0 wks	$8,000.00	80 hrs
5	Evaluate Total Available Marke	Wed 6/15/05	Tue 6/21/05	100%	0%	4.5 days	0 days	$12,060.00	36 hrs
6	Identify Driving Trends	Wed 6/22/05	Wed 6/22/05	100%	0%	8 hrs	0 hrs	$2,680.00	8 hrs
7	Analyze Overall Competition	Tue 6/21/05	Wed 6/22/05	100%	0%	1 day	0 days	$2,680.00	8 hrs
8	Identify Servicable Market Mtg	Wed 6/22/05	Fri 6/24/05	100%	0%	24 hrs	0 hrs	$8,040.00	24 hrs
9	Screening Completed	NA	NA	0%	0%	0 days	0 days	$0.00	0 hrs
10	⊟ **Market Evaluation Phase**	Wed 6/22/05	NA	10%	0%	1.65 days	15.35 days	$5,166.00	28 hrs
11	Gather Demographics	NA	NA	0%	0%	0 days	2 days	$0.00	0 hrs
12	Segment Markets	NA	NA	0%	0%	0 days	3 days	$0.00	0 hrs
13	Identify Competition	Wed 6/22/05	NA	50%	0%	1.75 days	1.75 days	$5,166.00	28 hrs
14	Select Targeted Markets	NA	NA	0%	0%	0 days	5 days	$0.00	0 hrs
15	Identify Appeals	NA	NA	0%	0%	0 days	2.5 days	$0.00	0 hrs
16	Finalize Product Criteria	NA	NA	0%	0%	0 days	2 days	$0.00	0 hrs
17	Market Evaluation Completed	NA	NA	0%	0%	0 days	0 days	$0.00	0 hrs
18	⊞ **Advertising & Promotions Ph**	NA	NA	0%	0%	0 days	29.33 days	$0.00	0 hrs
28	Adv & Promo Launched	NA	NA	0%	0%	0 days	0 days	$0.00	0 hrs
29	⊟ **Sales and Distribution Phase**	NA	NA	0%	0%	0 days	90 days	$0.00	0 hrs
30	Set Up Distributors	NA	NA	0%	0%	0 days	5 days	$0.00	0 hrs

Ready | | | | | | EXT | CAPS | NUM | SCRL | OVR

Figure 13.3

The Tracking table in the Task Sheet view makes fast work of entering Actual Work, Actual Durations, or Percentage of Completion.

When you enter a percentage of completion, Project 2003 calculates Actual Work and Remaining Work. First it calculates Actual Work as Work times the Percentage Complete. Then Remaining Work is calculated as Work minus Actual Work.

More Good Stuff

New in Project 2003 is the Physical % Complete. This field is for your estimate of percentage complete and is not connected with duration or % Complete calculations. You can use it to note progress discrepancies where the difficulty of work is not evenly distributed throughout the task's duration. For example, a duration completed to 95 percent might not have yielded 95 percent actual progress. The last 5 percent may hold the most difficult or risky work.

Summary task percentages of completion are calculated as the total Actual Work of the related subtasks divided by the total Work of the subtasks. In other words, subtasks are rolled up to calculate their summary task's percentage of completion. You can manually change the summary task's percentage of completion also. However, the subtasks are set as complete according to their listing order, not their actual completion. It looks nice, but don't rely too heavily on the information!

Another method of updating tasks is available directly from the toolbar. Place your pointer on the toolbar area and right-click. Select the **Tracking** toolbar from the pop-up list, as shown in Figure 13.4. You can click and hold on the toolbar handle to place the Tracking toolbar in any convenient location.

Figure 13.4

Open the Tracking toolbar to quickly mark the percentage of completion for selected tasks in any view.

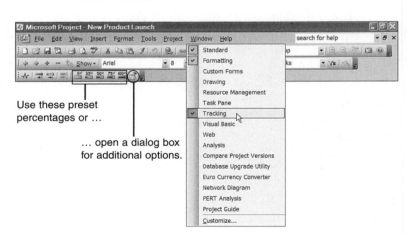

Use these preset percentages or …

… open a dialog box for additional options.

One of the great things about Project is that you can immediately see what effects your changes and updates make on the schedule. To view these effects when updating actuals, open the **Tracking Gantt** view and click the **Update Tasks** button on the Tracking toolbar. The Update Tasks dialog box may be used to change Percentage of Work Complete, Actual Duration, and Remaining Duration. In addition, you may change a task's Actual Start and Finish dates here, as shown in Figure 13.5.

Opens the Update Tasks dialog box

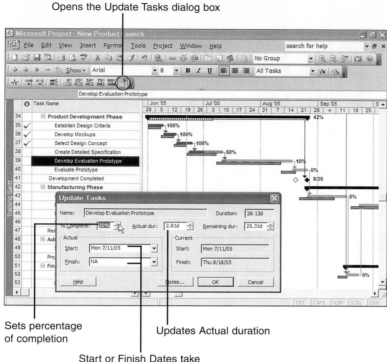

Sets percentage
of completion

Updates Actual duration

Start or Finish Dates take
precedence over other entries

Figure 13.5

The Update Tasks dialog box enables you to immediately see the results of your updates in the Tracking Gantt view.

When you don't need this level of detail in your actuals, use the Update Project dialog box to track progress. Select the **Tools** menu as shown in Figure 13.6. Then select **Tracking** and click **Update Project.** The Update Project dialog box shown in Figure 13.7 appears.

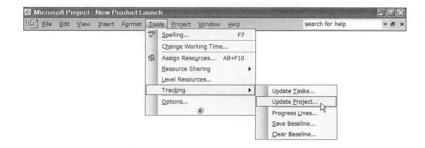

Figure 13.6

Select Update Project from the Tools, Tracking menu.

Figure 13.7

When your project is being completed exactly as planned or when greater accuracy is not needed, the fastest way to update is with the Update Project dialog box.

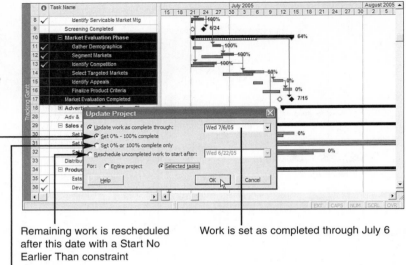

Percentage calculated based on start and finish

Remaining work is rescheduled after this date with a Start No Earlier Than constraint

Work is set as completed through July 6

Show only as 0% or 100% complete

Bringing Your Costs Up-to-Date

By default, costs are automatically updated for you in Project 2003 according to the baseline plan. As you update duration or work, costs are accrued as a percentage of task completion times the sum of the task's resource and fixed costs. This makes updating costs easy (and sometimes overly simplistic)!

It is rare that costs are actually incurred at the same rate as a task's completion. For example, consider the task of roofing a large building. The materials would probably be delivered (and the costs incurred) long before labor on the task begins. In this case, Project 2003 would accrue material costs, incorrectly, throughout their application (or at the beginning or end) rather than upon their delivery. Worse yet, if installation of the roofing were delayed, actual costs on this task would be understated for quite some time.

Although the costing method employed by Project is rudimentary, it provides adequate tracking capability for many projects.

If you decide to override the default cost accrual methods (and this is often wise), and enter your own actual cost information, the procedure is straightforward. First, stop Project 2003 from automatically calculating costs on an accrual basis. To do this, choose **Options** from the **Tools** menu to open the Options dialog box. Then click the **Calculation** tab and clear the check mark from the **Actual costs are always calculated by Microsoft Project** check box, as shown in Figure 13.8.

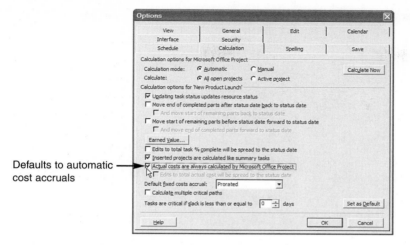

Figure 13.8

Clear the default, costs auto-matically calculated, before updating costs manually.

Defaults to automatic cost accruals

The easiest way to update costs depends on the type of cost involved. Methods for updating actuals for accrued resource assignment costs, per-use resource costs, and fixed task costs are described next.

Updating Actuals for Accrued Resource Costs

Accrued resource assignment costs are those costs that result from resource assignments. This includes labor, rent, or other costs that accrue as a function of the amount of work or duration the task requires. To enter actuals for these costs, select **Task Usage** from the **View** menu. Select **Table Tracking** from the **View** menu, and then select **Tracking** from the submenu that appears (see Figure 13.9).

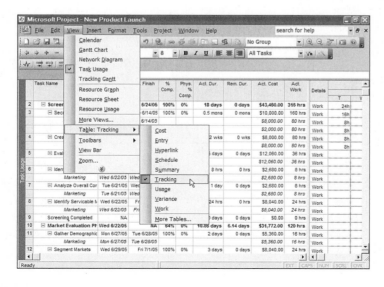

Figure 13.9

The Table Tracking and Task Usage options allows easy updates to actual costs for resources.

To update actual costs for the resource up to the current date, click the **Act. Cost** field and enter the total costs (see Figure 13.10).

Figure 13.10

To update an accrued resource assignment cost, use the Task Usage view.

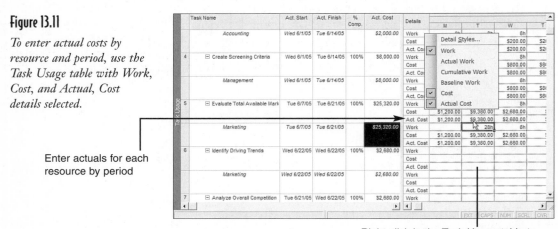

Enter the actual cost for the resource

To update the costs for a resource on a day-by-day basis, use the Task Usage pane. Drag open the pane until the dates are revealed. Right-click in the Task Usage table and add Actual Cost to the table from the pop-up menu, as shown in Figure 13.11.

Scroll to the dates and tasks you want to update and enter the actuals. Notice that the Act. Cost field changes as you enter the actuals. If the wrong timescale is showing (perhaps weeks rather than days), right-click the **Task Usage** table column heads and select **Timescale.** Change the scale to match your actuals data. Return to the Task Usage table and enter the actuals.

Figure 13.11

To enter actual costs by resource and period, use the Task Usage table with Work, Cost, and Actual, Cost details selected.

Enter actuals for each resource by period

Right-click in the Task Usage table to add Actual Costs to the fields shown

Updating Actual Per-Use Resource Costs

Per-use resource cost actuals are entered in the resource sheet. In the **View** menu, select **Resource Sheet,** point to **Table,** and then click **Entry.** Go to the Cost/Use field and enter the actual for the resources you want to change, as shown in Figure 13.12. The change is updated to all tasks that resource is assigned to as well as the project's total scheduled costs.

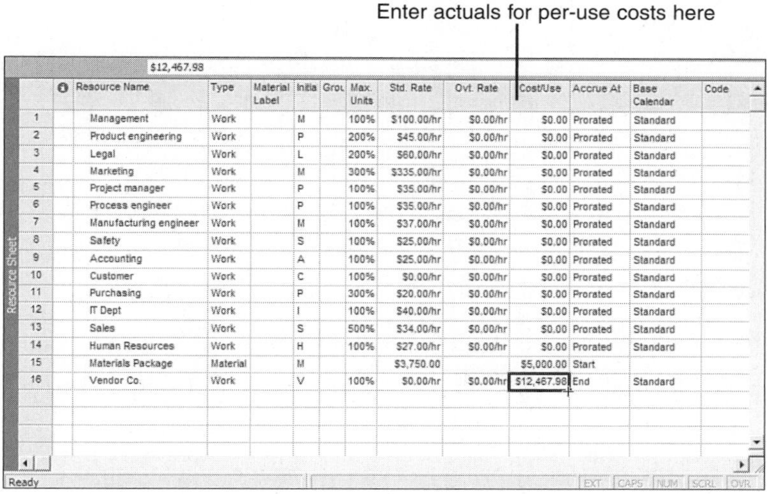

Enter actuals for per-use costs here

Figure 13.12

Use the Resource Sheet Entry table to update per-use actuals. Costs for all tasks using this resource are recalculated.

Updating Actual Fixed Task Costs

To update actuals for fixed task costs, use the task sheet. From the **View** menu, select **More Views,** and then apply the **Task Sheet.** Then point to **Table Tracking** from the **View** menu and select **Cost.** You're ready to enter fixed costs. Click in the Fixed Cost field and enter the actual value, as shown in Figure 13.13. Project recalculates the project's scheduled costs whenever the fixed cost is changed.

Congratulations! You've just mastered updating the project plan with actuals. In the next chapter, you'll learn how to turn all this new data into information you can use with Project's powerful analysis tools.

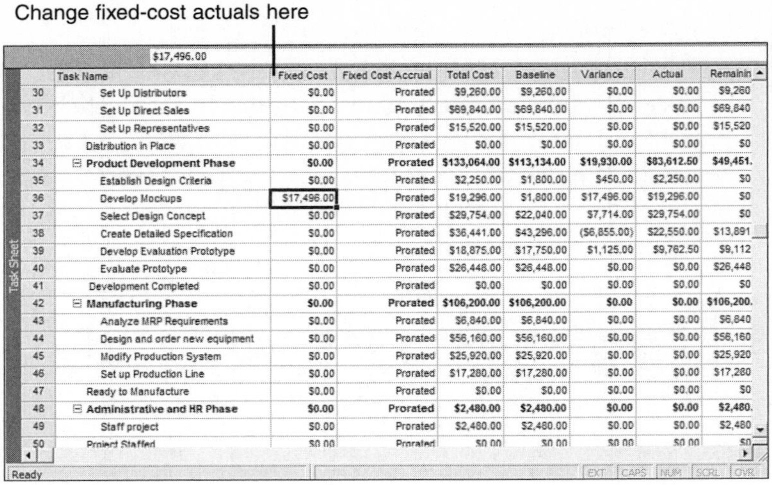

Figure 13.13

The Task Sheet Cost table provides the easiest way to update fixed-cost actuals.

Change fixed-cost actuals here

	Task Name	Fixed Cost	Fixed Cost Accrual	Total Cost	Baseline	Variance	Actual	Remainin
30	Set Up Distributors	$0.00	Prorated	$9,260.00	$9,260.00	$0.00	$0.00	$9,260
31	Set Up Direct Sales	$0.00	Prorated	$69,840.00	$69,840.00	$0.00	$0.00	$69,840
32	Set Up Representatives	$0.00	Prorated	$15,520.00	$15,520.00	$0.00	$0.00	$15,520
33	Distribution in Place	$0.00	Prorated	$0.00	$0.00	$0.00	$0.00	$0
34	⊟ Product Development Phase	$0.00	Prorated	$133,064.00	$113,134.00	$19,930.00	$83,612.50	$49,451.
35	Establish Design Criteria	$0.00	Prorated	$2,250.00	$1,800.00	$450.00	$2,250.00	$0
36	Develop Mockups	$17,496.00	Prorated	$19,296.00	$1,800.00	$17,496.00	$19,296.00	$0
37	Select Design Concept	$0.00	Prorated	$29,754.00	$22,040.00	$7,714.00	$29,754.00	$0
38	Create Detailed Specification	$0.00	Prorated	$36,441.00	$43,296.00	($6,855.00)	$22,550.00	$13,891
39	Develop Evaluation Prototype	$0.00	Prorated	$18,875.00	$17,750.00	$1,125.00	$9,762.50	$9,112
40	Evaluate Prototype	$0.00	Prorated	$26,448.00	$26,448.00	$0.00	$0.00	$26,448
41	Development Completed	$0.00	Prorated	$0.00	$0.00	$0.00	$0.00	$0
42	⊟ Manufacturing Phase	$0.00	Prorated	$106,200.00	$106,200.00	$0.00	$0.00	$106,200.
43	Analyze MRP Requirements	$0.00	Prorated	$6,840.00	$6,840.00	$0.00	$0.00	$6,840
44	Design and order new equipment	$0.00	Prorated	$56,160.00	$56,160.00	$0.00	$0.00	$56,160
45	Modify Production System	$0.00	Prorated	$25,920.00	$25,920.00	$0.00	$0.00	$25,920
46	Set up Production Line	$0.00	Prorated	$17,280.00	$17,280.00	$0.00	$0.00	$17,280
47	Ready to Manufacture	$0.00	Prorated	$0.00	$0.00	$0.00	$0.00	$0
48	⊟ Administrative and HR Phase	$0.00	Prorated	$2,480.00	$2,480.00	$0.00	$0.00	$2,480.
49	Staff project	$0.00	Prorated	$2,480.00	$2,480.00	$0.00	$0.00	$2,480
50	Project Staffed	$0.00	Prorated	$0.00	$0.00	$0.00	$0.00	$0

Ready   EXT CAPS NUM SCRL OVR

The Least You Need to Know

◆ Project actuals provide the information you need to keep a project on track.

◆ Actuals can be tracked for task start and finish dates, work completed, and costs incurred.

◆ Baselines can be set for the project to provide a comparison of actuals to the plan.

◆ At minimum, closely track start and finish dates on the critical path. When these tasks slip, the entire project may be at risk of not finishing on time.

◆ Carefully select and manage milestones. Trying to stay abreast of the minutiae can take your attention away from true achievement.

◆ Not all the information you need can be tracked with the project plan. Be observant, ask open-ended questions, and maintain high levels of communication with your team.

Managing Progress

In This Chapter

- ◆ Analyze project progress with charts, tables, views and reports
- ◆ Keep your team informed of commitments, schedules, and deadlines
- ◆ Identify project bottlenecks and problems before they occur
- ◆ Develop strategies to get a project back on track

The entire project management body of knowledge was created around the notion that a picture is worth a thousand words. Understanding workflow, time, resources, and costs requires a lot of data. Unfortunately, data isn't information. It's just detail: facts, figures, amounts, costs, dates, relationships, tasks ... well, you get the point. In most projects there is enough data to get lost in. And that's exactly what some project managers do. They're stuck in their offices until late at night, sorting through reams of meaningless data, trying to sort the good news from the bad. And while they're lost in all that data, the project is unmanaged, possibly wandering off course or, worse yet, grinding to a complete halt.

You, on the other hand, made the good decision to bring order and control to this chaos. You invested in Microsoft Project 2003 and this book. And now you get to cash in on all your work thus far. In this chapter, you get to turn all the data you've so meticulously created into the stuff success is made of: information! Get ready to be amazed. You're about to experience the primary benefits of Project 2003. You'll be able to monitor progress, analyze options, communicate with your team, and keep your boss smiling. You may even be able to make it home in time for dinner!

Analyzing Project Progress

Good project managers know exactly where their project stands every step of the way. Their fingers are on the project's pulse, monitoring progress, catching problems early, anticipating needs, and effectively using every resource at their disposal. Most of their information comes from the views, charts, and reports that are ready to use right out of the Project 2003 box.

If you need to emphasize key information, filter out unnecessary data, or highlight elements with special formatting, Project won't disappoint you. In fact, there are so many options that they can get in the way if you let them. Just remember, the idea is to make your job faster and easier, not more difficult. Learn to use the basics expertly, and leave the fancy window dressing to the rookies. You're seeking project success, not an award for best-dressed network diagram!

Project Statistics at a Glance

For a quick overview of your project, use the Project Statistics dialog box, as shown in Figure 14.1. This quick look describes the project in broad brushstrokes—start dates, finish dates, variances, duration, work, and cost. It is a good way for department heads or division managers to stay abreast of multiple projects within their areas of responsibility.

For example, if all project plans are accessible from the manager's computer (perhaps in one directory of a local area network), the manager can easily pop open this screen for each project and monitor progress. To view the Project Statistics dialog box, select **Project Information** from the Project menu and click **Statistics.**

This is a trick you may or may not want to teach to your boss!

Figure 14.1

The Project Statistics dialog box provides a quick look at project status.

Project Statistics for 'New Product Launch'

	Start		Finish	
Current		Wed 6/1/05		Mon 7/31/06
Baseline		Wed 6/1/05		Fri 3/24/06
Actual		Wed 6/1/05		NA
Variance		0d		90.83d

	Duration	Work	Cost
Current	303.83d	7,616h	$615,742.67
Baseline	213d?	7,467h	$591,673.67
Actual	44.99d	1,054.5h	$154,608.50
Remaining	258.84d	6,561.5h	$461,134.17

Percent complete:
Duration: 15%   Work: 14%

Close

Gantt Charts

The Gantt chart may be the most useful project management document ever developed. It has been around since the beginning of the twentieth century, and it's still going strong! (We should all be so lucky.) Its popularity is no doubt due to its power to communicate and its inherit ease to understand. With little instruction, even the most boneheaded member of your team (just kidding) can understand a Gantt chart. This is one useful, easy to read project document!

More Good Stuff

The Gantt chart was developed around the turn of the century (100 years ago, that is) by industrial engineer Henry Gantt. America was in the middle of the industrial revolution (the revolution just before the information revolution, that is). Complex manufacturing and construction projects abounded—skyscrapers, battleships, and new assembly lines were common projects. Mr. Gantt added greatly to the project management body of knowledge by developing his graphical representation of a project's tasks, duration, and sequence of work. His simple bar chart is so useful and easy to understand that I'll bet it'll be around for another hundred years! Thanks, Henry!

The Gantt chart is great because it shows task start and stop times, durations, and workflow sequences, all on a timeline. And if you hang a little more information on it, you can communicate resources, costs, completion, and other detailed information clearly. With the right formatting, the critical path is visible and kept in the forefront of your thinking. When time is of the essence (and it usually is), a Gantt chart is good to have around.

The Gantt Chart View

This is the default view for Project 2003, and for good reason. This view uses both text and graphics to communicate tasks, durations, and workflow sequence, as shown in Figure 14.2. The graphical depiction is created on a timescale where each task is represented as a bar whose length indicates the task's duration.

The right side of this view is displayed as a Gantt chart and the left side as a table. The table provides detailed information, such as (early) start and (early) finish dates, duration, predecessors, and resources assigned to the task. The table may be changed to other preset columns by selecting **View, Table.** Columns may be hidden or inserted by right-clicking the column header and selecting **Insert Column** or **Hide Column.** (When inserting, the new column appears to the left of the insertion point.)

Column widths may be adjusted by clicking and dragging the column head divider lines. The vertical divider between the sheet and the chart may be dragged to the left or right, providing additional space for the information you are interested in. To snap the column width to fit all data, in the header row double-click the right-side column divider.

Figure 14.2

The Gantt Chart view is the default view. Use it to set up your project's tasks, durations, dependencies, and resources.

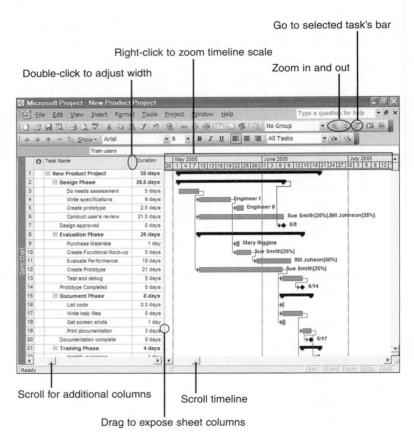

Go to selected task's bar

Right-click to zoom timeline scale

Zoom in and out

Double-click to adjust width

Scroll for additional columns

Scroll timeline

Drag to expose sheet columns

Finding the information you want in Project can be a little like looking at the world through a periscope. To quickly orient yourself and navigate to the information you want, right-click the timeline, select **Zoom,** check **Entire project,** and click **OK.** The timeline will fill all available space and will include the earliest through latest task in the project. To fine-tune the timeline, open the Timescale dialog box shown in Figure 14.3 by double-clicking the timeline header.

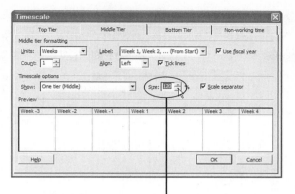

Compress or expand current scale

Figure 14.3

You can adjust the timescale's labels and range in the Timescale dialog box.

The Gantt view is good for

◆ Entering the work-breakdown structure and establishing tasks, summary tasks, and milestone tasks.

◆ Creating the initial workflow sequence by establishing task dependencies either in the predecessor column or by linking tasks in the Gantt Chart view.

◆ Entering estimated durations, and with the PERT Analysis toolbar activated, entering weighted average durations with PERT estimates.

◆ Establishing a project schedule and total project duration.

◆ Assigning personnel and other resources to the project, task by task.

◆ Communicating to project personnel when they will need to start and finish the tasks they are responsible for.

◆ Communicating an overview of the project's workflow and total duration to stakeholders.

Wow! No wonder this chart has been so popular all these years! To open the Gantt Chart view, click **Gantt Chart** from the View menu or from the view bar.

The Detail Gantt View

The Detail Gantt view is an important view for managing your project's scheduled completion dates. Slack and slippage is graphically displayed, alerting you to potential deadline problems. In Figure 14.4, the task Write Specifications started 4 days late and is approximately 75 percent done. This has forced out the early start of Create Prototype by 4 days, which in turn has rippled throughout the critical path causing the final milestone, New Product Delivered, to slip out by 4 days.

Figure 14.4

The Detail Gantt view reveals the critical path, schedule slippage, and slack.

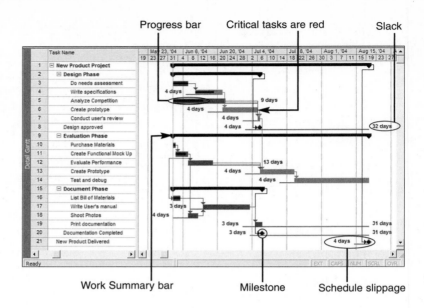

Progress bar   Critical tasks are red   Slack

Work Summary bar   Milestone   Schedule slippage

The alert project manager can see that to bring this project in on time, action has to be immediately taken to shorten the remaining critical path. In this project, only two viable options remain: Shorten by 4 days the total durations of Create Prototype and Test and Debug. With 20 percent of the project's duration already expended, this project manager has no time to waste! Presumably, applying additional effort to these tasks could shorten them. The problem is, where are the additional resources going to come from?

The Detail Gantt sometimes comes to the rescue as well as to the alert! Assuming that the resources assigned to Write User's Manual are qualified, they may be able to help out. According to the Detail Gantt, although Write User's Manual has already slipped 3 days, it isn't yet in danger of being late. In fact, it has total slack time of 31 days available. In other words, this task can be delayed up to 31 more days and not impact the project's deadline. Pulling the resources off Write User's Manual and using them on the Prototype and then on Test and Debug might do the trick!

Now that's putting the power of information to work—this time saving the project manager's reputation!

The Detail Gantt view is good for

 ◆ Everything the Gantt chart is good for, but because of the additional information it depicts, the Detail Gantt may confuse team members who do not understand the concepts of critical paths, slack, and slippage.

 ◆ Identifying task slack time and task slippage.

 ◆ Evaluating resource use options.

The Leveling Gantt View

When you have a limited supply of resources to cover all the work in a project, your favorite view is bound to be the Leveling Gantt. This view is used in conjunction with the robust leveling features of Project 2003. When a resource is scheduled for two or more tasks at the same time, leveling reschedules the tasks. That way, you don't have to clone people!

To open the Leveling Gantt view, select **More Views** from the **View** menu and apply the **Leveling Gantt.** As shown in Figure 14.5, the right side of the view is just like a Detail Gantt except for one thing: The task bars are split horizontally to indicate the before and after effects of leveling. In Figure 14.5, the effect of leveling workloads on the limited resources was modest. Even though Analyze Competition was delayed 20 days, by splitting tasks and applying resources first to the critical path, Project 2003 rescheduled without impacting the project's finish date. To learn more about leveling, refer to Chapter 12.

The Leveling Gantt view is good for

◆ Viewing the before and after effects of leveling resources.

◆ Understanding which tasks were leveled, the amount of delay used, and how those changes impacted the rest of the schedule.

◆ Reassigning resources to tasks in response to overallocations.

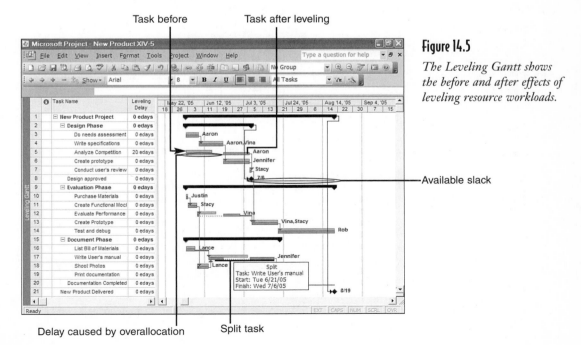

Task before   Task after leveling

Available slack

Delay caused by overallocation   Split task

Figure 14.5

The Leveling Gantt shows the before and after effects of leveling resource workloads.

The Tracking Gantt View

There should be a drum roll playing as this view opens! With one look at the Tracking Gantt, you can tell whether your project is behind or ahead of schedule. The Tracking Gantt chart displays two bars, similar to the Leveling Gantt. However, this time the lower bar is the plan you originally saved as the baseline. As you update progress, the actuals are shown as the top bar, giving you a task by task view of where you're ahead and where you're behind.

Secrets of Success

Timely progress updates are important. The first 15 percent to 20 percent of a project's total duration is an excellent indicator of project success or failure. Most project managers don't spot trouble soon enough and do too little when they finally decide to act. Early vigilance and aggressive corrective action is the sign of a project management professional.

To open the Tracking Gantt, click it in the view bar or select it from the View menu. As shown in Figure 14.6, task completion is indicated by a solid dark bar and a percentage. As you can see in the figure, this project's difficulties are immediately visible. The Write Specification task has gotten off to a slow start and the effects are felt all the way to the final milestone. The resulting delay will extend the project's completion by about a week.

Figure 14.6

The Tracking Gantt compares actual progress to the project's baseline and calculates a new schedule for all remaining tasks.

The Tracking Gantt view is good for

◆ Viewing actual progress compared to the project's baseline.

◆ Viewing actual start and finish dates and their impact on the reminder of the schedule.

◆ Managing the achievement of project milestones.

Enhancing Your View with Baselines and Progress Lines

You may enhance the communication capability of any Gantt view by adding a baseline or progress line. These enhancements use the project's planned data and actuals to make a visual comparison of progress.

Baselines

To use any of the features for comparing actuals to the baseline plan, as you saw in Figure 14.6, you first must set a baseline for your project. Do this when your plan is complete, just before you start the project. If you change the plan, you can always update the baseline and you can keep up to 11 separate baselines for each project. To set a baseline, select the **Tools** menu and point to **Tracking.** Then choose **Save baseline,** and select **Entire project.** Three sets of information are saved in the baseline data for later comparison:

◆ Task starts and finishes, durations, work, and costs

◆ Resources, work, and costs

◆ Assignment dates, work, and costs.

In addition to baselines information, Project 2003 can save up to 10 sets of task start and finish dates at any time. These can be compared to the baseline or current plan.

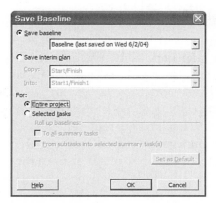

Figure 14.7

When you're satisfied the plan is ready for execution, save the baseline to monitor and control against. Multiple baselines can help you manage communications with diverse stakeholder groups.

Progress Lines

Progress lines provide a graphical representation of actuals to plan as of a given date. Project 2003 draws a vertical progress indicator line in any Gantt chart. As you can see in Figure 14.8, when it runs over task bars the line stretches to the left or right, connecting at the percentage of completion as of the progress date. For tasks behind schedule, the line stretches to the left; for tasks ahead of schedule, the line stretches to the right.

Figure 14.8

Progress lines add a graphic comparison of actuals to a given progress date on any Gantt chart.

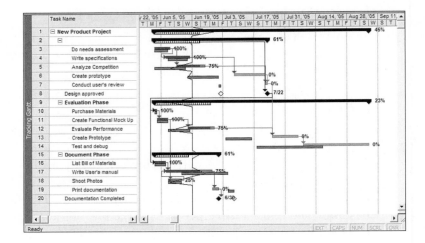

Multiple progress lines may be set to indicate key dates. To add a progress line to your Gantt chart, right-click the toolbar and select **Tracking.** Then, click the **Add Progress Line** button on the Tracking toolbar. Place the pointer on the Gantt chart where you want to insert a progress line and click. To change how progress lines display or to remove unwanted lines, select **Tracking** from the Tools menu and then click **Progress Lines.**

The Network Diagram View

Close behind the Gantt chart in popularity is the activity on node diagram. Project calls this diagram by its generic name, the network diagram. The name helps to explain its popularity. Network diagrams clearly display the sequence of workflow and task dependencies as a network of boxes and arrows. (Users of earlier versions of Project will recall that activity on node diagrams were called PERT charts.) See the example in Figure 14.9. Each task is represented as a node (a box), and the dependencies are shown with connecting arrows. To open a Network Diagram view, select **Network Diagram** from the View menu or from the View bar.

Hide Fields for maximum zoom out

Network Diagram toolbar

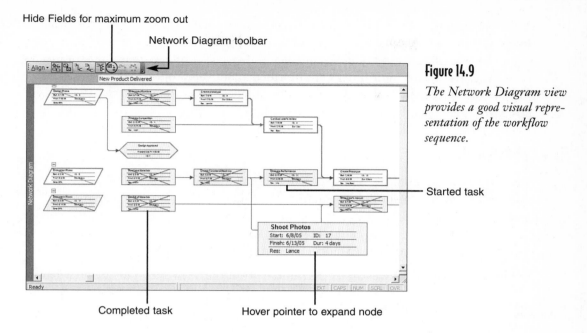

Figure 14.9

The Network Diagram view provides a good visual representation of the workflow sequence.

Started task

Completed task

Hover pointer to expand node

The Network Diagram view is good for

◆ Understanding complex workflow sequences.

◆ Graphically communicating how a task relates to the rest of the project.

◆ Locating strategically important tasks, such as those that must be accomplished before several other paths of work can begin (known as work bursts).

You can modify the contents, style, and layout of the network diagrams from the Format menu. The Network Diagram toolbar has several handy layout tools for aligning boxes. To zoom out and fit more boxes on a page, click the **Hide Fields** button.

Communicating With Your Team

Don't expect your team to automatically be able to decipher your project documents. Gantt charts and network diagrams can be confusing to the uninitiated. Instead, take some time and discuss each document with those who will be using it. Your project will do better if everyone understands how to use project information to his or her advantage.

Project managers use numerous conventions and vocabulary words to mean special things. These include *critical path*, *critical task*, *slack*, *float*, *lead*, *lag*, and *delay*, to name a few. Once again, those who don't understand the special project management meanings of these words will not be as well informed about the project as they should be. Make it a habit to establish an appropriate team vocabulary. The "Words at Work" glossary in the appendix can serve as an excellent reference.

The Calendar View

If you have to communicate a project schedule to anyone who isn't familiar with basic project management documentation, the Calendar view is just what you need! As shown in Figure 14.10, the Calendar view displays tasks as a bar spanning the days it is scheduled on. Everyone knows how to read a calendar, so communicating task responsibilities to even the least-informed teammate can be quick and mistake-free.

To display the Calendar view, select **Calendar** from the View menu or the view bar.

Figure 14.10

The Calendar view makes it easy to communicate the project's schedule.

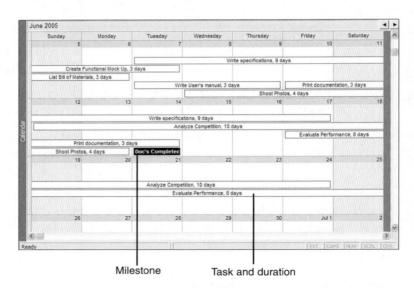

Milestone   Task and duration

Filtering Information

Information overload is a real possibility in project management. Sometimes it's important to be able to screen out unwanted information so you can focus on the important items. Whenever you find yourself in that situation, you can put Project 2003's filters to work and hold back the tide of information overload! Figure 14.11 shows filters in action.

You can use several predefined filters by filtering the entire project or one or more columns. To filter the entire project, click open the pull-down menu on the Formatting toolbar where it says All Tasks and click the filter you want. To remove the filter, select **All Tasks** from the list.

Clicking the **Autofilter** icon activates predefined filters on each table column header. You can apply multiple filters simultaneously. To apply, click open the pull-down menu and click one of the column's filter choices. To remove the filters, select **(all).**

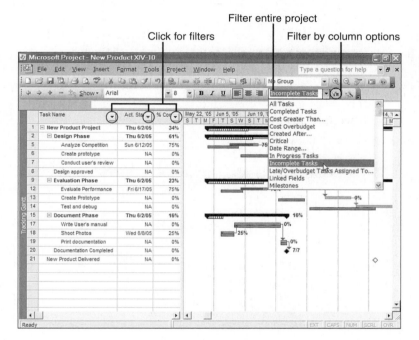

Click for filters   Filter entire project   Filter by column options

Figure 14.11

Filters limit the information in your sheet, table, or chart.

Project Reports

Project reports may not look as exciting as a Tracking Gantt or network diagram, but they serve up information by the page-full. There are 29 predefined reports in Project 2003, so you won't have any trouble finding what you need. If you must, however, you can create new reports or modify existing ones.

To print or view a report, open the Reports dialog box by selecting **Reports** in the **View** menu. The dialog box is shown in Figure 14.12. The most frequently used reports are accessed by selecting one of the categories and choosing a report from those graphically depicted. If you don't see what you need there, click **Custom** and browse all 29 reports. You edit a report, create a new report, or transfer a report from another project in the Custom dialog box.

Figure 14.12

Access all reports from the Report dialog box.

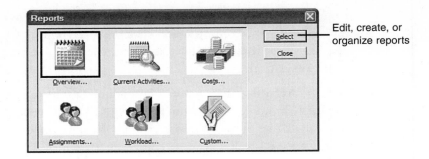

Edit, create, or organize reports

The Project Summary report is found in the Overview section. It lists key date, duration, work, cost, and status information on one sheet. When a report is selected, Project automatically takes you to a print preview screen, as shown in Figure 14.13. From there you can verify that the report is what you want before printing it.

Page layout preview

Zooms in or out   Shows multiple pages

Figure 14.13

The Project Summary report is one of 29 standard reports.

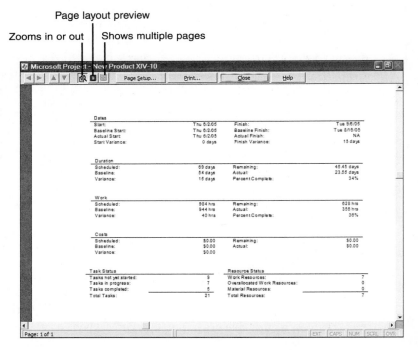

The first page of the Who Does What When report is shown in Figure 14.14. This report demonstrates the power of Project's cross-tab capability. Resources are listed by task and the number of hours they are assigned per day to each task. This is a perfect report to show how fairly you distributed roles, responsibilities, and workload.

Who Does What When as of Wed 6/2/04 New Product XIV-10	6/2	6/3	6/4	6/5	6/6	6/7	6/8	6/9	6/10	6/11	6/12
Aaron	8 hrs	8 hrs			8 hrs	10 hrs	10 hrs	8 hrs	8 hrs		
Do needs assessment	8 hrs	8 hrs									
Write specifications					8 hrs	8 hrs	8 hrs	8 hrs	8 hrs		
Analyze Competition											
Vina						8 hrs	8 hrs	8 hrs	8 hrs		
Write specifications						8 hrs	8 hrs	8 hrs	8 hrs		
Evaluate Performance											
Create Prototype											
Jennifer											
Create prototype											
Write User's manual											
Stacy		8 hrs			8 hrs	8 hrs					
Conduct user's review											
Create Functional Mock Up		8 hrs			8 hrs	8 hrs					
Create Prototype											
Justin	8 hrs										
Purchase Materials	8 hrs										
Rob											
Test and debug											
Lance	8 hrs	8 hrs			8 hrs			8 hrs	8 hrs	8 hrs	
List Bill of Materials	8 hrs	8 hrs			8 hrs						
Shoot Photos								8 hrs	8 hrs	8 hrs	
Print documentation											

Figure 14.14

Resource roles, responsibilities, and workloads are clearly reported with the Who Does What When report.

The Earned Value report is commonly required by a project's contract documentation. In many instances, progress payments are based on the earned value calculations. And if you've ever created this document by hand, you know what a chore that can be! Fortunately, an earned value report is ready and waiting for you. You can find the Earned Value report by choosing **Reports** from the View menu and then selecting the **Costs** reports category in the Reports dialog box. The first page of the report appears in Figure 14.15. The report is useful even when it isn't required by the project's contract documentation. It shows you how much of the planned expenditures should have been spent at this point of completion. Just update your actuals and print the report.

ID	Task Name	BCWS	BCWP	ACWP	SV	CV
3	Do needs assessment	$1,400.00	$1,400.00	$1,400.00	$0.00	$0.00
4	Write specifications	$4,860.00	$4,860.00	$4,860.00	$0.00	$0.00
5	Analyze Competition	$2,240.00	$2,100.00	$2,100.00	($140.00)	$0.00
6	Create prototype	$0.00	$0.00	$0.00	$0.00	$0.00
7	Conduct user's review	$0.00	$0.00	$0.00	$0.00	$0.00
8	Design approved	$0.00	$0.00	$0.00	$0.00	$0.00
10	Purchase Materials	$316.56	$158.28	$158.28	($158.28)	$0.00
11	Create Functional Mock Up	$960.00	$480.00	$480.00	($480.00)	$0.00
12	Evaluate Performance	$1,040.00	$1,040.00	$1,040.00	$0.00	$0.00
13	Create Prototype	$0.00	$0.00	$0.00	$0.00	$0.00
14	Test and debug	$0.00	$0.00	$0.00	$0.00	$0.00
16	List Bill of Materials	$960.00	$960.00	$960.00	$0.00	$0.00
17	Write User's manual	$0.00	$0.00	$0.00	$0.00	$0.00
18	Shoot Photos	$1,280.00	$320.00	$320.00	($960.00)	$0.00
19	Print documentation	$0.00	$0.00	$0.00	$0.00	$0.00
20	Documentation Completed	$0.00	$0.00	$0.00	$0.00	$0.00
21	New Product Delivered	$0.00	$0.00	$0.00	$0.00	$0.00
		$13,056.56	$11,318.28	$11,318.28	($1,738.28)	$0.00

Earned Value as of Wed 6/2/04 New Product XIV-15

Figure 14.15

Earned value reports are a snap with this ready-to-go report.

Earned value reporting is discussed more fully in Chapter 22 where I describe how to export this information to Excel for additional analysis, charting, and reporting.

Printing Project Documentation

To print any of the project views, select **Print** from the File menu and click **Preview.** You can see a Detail Gantt chart ready to be printed in Figure 14.16.

Figure 14.16

To print any chart, graph, sheet, or table you have on the screen and in the upper pane, click **Print Preview.**

Show single page

Show multiple pages

Zoom in or out   Page Setup dialog box

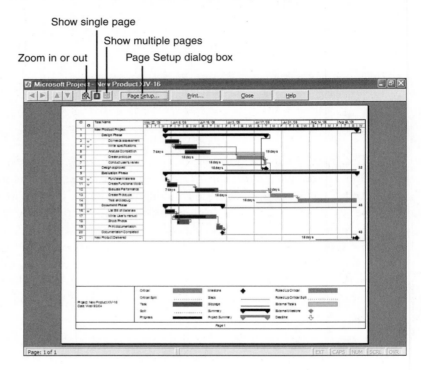

You can adjust the number of columns printed on each page, whether or not the ledger appears, as well as header and footer information in the Print Preview dialog box. To access these options from the Print Preview screen, click **Page Setup.** The Page Setup dialog box is shown in Figure 14.17. After you have modified the settings under any tab, you can review how the document will print by clicking **Print Preview** on the Page Setup dialog box. When you're satisfied, click **Print.**

Prints columns for selected table

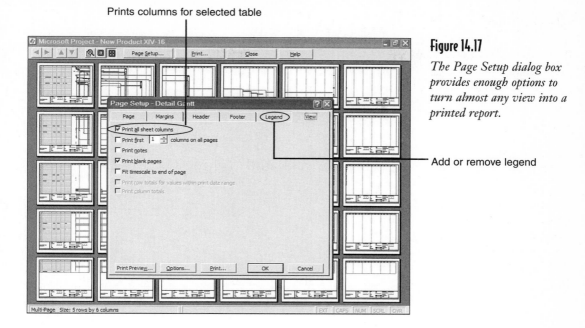

Figure 14.17

The Page Setup dialog box provides enough options to turn almost any view into a printed report.

Add or remove legend

The Least You Need to Know

◆ Project data isn't information until it's in a format you and your team can understand and use.

◆ Project 2003 provides a robust set of views, sheets, tables, reports, graphs, and filters to provide all the information you need to complete your project successfully.

◆ One of the essential duties of the project manager is to keep the project team informed. Be sure everyone who relies on your project documentation thoroughly understands it.

◆ Using a different baseline for each stakeholder group (for example upper management, vendors, and the core team) improves your ability to monitor and manage each group effectively.

When the Going Gets Tough, the Tough Get Creative

In This Chapter

- ◆ Using Project to identify and solve problems before they arise
- ◆ What to do when unexpected problems appear
- ◆ Decision making methods you can use to prioritize options and keep your project on the road to success
- ◆ The problem-solving checklist
- ◆ Using the triple constraints to protect your project's success

Every once in a while, a project is initiated, implemented, and completed without its success being threatened. Problem-free projects, although rare, do exist. However, for the most part, you'll have to deal with at least some problems on every project. Problems are an integral part of accomplishing that which has not been done before.

But with good planning, an experienced team, and the strategies and techniques in this chapter, coupled with timely action, you'll be able to fix, avoid, or rightfully ignore just about any problem that comes your way!

Identifying Potential Problems

The earlier you spot a problem, the more options you have to do something about it. The earlier you deal with a problem, the less likely it will have a negative impact on your project's success. Therefore, the best time to avoid problems is always in the project initiation or planning phases.

Spotting Problems During Planning

In this early phase of the project, watch for the killer problems—those that could prevent the project from achieving success. Many of the major risks your project faces are not unknowns. When trying to decide what could go wrong in a project, you and your project team's collective experience is your most important asset.

When you first start planning the project—thinking through execution options, creating the work breakdown structure, and establishing the initial schedule—stay constantly alert for problems. It's impossible to avoid or even detect all of them, but that's okay. You're looking for the big ones. The problems that could turn your project (and possibly your reputation) into toast. To uncover killer problems in the planning phase, ask the following questions:

◆ **Of all that could go wrong, what do you fear most?** Trust your experience and intuition. No one is in a better position than you to assess threats to your project's success. Guard against everything your hunches tell you are potentially large problems.

◆ **How do the triple constraints stack up?** Are all of them highly important, or are one or two of them flexible? Be especially alert for anything that might impact the driving constraint. If the driving constraint is not met, the project is a failure. Having at least one constraint that is flexible greatly reduces project risk. Where there is flexibility, there are alternatives. Moreover, when you have alternatives, your risk is reduced. (For more information on the triple constraints, see Chapter 3.)

◆ **Is the project goal overly optimistic?** Is the time available adequate? Are all the resources you need readily available? Do you have access to all the people, money, equipment, facilities, materials, information, and technology required by the project?

Of all the mistakes project teams make, overoptimism is not only the most common, it's also the most deadly. Too many project managers base their assumptions on how they want their project's operational environment to be, rather than on how it actually is. In the early stages of planning, you should tend toward pessimism rather than optimism. The goals you set now are the goals you'll be judged by later. Make it as easy as possible to be successful! Bosses never care how difficult the project is, they just care how successful it is.

Secrets of Success

There's a growing trend in many industries toward a shortage of trained workers. Don't assume that all the resources you will need will automatically be available. Rather, assess your resource needs with Microsoft Project as early in the planning stage as possible. Create a preliminary schedule and load it with resources as described in Chapter 9. The preliminary schedule can help you identify the areas that are understaffed and therefore at risk.

Using Microsoft Project to Deal With Potential Problems

Microsoft Project can be a valuable tool for assessing potential problem areas. Whenever a proposed project appears difficult, complex, or time sensitive, create a preliminary project plan. Even a roughly estimated plan greatly improves your understanding of the required tasks, sequence of work, and resource requirements. Creating the preliminary plan is a learning process. It often reveals many of the challenges that lie ahead.

Workflow Considerations

Experienced project managers are alert to potential workflow sequence problems. As discussed in Chapter 5, every task in the project is important and must be accomplished for the project to be a success. Many tasks depend on the completion of others before they can begin. In some cases, if a task is delayed many others will be adversely affected. Some tasks have no flexibility as to when they may be accomplished—they have no slack. Others lie on the critical path and, if delayed, the entire project will be delayed. For all these reasons, it is important to understand the workflow sequence and how to identify potential trouble spots.

The best way to understand the workflow sequence is with Microsoft Project's Network Diagram view, as shown in Figure 15.1. To open this view, click **Network Diagram** from the View menu. For an overview of the project, zoom out by clicking **Zoom** from the View menu, check **Entire project,** and click **OK.** The maximum reduction is 25 percent, so you may either have to drag the view bar and scroll to view large projects or turn the details off with the Hide Details button on the Network Diagram toolbar.

Secrets of Success _____

Network diagrams make it possible to identify points that are strategically important to the workflow. Tasks that have many successor tasks are called *work bursts*—many new paths of work burst open when these are accomplished. Conversely, any delay on or before a work burst will block the start of many tasks. Tasks that have many predecessor tasks are *work merges*—before they can begin, several tasks must be accomplished within the same time frame. To accomplish a work merge, many predecessor tasks must be undertaken in unison. To keep your project in a normal state of forwardness, manage work bursts and merges carefully.

A long critical path exposes the project to many potential delays

Figure 15.1

For a strategic understanding of the project's workflow, use the Network Diagram view.

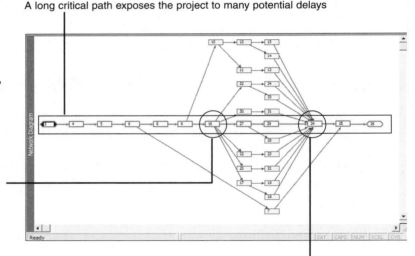

Work burst delays can create a bottleneck

Work merges require much coordination before progress can continue

Every project has an optimum sequence of work, depending on the available time, resources, and desired level of risk. The Network Diagram view helps you understand the strategic importance of each task and its relationship to the whole project. For example, after viewing the network diagram for the project in Figure 15.1, the project manager might decide the project's completion date is overly optimistic. The project has a very long critical path, and if anything delays any of these tasks, the due date may be in jeopardy. A cushion of additional resources or a time extension may be in order.

Resources Versus Time Considerations

Generally speaking, the faster a project must be accomplished, the more resources are required. Conversely, the fewer resources available for a project, the longer the project will take. It is therefore important to assess the intended duration of the project in conjunction with resource availability. Once again, the best way to do this is with a preliminary plan.

When time and resources are both in short supply, create the plan with the **Schedule from: Project Finish Date** option selected in the Project information dialog box. You may want to review the section "Start Date or Finish Date Scheduling" in Chapter 10 for more information. Create a resource list as described in Chapter 8. Then assign resources to the tasks as described in Chapter 9. The final step is to level resource allocations with the option **Level only within available slack** selected in the Resource Leveling dialog box. If resource overallocation warnings appear as Microsoft Project levels the project, select **Skip All.** Presto! You now have a schedule that finishes within the given time and exposes any resource shortages as overallocations.

To find the resources shortages, select the **Resource Sheet View** from the View menu. As shown in Figure 15.2, overallocations that remain after leveling are tagged with a yellow exclamation point icon in the indicator column. These are the resources your project is lacking. To quantify the shortage, increase the **Max. Units** for each overallocated resource until the warning icon is gone. (After each change, click outside of the field to make Project recalculate.) Although this process is not exact, it is a good preliminary method to estimate the number of required resources.

If resources are only 10 percent or 20 percent off, small adjustments in the schedule may compensate for the shortages. On the other hand, if the required resources fall short by 100 percent or 200 percent, serious problems are likely to occur. Proceeding without substantial changes in resources, time, or project scope would be risky.

To determine exactly where your resource shortages are and how they relate to the workflow, the combination view shown in Figure 15.3 is a powerful tool. With it you can find each overallocation and drill down to the detail on a task, resource, or time-period basis.

To create this view, select **Network Diagram** from the View menu. Then open the lower pane by clicking the pane bar (found just below the vertical scrollbar) and dragging it up. Now make the lower pane current by clicking in it, and then select **Resource Usage** from the View menu. Right-click the right side of the Resource Usage sheet, and from the pop-up menu select **Detail Styles.** Choose the **Usage Details** tab and select **Work, Overallocation,** and **Percent Allocation** from

Available fields and add them to **Show these fields.** Click **OK**—your crystal ball, er, combination view, is complete.

Figure 15.2

Locate resource shortages by allocating available resources and then leveling within available slack.

Resource overallocations

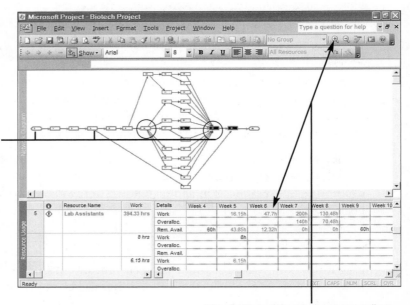

Adjust the units available to estimate
required staffing levels.

Chapter 12 has additional information on finding and reducing resource problems.

Figure 15.3

Scroll through the network diagram with the arrow keys to find potential resource problems.

The combined effects of
critical path, work burst,
work merge, and resource
shortage reveal a potential
disaster

After finding resource shortages, adjust
the timescale to reveal greater detail

A good preliminary plan coupled with this combination view is the closest thing there is to predicting the future! When the stakes are high, use this technique to minimize your risk.

Presuming you've spotted a few problems, let's see what you can do about them.

Problem Analysis

At the first sign of trouble, don't panic. In fact, don't do anything yet. Problems will undoubtedly arise in your project, but not all of them are worthy of your attention, time, or resources. Remember, you're seeking success, not perfection. To stay on the path to success, save your limited resources for the serious problems. Sometimes you just have to ignore the little problems and save all your energy for the big ones!

To decide which problems to ignore and which to address, use the following problem-analysis checklist:

♦ **Will it impact the critical path?** Problems that threaten the start or finish of any task on the critical path will threaten the project's scheduled completion date. Time is usually very important, and if it happens to be the driver of your project, the project's success is seriously threatened. When a problem is "on the path," move quickly and forcefully to resolve the issues. These problems need your immediate and full attention. For more information, on managing the critical path, see Chapter 11.

♦ **Will it impact the driver?** The driving constraint must be protected at all costs. If the driving constraint is not achieved, the project is a failure. Don't do anything your mom wouldn't approve of; but otherwise, do whatever you have to do! Your project, your team, and your reputation are at stake. When the driver is at risk, take decisive action immediately. For additional information on this important concept, in Chapter 2.

♦ **Who will be affected?** When problems arise, people can get hurt. One of the responsibilities project managers have is to make sure no one gets hurt on their projects. Never blindside a teammate, never hurt the project's customer, and never surprise your boss (negatively, of course). As soon as you realize the potential for harm is present, advise all parties who may be affected. There is another reason besides "It's the right thing to do." When you've found and informed all the stakeholders who could be negatively affected, you've just populated and motivated a problem solution team! These individuals are most likely to help you solve the problem.

You've Got a Problem—Now What?

When problems that require your attention arise, don't try to solve them alone. You have a team, and now is the time to rely on it. Also, solicit help from everyone who is likely to be affected by the problem. Those who are in harm's way, even though they are not official members of your team, will be motivated to help solve the problem!

Brief this problem-solution team on the importance of the problem. Now is not the time to be diplomatic. State the nature of the risk frankly and honestly. Don't underplay or overplay the significance of the situation.

Then define the apparent problem. Take nothing for granted. Don't assume you completely understand the problem. You want to have a good definition of the problem, because with the definition lies the solution strategies you're seeking. State the apparent problem from your team's points of view as well as your own.

Creative Thinking When Your Job Depends on It

The ability to be creative is a function of how willing one is to take a risk. When you have an organizational climate of risk aversion, creativity is stifled. Always strive to maintain a nurturing, rather than criticizing climate in your project team. That way, when you need creativity to solve a problem, you're halfway home!

The best way to get a good idea is to get a lot of ideas. There is always more than one solution to every problem. Our job is to find the best one for now. The goal when seeking solutions is to create as many ideas as possible. Project managers often use brainstorming techniques to find solutions.

Secrets of Success

If your proposed solutions involve schedule, resource, or scope changes, be sure to check out the effects in Microsoft Project before implementing the changes. Make sure your plan is current, save it, and then make the proposed changes in a copy of your plan. Carefully explore the effects of your changes and be alert for any unwanted ripple effects.

Finding solutions can be difficult, so the tendency is to stop at the first idea that comes along. Don't do that, because you need options! In fact, don't even consider the first idea. Just make a note of it and continue the search. Tell your team to turn their creativity throttle up and their evaluation throttle down. Create as many new ideas as possible. When some are truly ridiculous, that's good. You know the team is comfortable enough with one another to be playful, take a risk, and be genuinely creative.

Even with creative people who work well together, you'll usually find a long gap between the first idea and the second. And usually there is an equally long gap between the second and third. However, somewhere along the line, the flow of ideas picks up noticeably. When that happens, it's a good sign that the team is focused on the task at hand, not on their last phone call or yesterday's meatloaf. Collect all the ideas you can and then begin the evaluation process.

More Good Stuff

Some of the most creative people I know are playful, incorrigible rule breakers. They probably spent most of their school days in the principal's office, explaining why their idea was better than the teacher's. When you're faced with a tough problem (and they're all tough until you find a solution), ask your team this question: What rules can we break? Now is not the time to be compliant! Hopefully that unruly student has grown up and is now on your team. So long as you protect the driving constraint and achieve the project's ultimate goal, break any rule you must. It's best if you don't bend or break any of the triple constraints, but when necessary, break the weak constraint first. This way, the project can still be a success. What rules can you break? All of them, as long as your mother approves.

The team should also evaluate the ideas. What may seem like an impassable roadblock to one person may be easily solved by another. After you've considered the options and examined their effects on your schedule, seek consensus from the group. Although everyone may not agree that any given solution is the best choice from his or her point of view, everyone can agree to support the idea.

Now it's time to implement the solution. This may be done by the team as a whole or (more likely) by one or two individuals. And when the solution is being implemented by a few for the good of the whole, it is important to remember that they are part of the team. Should things not work out as planned, don't allow them to take the heat for the team. On the other hand, when the implementation is successful, don't allow them to bask in all the praise, either. (If your organization is like most, very little praise basking is done. You probably won't have to worry about that one!) Good teams hold themselves equally and mutually accountable in all situations.

More Good Stuff

Consistently use the same phrase to gain consensus in collaborative work groups. This helps everyone understand that you're trying to gain group support for a decision. When the team's communication is good, use these words: "Is there anyone who cannot support this solution (idea, approach, method …)?" When communications are poor, ask each person individually, "Will you support this decision?"

> ### More Good Stuff
>
> It's not *my* idea or *your* idea, it's *our* idea or *the* idea. Leave all the personal, singular, possessive pronouns out of your language and out of your thinking. To remind yourself to use good team language and thinking, before you enter team meetings, leave all your personal possessions in the hallway—your personal possessive pronouns, that is. You'll see an immediate effect in your team's attitude and behavior.
>
> And while you're leaving things in the hallway, leave all your *buts* out there, too. Replace them with *and.* Which is better, "Yes I heard what you said, and …" or, "Yes I heard what you said, but …"? Using *but* negates everything that comes before it. When you replace *but* with *and,* trust and respect is higher because the other person's point of view is accepted as valid, not rejected out of hand. These simple changes (with genuine trust and respect) can dramatically improve a team's communication effectiveness.

You've already determined the problem is an important one to solve, so make sure the intended solution is rapidly put into effect. The only thing worse than getting bitten by something you didn't see is being bitten by something you did see. Monitor execution closely!

Bright Ideas for Dark Times

Your best insurance against success-threatening problems is flexibility. Knowing how to adapt, how to move fast, and how to bend without breaking are essential skills if you want to build a reputation as a successful project manager.

Paradoxically, flexibility comes from tight control—an accurate schedule and close monitoring of actuals versus planned durations, costs, start and finish times—and milestone achievements. Knowing where you can slow down or let tasks slip out in time (using slack), thereby releasing resources for other work (resource leveling), is also determined only with an accurate plan. In fact, flexibility is revealed only with an accurate plan as your guide.

> **Secrets of Success**
>
> The biggest hidden resource in every project is slack—the amount of time a task can slip without affecting the project's completion. Knowing where slack is hiding is knowing where there's flexibility. To learn more about this hidden resource, see Chapter 11.

Most problems we deal with have to do with not meeting the project's time, cost, or performance requirements—any one of the three puts your project in jeopardy. It's increasingly more difficult to save a troubled project if all three constraints are threatened. When you're behind schedule, over budget, and the deliverable isn't deliverable … it may be time to dust off your resumé or add a helmet and flak jacket to your wardrobe!

CAUTION   Project Pitfalls

Before charging into a solution, verify that the triple constraints are still prioritized as they were at the beginning of the project. A rapidly changing competitive marketplace, changes in ownership, changes in leadership, or other such external forces can change your project's triple constraints. Be sure you've properly identified the drivers and know how flexible the other constraints are. When problems arrive, you need flexible constraints the most.

Projects facing trouble on three fronts are suffering from poor initiation and planning, to say the least. Goals were overly optimistic. Assumptions were incorrect. Stakeholders were never truly committed. Resources weren't forthcoming. Information was lacking. Alas, the vampire project was born!

When you find yourself in a situation like this, the first job of a team leader is to save the people. All too often the team takes the heat for management's overly optimistic (or overly simplistic) view of the world. The second job is to save as much of the project as possible, knowing that you've likely missed the only real opportunities for success long ago. Focus all energies on salvaging the driving constraint and the people. It's about all you can do.

Fortunately, you now have this book to guide you through the danger-wrought early stages of project management. So from here on out, the problems will be fewer and less pervasive.

The following list can be used as a checklist of possible solutions.

- **Parallel more tasks or paths.** When you're finishing too late, a good solution to consider is to parallel more tasks. Of course, you must shorten the critical path in the process. One way of doing this is to examine every task on the critical path and see whether any of them could be split off into a parallel path.

- **Add resources.** Managers often resort to piling on more resources. But unless the resources are taken from tasks that might be delayed (using their slack time), and the resources were assigned for the duration of the project, this option may get expensive quickly. In some cases, you may be able to spend the same amount of money in a shorter time, and that's great. But all too often, you reach a point of diminishing returns—overtime, double time, or just-too-tired-to-think time—and costs go up.

◆ **Make or buy considerations.** In some situations, you may be able to buy or hire out work segments you originally planned on doing with your own resources. Don't decide to reject this option until you've researched the situation. Send out a request for proposals and see what rises to the opportunity! You may be surprised that someone is willing and able to do the task better, faster, and cheaper than your own workforce.

◆ **Use incentives and disincentives.** These can be a powerful way to motivate vendors and subcontractors to prioritize the use of their resources in your project's favor. When all else is equal, limited resources will be loaded onto those tasks (or projects) where there is the largest penalty for late completion or the greatest reward for early completion. Be sure all rewards or disincentives are agreed to before the project begins.

◆ **Substitute alternatives.** As a reminder, the spirit of competition is alive and well. Chances are, there is a second source for almost everything you need on your project. Shop around.

◆ **Go for substantial completion.** If the project's main goal can be achieved without finishing all tasks, focus on those tasks that produce a usable, although not complete, project.

◆ **Narrow the scope.** When there have been major changes in project assumptions it's wise to return to the definition stage and narrow your project's scope. Salvage as much progress (not work, but progress) as possible, and set a new, more realistic goal.

◆ **Renegotiate.** When worse comes to worst, beg for mercy. Call in favors, beg for forgiveness, or just plan grovel. If you have something you can negotiate with (that is, throw in for reconsideration of the agreement), now's the time to do it. This is not always a pleasant task, but renegotiating beats failing.

◆ **Expedite.** If the project is running over schedule and the budget is not the driver, consider expediting the project. This is also called crashing the schedule. (I've found owners and originators get a little nervous when project managers use the word *crash*, so save yourself some trouble and always refer to crashing as expediting.) This is a formal technique in which you consider how to shorten the duration of each task and at what cost. It is an important tool to understand, so Chapter 16 is devoted to it.

Murphy reminds us that things always look darkest just before they turn totally black. But that's okay. With your new problem analysis and solution tools, you'll never have to be afraid of the dark, or vampire projects, again.

The Least You Need to Know

- An understanding of the triple constraints is essential to prioritize solution options. Since they can change, always reassess before implementing solutions.

- An accurate plan and tight monitoring provides the impetus and the alternatives you need to solve difficult problems successfully.

- Use Microsoft Project to identify potential problems and test proposed solutions.

- Not all problems are worthy of your attention. If they do not affect the critical path, the project's goal, or the driving constraints, ignore them. Save your attention, energy, and resources for the important problems.

- Break whatever rules you must to protect the project's goal and its driving constraints—just don't embarrass your mother.

16

Expediting (Crashing) a Project

In This Chapter

- ◆ Determine the cost of using additional resources to compress a project's schedule
- ◆ Create documentation in advocacy or defense of contract claims
- ◆ Determine the most cost effective duration for any project
- ◆ Optimize the project's costs against time for any situation

The old saying "Time is money" goes a long way in describing the time/cost analysis tools in this chapter. Knowing how to squeeze a schedule into a seemingly impossible timeframe is an important skill, especially when you can determine the most cost effective way of doing it.

The principle of expediting also provides a solid financial footing when making project decisions. You'll be better able to discuss issues that affect durations in tasks or projects; better prepared to negotiate changes in budgets and contracts.

This chapter provides the methodology and procedures to analyze cost/time relationships in any project.

When Crashing Is a Good Thing

Expediting is more commonly referred to as *crashing* the project or timeline in the project management profession. And like many of the terms project managers use freely, your customers, project originators, and team members won't always understand what you mean. Crashing is a good thing when you need to speed up the completion of a project. However, it is the rare customer who wants to have anything they care about crashed. Save yourself some trouble. Refer to crashing the project as expediting. Everyone knows that expediting makes things happen faster. Moreover, everyone understands that expediting usually comes at a premium price.

Buying Time

Essentially, expedite analysis reveals what additional costs are incurred when shortening the duration of a task (see Figure 16.1). When the task was originally planned, certain assumptions were made. I call these the normal assumptions. Under normal conditions, what costs are incurred and what duration is required? This is Your preferred method of completing this task.

Figure 16.1

Expedite (crash) analysis requires estimating the cost of reducing each task's duration from a normal approach, and then applying these changes to the project schedule.

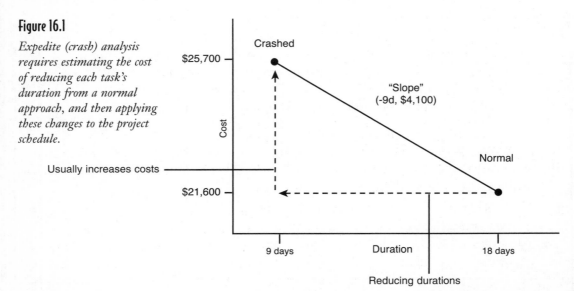

For some reason, however, it may become necessary to complete the task in a shorter timeframe. In project management terms, the priority of the triple constraints has changed. For whatever reason, time has become a driving constraint, performance remains unchanged, and cost has become the most flexible.

More Good Stuff

Two popular methods of shortening a schedule are expediting (commonly known as crashing) and fast tracking. Crashing compresses the schedule by applying more resources to tasks to shorten their durations. Crashing typically increases the project's costs but produces reliable results. Fast tracking alters the workflow logic by running tasks in parallel that would normally be run in finish-to-start sequence. Examples of this include writing software before the needs analysis is complete, and building a payload module before the launch vehicle's lifting capacity has been verified. Fast tracking therefore compresses the schedule by assuming additional risks—cost, time, quality—and results may all be adversely affected (or not). When compressing a schedule, choose your method carefully. The crash course is probably safer than the fast track!

Project Pitfalls

When projects don't have adequate staffing, many organizations rely on their salaried employees to make up the difference. Hiring temps, working hourly employees overtime, and hiring additional people add to the cost of a project. On the other hand, the more fixed-salary employees are worked, the lower their effective hourly rate becomes! This tactic can be effective for resolving short-term situations or problems. However, working salaried staff excessively over the long term will probably result in lowered productivity, bad decisions, poor morale, and a loss of your most capable team members. Don't let short-term tactics become long-term problems.

To expedite you may need to work overtime, hire temporary employees, or buy rather than make certain work components. A commonly used expedite method is the purchase of overnight air delivery. If you had the time, ground shipping would be much cheaper. Usually these options are more expensive. To understand exactly how much more expensive expediting a task is, project managers use expedite analysis.

Note that expediting a project doesn't always cost—sometimes it pays! Anytime there is large capital equipment involved, expediting may yield positive financial benefits. Consider the semiconductor facility shut down for equipment repairs, construction machinery needed for five weeks but rented by the month, or a project that when completed will begin producing revenues or beat the competition to market. Or consider contracts that contain penalty clauses—expediting may be the cheapest solution! To improve vendor performance, an increasing number of organizations are including penalty clauses in their contracts.

Expedite analysis can also build a case for additional compensation. If on a long project the first team unnecessarily slowed the project, the last team might face large expedite costs to meet the deadline. If you're frequently "the last one in," consider providing a (normal) schedule with your proposal that clearly states shortening the project duration requires additional compensation. (Be sure to check with your legal advisor before implementing this).

I was once asked to expedite the installation of a series of 13 telecommunication relay sites across a remote stretch of the Rocky Mountains. A tax law had changed, making it desirable for the owner to complete construction before year-end. Rather than waiting for spring and better weather (when the cost and durations had been planned), an immediate start was agreed upon.

In some cases, the remoteness of the sites required over-snow vehicles to transport crews, materials, and equipment. The cold weather slowed crews as they struggled to stay warm and safe. Sites that would normally be worked with standard excavating equipment and techniques had to be blasted into submission with high explosives. Concrete had to be prepared, poured, and cured in subzero temperatures with small onsite mixing systems. It was obvious that every step of the process would be more costly, but how much more costly was the question. To identify the additional costs, we preformed an expedite analysis.

Expedite Analysis

Fortunately, half the work of every expedite analysis is already done, assuming you've already estimated the project's normal duration and costs. All you need to do is re-estimate each task remaining on the project and compare the crashed duration and costs with the original durations and costs. This process of comparison yields the difference (known as the *slope*) between the normal and expedited costs and durations. The math can be done by hand or with a spreadsheet program.

After the slope has been identified for each of the remaining tasks, you'll want to transfer it into Microsoft Project 2003. You can then display the slope on the Detail Gantt chart and have a better understanding of the expedite options available.

Words at Work

Slope is a word project managers borrow from mathematics and (shame on us) we abuse! In mathematics, slope is a ratio of the vertical distance to the horizontal distance of a straight line. It implies that for any incremental change in one factor, the other factor is directly and proportionally changed. In project management, slope describes the difference in the two points, not the ratio. Project managers aren't always able to make the smooth, incremental changes that the word *slope* implies. The choices may be all or nothing, whole units only, or for other reasons, unrealistic. For example, if expedited shipping cuts three days out of a task but only one extra day is needed, paying for only the day needed is not an option—it's all or nothing.

Putting Expedite Analysis to Work: An Example

Consider the Telecom System project shown in Figure 16.2. As originally planned, each of the 13 sites was expected to cost $97,800 and require 49 days to complete. The project sponsor requested an expedite analysis to consider what a shorter project duration would cost.

	Task Name	Duration	Total Cost
1	⊟ Site #1	49 days	$97,800.00
2	Survey Site	5 days	$2,000.00
3	Prepare Site	18 days	$21,600.00
4	Erect Tower	15 days	$15,500.00
5	Install Antenna	6 days	$4,700.00
6	Erect Equip Bldg	5 days	$7,700.00
7	Install Power Sys	5 days	$11,300.00
8	Install RF Equip	10 days	$31,500.00
9	Tune and Test	5 days	$3,500.00
10	Site #1 Operational	0 days	$0.00

Figure 16.2

Under normal conditions, each site required 49 days to complete at a cost of $97,800 each.

The project manager needed to analyze how much it would cost to expedite each task in the project. The easiest way to do that is in a spreadsheet such as Excel. The result is shown in Figure 16.3.

When creating an expedite analysis, ask yourself this question: "If money were no object, how could I shorten the duration of this task?" Although there are usually limits to the money, asking this is a good way to stimulate your creativity. Consider every available option. This may include working overtime, adding additional resources, requiring subcontractors to complete their assignments earlier (which might involve a bonus or other incentive), using faster equipment, purchasing rather than making, and any other strategy you can come up with. After you estimate the expedited durations and costs, compare them to the normal durations and costs. The difference is the slope.

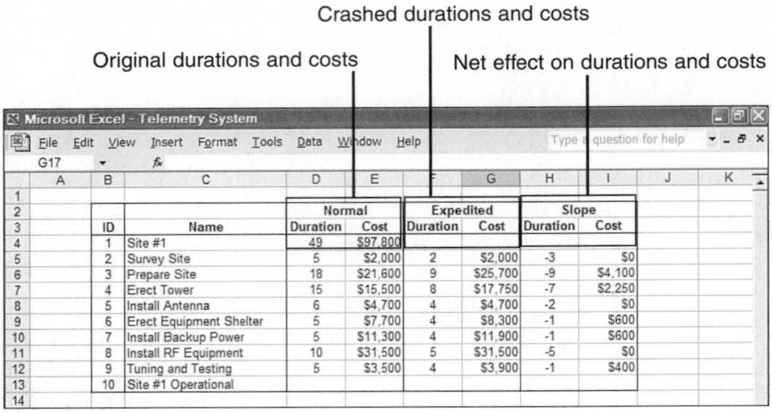

Figure 16.3

A spreadsheet facilitates determining the slope for each task.

Crashed durations and costs

Original durations and costs

Net effect on durations and costs

	ID	Name	Normal		Expedited		Slope	
			Duration	Cost	Duration	Cost	Duration	Cost
	1	Site #1	49	$97,800				
	2	Survey Site	5	$2,000	2	$2,000	-3	$0
	3	Prepare Site	18	$21,600	9	$25,700	-9	$4,100
	4	Erect Tower	15	$15,500	8	$17,750	-7	$2,250
	5	Install Antenna	6	$4,700	4	$4,700	-2	$0
	6	Erect Equipment Shelter	5	$7,700	4	$8,300	-1	$600
	7	Install Backup Power	5	$11,300	4	$11,900	-1	$600
	8	Install RF Equipment	10	$31,500	5	$31,500	-5	$0
	9	Tuning and Testing	5	$3,500	4	$3,900	-1	$400
	10	Site #1 Operational						

Comparing Options and Paths

After the slope for each of the individual tasks has been established, it is necessary to use the Detail Gantt chart to understand how each of the alternative approaches would fit into the schedule. If all tasks were in a finish-to-start sequence without parallel paths, the project manager could simply select which tasks to expedite to get the intended results. More frequently, the project manager will want to see how each of these proposed changes is integrated into the workflow sequence: Shortening a task may change the critical path; parallel tasks may increase the cost of shortening a given path segment.

To facilitate your analysis, add the slope information to the Detail Gantt view. As shown in Figure 16.4, right-click the column head titled **Start** (your new column will be added to the left of this point), and select **Insert Column** from the pop-up menu. Scroll down to **Text1** and highlight it. Rename this text column by entering **Slope** into the **Title** field and click **OK.**

After the column has been inserted, enter the duration and cost for each task from your expedite analysis. Traditionally, the slope is noted within parenthesis as the change in duration and change in cost separated by a comma. Now right-click in the Detail Gantt view and select **Bar Styles** from the pop-up menu. As shown in Figure 16.5, select the **Text** tab and select **Text1 (Slope)** from the list of available fields for placement to the left of each bar.

The resulting view enables the project manager to fully understand the costs associated with expediting any task or group of tasks. This view is shown in Figure 16.6. For example, by choosing to expedite those tasks with zero increases in costs, the project manager could reduce overall project duration by a total of five days. By choosing to expedite task number four, Erect Tower, the project could be shortened to 37 days at an additional expense of $2,250.

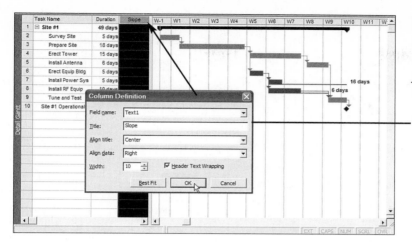

Figure 16.4

Insert a text column into the Gantt Chart Entry table for your expedite analysis slope results.

———— The new column is shown

Add text to all other tasks

Add text to critical tasks

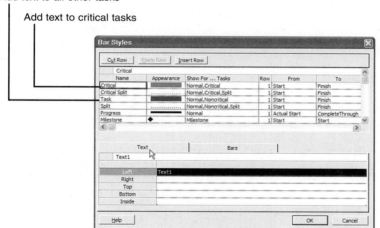

Figure 16.5

Place the results of your expedite analysis on the Gantt Chart by adding a text field to be displayed to the left of each task's bar.

With the Detail Gantt chart and the slope data clearly visible, the project manager can get to work. First shorten all tasks with zero cost of expediting. Then apply reductions to tasks on the critical path and observe the changes in project duration and the critical path. Through trial and observation, 22 total days can be cut from the project's critical path. Any tasks that have total slack remaining would not shorten the critical path, so incurring these expedite costs is not necessary. Overall, each site was shortened by 22 days at an increased cost of $6,750.

Figure 16.6

The cost of expediting a project can be carefully analyzed by posting the slope next to each task.

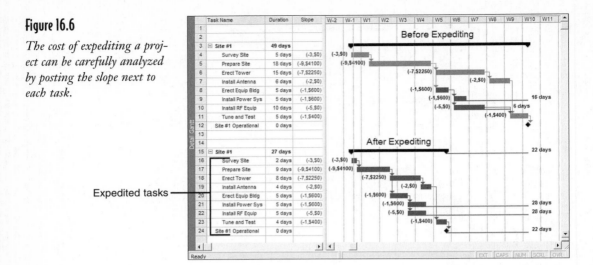

Do you think the person who coined the expression "Time is money" was a project manager?

The Least You Need to Know

◆ Expedite analysis provides the information needed to make sound decisions on shortening a project with the least expense.

◆ Alternative methods of schedule compression can be compared for cost and time effectiveness.

◆ Expedite analysis can be used to quantify contract compensation claims.

Whew! Wrapping Up the Project

In This Chapter

- ◆ Checklist for closing your project down and moving on
- ◆ Preparing final project reports
- ◆ Capturing the lessons only experience can teach
- ◆ Releasing the project team for other duties
- ◆ Pulling the life-support plug on projects that just won't go away

"Are we there yet?" Some projects seem like a journey that lasts forever. Hopefully you took the advice of this book when planning your project. If you did, chances are good that your project has steadily picked up speed on its journey to completion. Rather than grinding to a lurching, stumbling halt, project completion has arrived as expected—on time and in good order by all accounts.

In any case, the project manager has several closing responsibilities to the project and the stakeholders of the project. No matter if the project falls short, meets, or exceeds expectations, this chapter shows how to bring a professional closure to the endeavor.

Gaining Project Acceptance

Your first goal (and responsibility) in project closure is to make sure that the project is accepted as complete. The project must meet its specified goals and objectives.

Oddly enough, the most important step you'll ever take toward the completion of the project is in the initial stages of the project—in the definition stage. That's when you set the rules that your project's success will be judged by. That's when you set the expectations that must be met for the project to reach a successful conclusion. It is here that the specific, measurable project outcomes are documented and agreed on by all stakeholders. Trying to negotiate a completion agreement at the end of a project is at best frustrating and at worst suicidal.

Many organizations have a formal procedure for documenting project acceptance. If you do not have a formal procedure or if the project documentation does not specify a procedure, use Table 17.1 as a guide.

Table 17.1 Project-Acceptance Checklist

Procedure	Description
Notice to Complete Project	At the 80 percent to 90 percent completion point, send a notice that you are about to complete the project. This alerts the project's owners or end users to be ready for the deliverables. It alerts the project's sponsor that this stage is about to conclude and accordingly, prepare for whatever is next on the agenda. It also puts the team on notice that the final push is on and a transition to other duties is coming soon.
Substantial Completion Review	Identify and list all work that has been successfully completed to date. Then identify and list all the remaining work items. The original definition of the project and any agreements made during the project should be used as the baseline for this review.
Remaining Work Identified	Any remaining work needs to be explicitly identified. If possible, gain stakeholder signatures at this point so that work that does

Procedure	Description
	not appear on the list can't be demanded at some indeterminate point in the future. Frequently called a punch list, the identification of remaining work can help to successfully bring even troubled projects to a satisfying close for all parties.
Final Completion Plan	The final push to completion can be facilitated with a good completion plan. This important, time sensitive stage of the project must be closely managed. Don't let down your guard at this point. Many things can derail your project's success if you ignore this step: Team members may lose focus, owners may be overly anxious to accept the deliverables, and many people's lives will change as they move on in their professional endeavors and personal relationships. Stay alert and stay in close contact with all stakeholders.
Notice of Completion	After the final items have been delivered and the project has been completed according to the documentation, send a written notice of project completion to the stakeholders. Contractual responsibilities, ownership, and authority likely changes at this point. Check with your legal and financial team to make sure all your i's are dotted and your t's are crossed.
Formal Acceptance	This may come as a legal document, a letter of acceptance, or a thank you note. If a legal document is required by the project's documentation or your organization's policies, don't ignore this final task. Regardless of how well the project went, you haven't succeeded until the paperwork is signed, sealed, and delivered (and the check clears the bank).

Final Project Reports

Often times a specific set of final reports are required by the project owner or sponsor. These may include quality assurance audits, specification compliance results, engineering documentation, training manuals, or as-built drawings. It's not unusual for project documentation to include union, state, or federal labor-compliance reports as well.

Although not always required, some project managers create a wrap-up report for their management. This is a perfect opportunity to communicate to your principals the project's accomplishments, challenges, and lessons learned. It is also a good time to publicly thank key contributors, team players, and others who made your job a little easier or more successful.

Writing the Final Report

The wrap-up report may be as brief as an interoffice memo or as lengthy as a total project review. Regardless of the size, write the report with a professional, objective tone. Keep your report as brief as possible. The longer the report, the less likely it will be read! Focus on the reader's point of view, and make sure the report is appropriate for everyone who will have access to it—upper-management's report is probably not appropriate for the project team or the customer. Handle all sensitive information carefully.

Report Content

At a minimum, include the following five sections in every final report. This format sets the stage for objective, positive, and professional renderings of your projects. Each section's length and exact content can be altered depending on your audience.

- **Executive summary.** A short, written overview of the project's goals and achievements, a summary of the project's implementation process, and an overview of how well the project met the performance, time, and cost constraints. The Project Summary report shown in Figure 14.13 of Chapter 14 is an excellent report to include in this section. The project's baseline, actual, and variance is reported for start and finish dates, duration, work, and costs in an easy-to-read format. By adding one or two written paragraphs, you've got a great executive summary.

- **Achievements.** A complete listing and analysis of the project's goals and objectives. Refer to the project initiation document, statement of scope, and any amendments made to these during the project. For larger projects, add the required test, audit, or inspection documents.

♦ **Implementation analysis.** A detailed analysis of how well the project met performance, time, and cost objectives; and how well the project used resources, met financial objectives, and attained quality objectives. The Tracking Gantt chart and two Task Usage combination views can add communication punch to this section of your report. One task chart shows the Work table and the other shows the Cost table. These views are described in the next section.

♦ **Recommendations.** Report any new issues or tasks that need future consideration. Recommend changes to methodology, staffing, administrative procedures, technology, resources, and any other issues that can make the organization more productive or cost effective.

♦ **Special acknowledgments.** You didn't do it alone, so give credit to those who made the project a reality.

Key Final Reports

An excellent overview of the project's planned and actual progress is provided by the Tracking Gantt chart. Figure 17.1 provides an example. To access and print this report, choose **Tracking Gantt** from the View menu. Click and drag the vertical divider until only the Gantt Chart and the Task Name column is shown. Select **Print Preview** from the File menu. To adjust how the page will print, click **Page Setup.** If this is the first time you've used Page Setup, select each of the tabs in the Page Setup dialog box and investigate the available options. When you're satisfied with the look of your page, click **Print.** The Tracking Gantt is ready to include in your final report. (See Chapter 14 for additional views and printing tips, and Chapter 22 for exporting views to PowerPoint presentations).

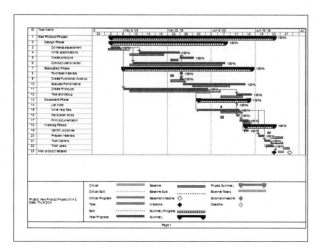

Figure 17.1

The Tracking Gantt provides an excellent overview of the project's actual versus baseline progress.

The Task Usage chart compares baseline versus actual work (or costs) by task. Figure 17.2 shows the Task Usage view using the Work table with the Actual, Baseline, and Accumulative work details selected. Figure 17.3 shows the Task Usage view with the Cost table and the Cost and Actual Cost details selected. You can zoom to the entire project or any other time period you want by right-clicking the timescale. To print these reports, click **Task Usage** from the View menu, **Table** from the View menu, and then select either the **Work** or **Cost** table. Right-click the details area to select the information you want. Then select **Print Preview,** and if you like what you see, click **Print.**

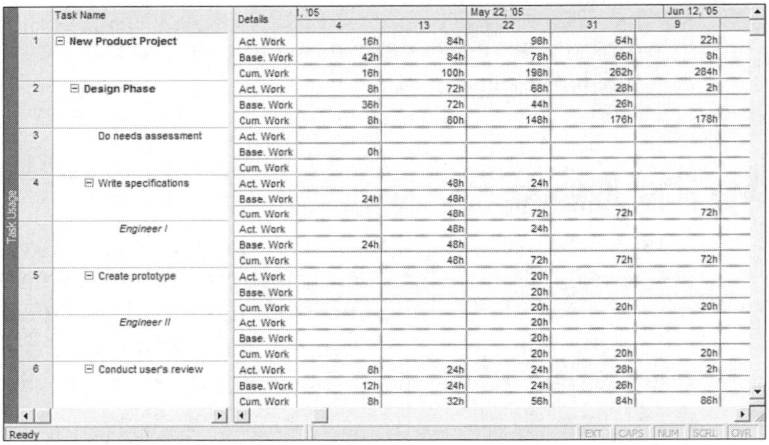

	Task Name	Details	, '05 4	13	May 22, '05 22	31	Jun 12, '05 9
1	New Product Project	Act. Work	16h	84h	98h	64h	22h
		Base. Work	42h	84h	78h	66h	8h
		Cum. Work	16h	100h	198h	262h	284h
2	Design Phase	Act. Work	8h	72h	68h	28h	2h
		Base. Work	36h	72h	44h	26h	
		Cum. Work	8h	80h	148h	176h	178h
3	Do needs assessment	Act. Work					
		Base. Work	0h				
		Cum. Work					
4	Write specifications	Act. Work		48h	24h		
		Base. Work	24h	48h			
		Cum. Work		48h	72h	72h	72h
	Engineer I	Act. Work		48h	24h		
		Base. Work	24h	48h			
		Cum. Work		48h	72h	72h	72h
5	Create prototype	Act. Work			20h		
		Base. Work			20h		
		Cum. Work			20h	20h	20h
	Engineer II	Act. Work			20h		
		Base. Work			20h		
		Cum. Work			20h	20h	20h
6	Conduct user's review	Act. Work	8h	24h	24h	28h	2h
		Base. Work	12h	24h	24h	26h	
		Cum. Work	8h	32h	56h	84h	86h

Figure 17.2

The Task Usage view with the Work table selected provides a comparison of baseline versus actual work data for the project and each task by resource and date.

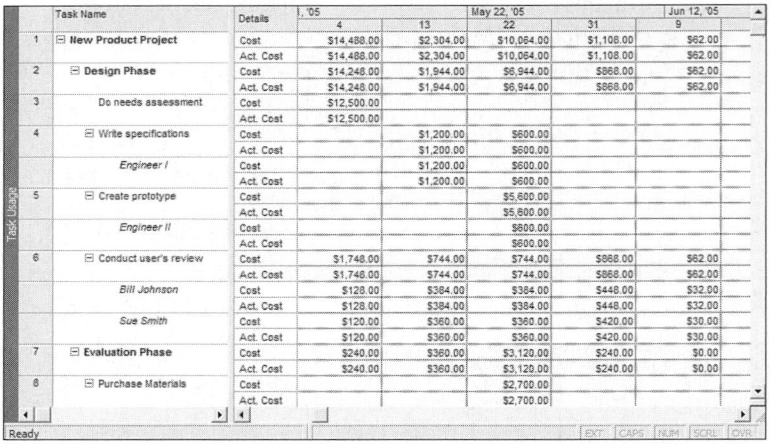

	Task Name	Details	, '05 4	13	May 22, '05 22	31	Jun 12, '05 9
1	New Product Project	Cost	$14,488.00	$2,304.00	$10,064.00	$1,108.00	$62.00
		Act. Cost	$14,488.00	$2,304.00	$10,064.00	$1,108.00	$62.00
2	Design Phase	Cost	$14,248.00	$1,944.00	$6,944.00	$868.00	$62.00
		Act. Cost	$14,248.00	$1,944.00	$6,944.00	$868.00	$62.00
3	Do needs assessment	Cost	$12,500.00				
		Act. Cost	$12,500.00				
4	Write specifications	Cost		$1,200.00	$600.00		
		Act. Cost		$1,200.00	$600.00		
	Engineer I	Cost		$1,200.00	$600.00		
		Act. Cost		$1,200.00	$600.00		
5	Create prototype	Cost			$5,600.00		
		Act. Cost			$5,600.00		
	Engineer II	Cost			$600.00		
		Act. Cost			$600.00		
6	Conduct user's review	Cost	$1,748.00	$744.00	$744.00	$868.00	$62.00
		Act. Cost	$1,748.00	$744.00	$744.00	$868.00	$62.00
	Bill Johnson	Cost	$128.00	$384.00	$384.00	$448.00	$32.00
		Act. Cost	$128.00	$384.00	$384.00	$448.00	$32.00
	Sue Smith	Cost	$120.00	$360.00	$360.00	$420.00	$30.00
		Act. Cost	$120.00	$360.00	$360.00	$420.00	$30.00
7	Evaluation Phase	Cost	$240.00	$360.00	$3,120.00	$240.00	$0.00
		Act. Cost	$240.00	$360.00	$3,120.00	$240.00	$0.00
8	Purchase Materials	Cost			$2,700.00		
		Act. Cost			$2,700.00		

Figure 17.3

The Task Usage view used with the Cost table provides a comparison of baseline versus actual cost data for each task by resource and date.

Preparing for the Future

Every project is a learning experience; to make the most of it, create a project archive. To borrow a few words, you never know when you may pass this way again!

Creating a Project Archive

Some of the most important bits of information to collect (before it's thrown out by the cleaning crew) are all records of time spent on tasks. As you have seen, accurate duration estimating is key to creating an accurate schedule. And an accurate schedule is the project manager's best (and sometimes only) friend! So even if you have to dig through the trash to get them, save all the time records for every project you work on. You don't have to compile or evaluate the data right now. Just save it. If a similar project is in your future, you'll be glad you turned into a timecard collector!

If you've tracked actuals against your baseline plan in Project 2003, you're way ahead of the game. The timecard information has already been applied to each task. The information you need to evaluate the actual versus estimated durations is ready and waiting in Project 2003! All you need to do is make an archival copy of the project data file and store it in a safe place. Just save your project onto a CD or other removable media and place it with the hard copies of your project documentation. If and when it's needed, you'll be ready!

Creating a Project Template

If you're likely to do a similar project in the future, create a project template. The work breakdown structure, workflow logic, duration estimates, and resources can all be ready to go with minor edits. To create a template, select **File, Save As,** and at the bottom of the Save As dialog box in Save as type, select **Template.** Type in a name for the template and click **Save.** In the Save As Template dialog box, shown in Figure 17.4, choose which data you want to remove from the file before saving it as a template. For example, you may want to remove baselines, actuals, resource rates, or fixed-costs items, because they may change on the next project. The template is stored with an .mpt extension in the Microsoft Templates directory by default.

Figure 17.4

Saving project templates makes planning similar projects faster, easier, and safer.

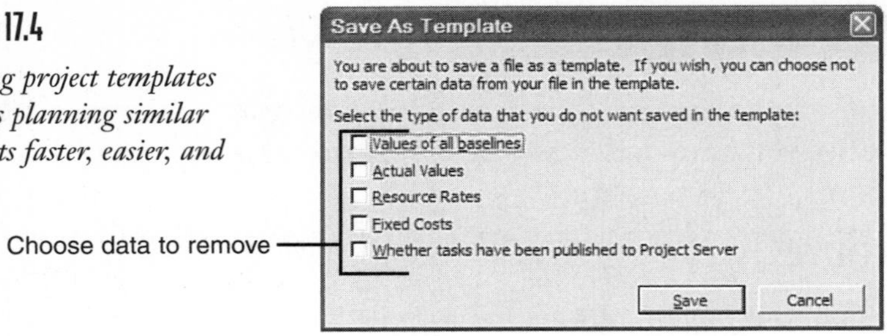

Choose data to remove ——

Capturing Historic Information

It's also a good idea to maintain a complete set of project communication documents. On rare occasions I've been asked to explain what happened or who did what several years after a project has been completed. It's amazing how much you can recall with a few dated meeting notes, memos, or archived e-mail messages to jog your memory.

If you've been using project control documents as recommended in Chapter 2, now's the time to gather them all up and store them in a safe place. Depending on the size of the project, you may want to use a clear plastic file folder, a three-ring binder, or perhaps cardboard file boxes. Whatever you do, keep it in one place and mark the outside with the contents and a shred date. In addition to a copy of your project journal gather the original concept checklist, project charter, statement of work, project initiation document, scope statement, baseline plan, and all scope-change requests. Gather any pictures of the project or the project meeting notes for the archive. You can also sort your e-mail archives by name or content to find project related e-mails. And finally, if you keep a phone log, you'll want a copy of it in the archives as well. Okay, call me a pack rat, but I would rather have it and not need it than need it and not have it! Case in point, four years after completion of a project my firm successfully defended itself with a note that had been scrawled on a paper napkin and saved in the project archives. A short note really is better than a long memory!

Capturing Lessons Learned

The difference between good project managers and excellent project managers is often surprisingly small. Take some time at the end of the project to survey your team. Ask them what went well, what they learned, and what they would do differently next time. Ask them how you could help them be more successful on the next project. Small lessons can turn into big wins on the next project.

Reassigning Project Personnel

Some projects grind to a halt as they approach completion. Most of the time, these problems are a direct result of poor definitions or a lack of stakeholder buy-in. Other times the resistance to completion comes from within the team. For many reasons, some teams just don't want to finish up and move on. If you find yourself (or your team) trapped in a self-imposed never-ending project, you need to be ready to provide some nurturing leadership.

Personnel problems come disguised in excuses and ambiguity, so they can be hard to identify. When nearing the completion of a project, be on the alert for these people problems.

Woe Is Me—The End Is Near!

You can expect two kinds of personnel problems when nearing the end of a project. In one case, team members are abandoning the project like it was a ship on fire. They're doing just enough to get by and the bulk of their energies are spent finding their next landing spot. You can expect a few of these nervous types on every project. As they realize the end is near, they're panic stricken! "What next? How am I going to make my mortgage?" Their fears are understandable.

The best course of action with them is one of reassuring leadership. Stay with them emotionally. Let them know they've done a good job, they've been noticed, and that you'll hate to see them go. A little honest respect goes a long way in reassuring these folks that it will all work out in their best interest. Your confidence in their abilities is a powerful stabilizing force. Keep them focused and informed. Help them understand the situation, the wrap-up process, and the timeline involved. These folks need to be in control of their own destinies, so the more forthcoming you are with the facts, the better off you'll both be.

Secrets of Success _____

When the project is over, refrain from complaining about a team member's behavior. Little can be improved after the fact, and no one responds to whining. Drop the past and focus on the future. What's important now is to spend your energy celebrating the success of those who contributed to the success of the project.

Then there are those who don't want the project to end, no matter what. They like it here. From these types, stretching the job out or downright sabotage can be a real threat. Be on the alert for work slowdowns. Don't wait for the first sign of trouble.

Expect it and take preemptive action. You see, the folks who are afraid to move on need exactly the same reassurance and leadership as the group that is already running for cover. They have the same fears; they're just acting them out in a different way.

If you can, help them find another role, write a sparkling letter of recommendation, or put in a good word to a colleague. Your team took care of you; now it's time to take care of the team. What goes around comes around!

Following Your Mother's Advice (Again)

It seems like moms are getting a lot of good press in this book. You have to admit, they've usually got some pretty good advice. Earlier, it was scheduling every task as soon as possible—never putting off until later what we could do now.

Well, here's another: Don't forget to say thank you! These are probably the most powerful words in a project manager's vocabulary (and on some projects, the least frequently heard). Not only do these simple words make people feel good, they also send a powerful message. Recipients know that you understand the contribution, risk, hard work, and occasional sacrifices they've made for the good of the project.

More Good Stuff

Some organizations maintain a budget for bonuses, incentives, and rewards. If yours does, use it! But take care. In some industries (such as defense contracting), there are strict rules on compensation and gifting. Also, if there's one secret that's impossible to keep in any organization, it's who got the biggest bonus (or no bonus at all). Parties or celebrations often have a better team-building effect. If you don't have a budget, get creative! Have a potluck lunch in the conference room or order in pizzas. Make certificates of appreciation on your computer. The important thing is to acknowledge contributions. No matter how modest the embellishments may be, it's the thank you and recognition that counts the most.

Personal recognition is a powerful leadership tool. Put it to work; it's effective. Moreover, I guarantee your mother will approve!

The Least You Need to Know

◆ The best way to close a project is determined in the initial planning stages by carefully defining the project's goals and objectives in measurable terms.

◆ Ideally, progress quickens from initiation to planning to execution to completion. When projects falter in late stages it is symptomatic of inadequacies in the earliest stages.

◆ Project success depends on how well the stakeholder's expectations are met. It is difficult, if not impossible, to change stakeholder expectations late in the project.

◆ Personnel issues frequently arise in the late stages of a project. Astute leaders deal with these transition issues preemptively.

Part 5

Beyond the Basics with Project 2003

Fasten your seatbelt. In Parts 1 through 4 you learned how to use planning skills with Microsoft Project 2003 to fly a project on the straight and level. In Part 5, you'll learn how to do a few really cool, high-speed aerobatic maneuvers. (I hope you aren't a white-knuckle flyer.)

You'll learn how to control and manage multiple projects, how to share resource pools across the organization, and how to consolidate project information to make managing your project portfolio easier than you ever thought possible. You'll learn the easiest ways of importing and exporting information to any program or format. You'll see how you can publish your plan to the web, and how to keep a virtual team in perfect sync with e-mail. You'll learn how Project 2003 fits into the Microsoft Enterprise Project Management system. And finally, you'll learn how to get your project ready for prime time and present to anyone with credibility, confidence, and persuasive clout. In short, this is where you become a project ace!

Too Many Projects, Too Little Time

In This Chapter

- ◆ Managing multiple projects and project portfolios
- ◆ How to use master projects and subprojects
- ◆ How to prioritize projects in any organization
- ◆ Using a common resource pool to facilitate resource sharing
- ◆ Consolidate project files for reports, scheduling, or coordination purposes

One of the benefits of being a capable project manager is that the projects never stop coming—well, it's nice to know you're appreciated, isn't it? Dealing with multiple projects is challenging. This chapter teaches you how to expand the number of projects you can effectively (and more comfortably) manage.

Managing Multiple Projects

There's one fundamental problem with managing multiple projects—it's hard! You just can't do two projects at a time as well as you can do one. And, you certainly can't do three as well as you can do two. And you … well, you get the point. The more projects you manage at one time, the more difficult it is to manage any of them successfully. Everyone has a limit. Unfortunately, the next project added to your portfolio might be the one that puts all your projects at risk. In short, your risk as a project manager goes up in direct proportion to your project management workload.

Secrets of Success

If you're faced with a project priority dilemma, don't go it alone. Anything you decide will almost certainly affect someone adversely. It's likely that someone at a higher level in the organization has either missed or ducked the issue. Your peers are probably facing the same issues, so team up and help your boss decide. If it falls on your shoulders, facilitate consensus based on the higher good for the organization as a whole, not one project or another.

In addition, when conflicts occur in a multiproject environment, there are always questions about which project should take priority. This decision should be left to the project manager. These issues must be decided at a higher level in the organization. Otherwise, the organization sets competing groups at odds with one another. Eventually, the organization as a whole suffers.

Finally, the most divisive issue confronting project managers in a multiproject environment is one of resource allocation. There's never an abundance of resources. Scarcity is the rule. And when two project managers need the same resource at the same time, the situation is frustrating at best. Consequently, it's important to carefully manage all scarce resources that are used across several projects. As you'll soon see, Project 2003 comes to your rescue in a big way here!

More Good Stuff

The first step in learning how to manage several projects at a time is to learn how to manage one project more effectively. That of course, takes an effective planning process. As the project portfolio increases, more planning and greater detail is required to coordinate work, share resources, and avoid conflicts. Consequently, one of the keys to managing many projects is being able to plan rapidly, with high levels of detail. Microsoft Project provides an excellent platform for this purpose.

Working On the Right Projects

If there is one thing most organizations could do to achieve more, it is to attempt less. Too many organizations dilute their ability to accomplish important projects by taking on too many. Every additional project brings greater complexities, increased risk, and as systems are overly taxed, a reduction in effectiveness.

Beyond these obvious issues lurks another: every project inflicts a communication burden on the worker. Daily meetings, e-mail, and reporting takes a toll. Assuming only twenty minutes per project, per day were required (meetings, phone calls, and e-mail), an involvement in six projects slashes productivity by twenty-five percent! Each project on average, could receive only five hours of attention per week and a one-month project couldn't be completed for eight months.

To better manage multiple projects, do less! Focus your resources on the right projects. Complete them quickly, then move on.

Project Portfolio Management

Ultimately, the goal of managing a project portfolio is to support the organization's mission as efficiently and effectively as possible. Consequently, one of the biggest mistakes made when managing multiple projects is in ignoring how each project relates to the organization's goals and objectives. Without this understanding, no meaningful project prioritization can take place.

This brings us to a salient point: Project managers cannot prioritize projects or the use of shared resources, without the participation of upper management. If you're not sure which project should get the green light and which should get the red, insist on upper-management's participation.

Ideally, managing multiple projects starts with senior management. Only with their participation can there be a project environment that

- ◆ Keeps the organization's mission, goals, and objectives at the center of effort.

- ◆ Integrates project portfolio management with the organization's strategic planning process.

- ◆ Maintains a comfortable level of resource flexibility above the minimums required for ordinary operations.

An effective way of facilitating these strategies is to expand the earliest phases of the project process framework to include project proposal, investigation, and screening functions.

Project-Screening Checklist

One of the most effective tools for managing a portfolio of projects is a well-thought-out project-screening checklist. It sounds overly simplistic, but the process of creating one challenges project leadership and upper management to come to grips with the organization's core strategies and objectives.

The selection criteria must yield projects that

- ❏ Provide real benefits supporting the organization's mission, goals, or objectives.
- ❏ Are within the organization's project abilities.
- ❏ Are a good strategic fit within the project portfolio.
- ❏ Improve the organization's return on investment.
- ❏ Measurably add to the delivery of value.
- ❏ Reduce costs or improve operational efficiencies.
- ❏ Increase strategic growth and improve the organization's overall strength and resiliency.
- ❏ Do not detract from any of the above.
- ❏ Do not adversely increase risk.
- ❏ Do not deteriorate necessary capacities, systems, and resources.

The first step in managing multiple projects is to make sure you're managing the right projects!

Multiple-Project Success Rules

Managing multiple projects is no easy task. Moreover, without the cooperation of the entire organization, it is almost impossible to do well. When managing multiple projects, keep these basic tenets in mind:

- ◆ The better your project management skills and techniques, the larger portfolio you can effectively manage.
- ◆ The more prevalent the project management process, vocabulary, and skills are in your organization, the larger portfolio it can effectively undertake.

- In the multiple-project environment, conflicts revolve primarily around shared resources. Therefore, the organization and project managers must always endeavor to optimize scarcity.

- Recognize that everyone has a limit.

- One too many projects may result in the failure of several others.

- When all projects are the "top priority," all projects will suffer.

- Don't prioritize alone, insist on upper-management participation.

- Neither skill nor effort nor Microsoft Project 2003 can completely compensate for a fundamental lack of resources.

To make the most of what you have to work with, consolidate project information, use compatible project management methods throughout the organization, and plan at greater levels of detail. Microsoft Project 2003's information management capabilities can help you succeed in this challenging, multiple project environment.

Consolidating Project Files

Maintaining a perspective of the entire project portfolio is difficult without a system to consolidate projects, workflow, resource requirements, and resource availability. Microsoft Project brings many capabilities to this issue. One of the easiest and most useful of these is its ability to create master projects and then insert subprojects. This simple notion rolls great quantities of information into one easily accessed information hub.

The projects rolled into a master project may or may not be related. It can bring order to many projects or it can greatly simplify the managing of large projects. For example, a large project can be broken into subprojects by project manager, major objective, phase of work, budget, responsible team, or any other division your organization needs. In addition, the master project can be expanded or contracted just like any project file to limit what is shown on the screen. This enables you to coordinate an entire set of projects from an overview perspective and still drill down for complete detail at any time. Now, that's living!

To create a master project, open the file you want to be the master project. This may be an existing project or a new file. On the View menu, choose the **Gantt Chart** view. Now click the row where you want to insert the subproject, and choose **Project** from the Insert menu. Figures 18.1 and 18.2 illustrate this process.

Figure 18.1

Open the file you want to be the master project and click **Project** *in the Insert menu.*

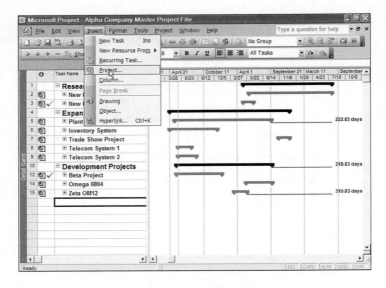

Figure 18.2

Choose the project you want to insert into the master project and click **Insert** *or* **Insert Read Only.**

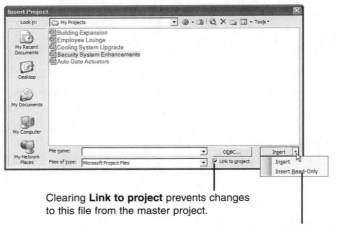

Clearing **Link to project** prevents changes to this file from the master project.

You may insert a project as read-only.

More Good Stuff

When working with master projects, carefully consider the effects of linking inserted projects. Subprojects inserted with **Link to project** checked (found at the lower right of the Insert dialog box) will be leveled as an integral part of the master project. On the other hand, when **Link to project** isn't checked, leveling the master project has no effect on the inserted subproject. In a like manner, changes made to linked subprojects are reflected in the master project even when the modifications are made outside of the master project. Subprojects that are not linked may be opened and modified without changing the master project in any way.

After the projects have been added to the master project, you can work with them just like they were still separate projects. Unless you inserted them as read-only, all changes made to these files will be saved in the individual project files as well. If you don't want to update the subproject files from the master file, clear the **Link to project** check box before inserting the project file.

Subprojects are treated like summary tasks in the master project so you can indent or outdent tasks. Be careful, however; these changes will be shown in the original project file as well. For this reason, it is usually best to refrain from changing the task hierarchy in the master project file.

By clicking the plus or minus signs next to the tasks, you can hide or show the subproject's tasks. You can also link tasks just as you would normally. The easiest way to do this in the master project is to click the predecessor task and drag the new link to the successor task. As you link tasks between subprojects, the new critical path is calculated and the project's schedule automatically adjusts, as shown in the Detail Gantt Chart view in Figure 18.3.

A master project with four subprojects is shown in Figure 18.4. Clicking the outline symbol reveals all the tasks within the subproject.

Click the outline symbol
to hide or show subtasks

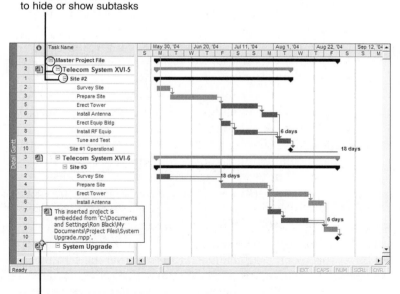

Figure 18.3

The critical path, slack, and delay are automatically calculated for the master project when you modify task dependencies.

Hovering over the inserted project icon displays
the subproject's source information

Figure 18.4

Each subproject appears as a summary task in the master project.

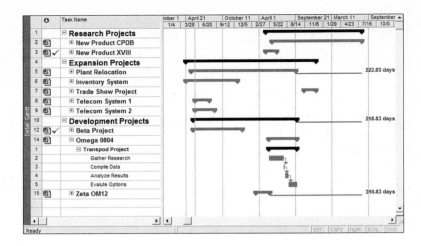

Using a master project file to coordinate your projects is helpful for several reasons. Some of the most important ones are described in Table 18.1.

Table 18.1 When to Use Master Projects

Situation	Comments
Complex projects	Breaking a large project down into smaller subprojects that are more manageable is one of the most valuable uses of master projects. Simplifying complex projects makes them easier to understand, monitor, and control.
Multiple projects	When you or your organization has multiple projects, it can be helpful to combine them into a master file even if they are not directly related to one another. Viewing all the subprojects, their start dates, and completion dates on one screen provides an important perspective for top level management. Project priority can be shown in the master project file. In addition, organization-wide reports can be created from the master file.
Multiple stakeholders	One project file can be used to create several master project files. Each master file can then be set up to meet the needs of the various stakeholders. Modification to project data in any of the master files is captured in the subproject file.

Situation	Comments
Shared resources	One of the most important benefits for combining files into a master file is the ability to use a common resource pool. Resource information can be stored in a central location, and master projects or subprojects can draw on this pool for resources. Resource leveling, resource allocation, and resource priority problems can be effectively dealt with using a common resource pool.

Sharing Resource Pools

To share resources between projects, it is necessary to create a common resource pool. The easiest way to do this is to set up a project without any tasks to hold all your resources. You can start from scratch and enter all the resources, costs, and pay rates as you would for any new project. However, there is no need to work that hard if you already have the resources you want in the pool in another project. Here's what you do:

1. Open the files that have resources you want to place in the resource pool. On the View menu, select **Resource Sheet,** as shown in Figure 18.5.

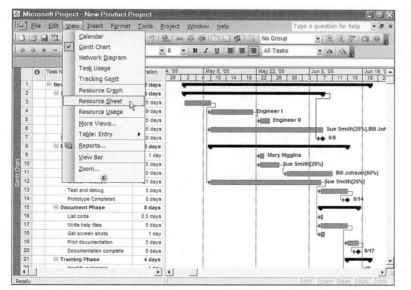

Figure 18.5

*Open each file that has resources you want to add to the resource pool and select the **Resource Sheet** view.*

2. In the Resource Sheet view of each project, check that no two resources have the same name and that no one resource has different names. Edit any conflicts before continuing.

3. In the Project Information dialog box, check the project **Start date** or **Finish date** fields for each project, and make a note of it. You will use the earliest or latest of these dates in Step 5 when creating the new resource pool project. The Project Information dialog box is found on the Project menu and is shown in Figure 18.6.

Figure 18.6

Make a note of each project's start or end date before creating the new project that will be used as a resource pool.

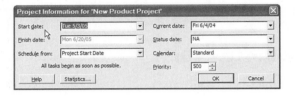

4. Create a new project by clicking **New** in the File menu and selecting a **New Blank Project** from the New Project pane.

5. In the Project Information dialog box, type a start or finish date that is early enough or late enough to make the resources available for all open projects. Now save the project with a representative name such as **Master Resource Pool.**

6. In the Window menu, select the first project whose resources you want to add to the resource pool. In the Tools menu, choose **Resources,** and then select **Shared Resources**, as shown in Figure 18.7.

Figure 18.7

*Select the project whose resources you want to add to the resource pool and click **Shared Resources**.*

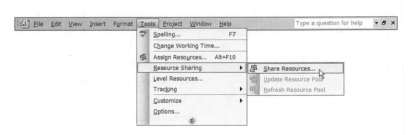

7. When the Shared Resources dialog box appears, check the **Use resources** box and then choose the resource pool file in the From box. This process is illustrated in Figure 18.8. In this way, add each project file you want to connect to the resource pool. Leave the default, **Pool takes precedence** box selected to prevent sharing projects from overallocating or modifying the pool's data. Save each of the files before closing them.

Pool file overwrites sharing file

Sharing file overwrites
the resource pool

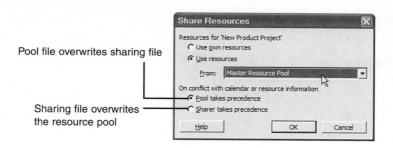

Figure 18.8

Choose the resource pool file-name from the list in the From field.

The resources are now available for use in any of your projects from the master resource pool as shown in Figure 18.9. You may also add resources directly into the master pool as you would with any project file.

Figure 18.9

When key resources must be shared between many projects, a master resource pool helps to centralize your control.

	O	Resource Name	Type	Material Label	Initials	Group	Max. Units	Std. Rate	Ovt. Rate	Cost/Use	At
1		Engineer I	Work		E I	Staff	100%	$25.00/hr	$35.00/hr	$0.00	Pr
2		Engineer II	Work		E II	Staff	200%	$30.00/hr	$40.00/hr	$0.00	Pr
3		Soft Analyst	Work		S	Staff	200%	$30.00/hr	$40.00/hr	$0.00	Pr
4		Electrican	Work		P I	Staff	550%	$15.00/hr	$22.50/hr	$0.00	Pr
5		Apprentice Elec.	Work		P II	Staff	300%	$20.00/hr	$30.00/hr	$0.00	Pr
6		Subcontr 1	Work		Sub 1	Vendor	100%	$0.00/hr	$0.00/hr	$1,386.00	Er
7		Installer	Work		I	Staff	200%	$17.50/hr	$26.25/hr	$0.00	Pr
8		Test Equip	Work		TE	Equip	100%	$0.00/hr	$0.00/hr	$100.00	St
9		Install Equip	Work		Tools	Equip	100%	$0.00/hr	$0.00/hr	$25.00	Pr
10		Vendor Co.	Work		V	Vendor	100%	$0.00/hr	$0.00/hr	$1,200.00	Er
11		Bill Johnson	Work		BJ	Staff	0%	$28.00/hr	$42.00/hr	$0.00	Pr
12		Sue Smith	Work		SS	Staff	100%	$30.00/hr	$45.00/hr	$0.00	Pr
13		Tech Trainers	Work		TT	Vendor	250%	$0.00/hr	$0.00/hr	$1,500.00	St
14		Conference Rm	Work		C	Facility	25%	$0.00/hr	$0.00/hr	$0.00	Pr
15		Cable Supplies	Material	CBL		Material		$0.00		$0.00	Er
16		Connectors	Material	CON		Material		$0.00		$0.00	Pr
17		n	Work		n		100%	$0.00/hr	$0.00/hr	$0.00	Pr
18		Ron Black	Work		R		100%	$0.00/hr	$0.00/hr	$0.00	Pr
19		Mary Higgins	Work		M		100%	$0.00/hr	$0.00/hr	$0.00	Pr
20		Bill Johson	Work		B		100%	$0.00/hr	$0.00/hr	$0.00	Pr

To access these resources from another project, make sure that the share-from file can be seen in the Windows menu. (If it isn't, just open the file.) Then in the Share Resources dialog box, check **Use resources** and choose the share-from file in the **From:** pull-down menu, as shown in Figure 18.10.

Figure 18.10

Any project file that you have access to can act as a resource pool.

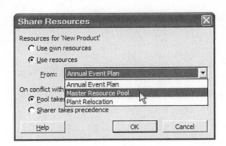

Getting Speedy with Project Templates

When managing multiple projects, greater planning detail helps alleviate resource conflicts and other potential issues. If many of your projects are similar, you can use templates to speed planning and improve the level of detail. A well-thought-out template can save hours of planning and data entry. Wouldn't it be nice not to have to start from scratch on the work breakdown structure, duration estimates, task dependencies, cost information, and resource assignments? Even if your next project isn't exactly like the template, you could still be hours ahead of the game.

Templates serve two other important functions: First, they help prevent leaving out essential items; second, templates can help transfer knowledge throughout your organization by helping others replicate proven project methodologies. When multiple projects make you too busy to plan, turn to templates for a planning productivity boost!

For complete instructions on how to create a template, see the section "Preparing for the Future, Creating a Project Template" in Chapter 17. Then the next time a project like this one comes along, you'll be ahead of the game! To use your new template select **New** from the File menu. In the New dialog box, select the **Template** tab and double-click the desired template. Voilà! You're off to a running start!

Project Pitfalls

Several templates install with Microsoft Project 2003 and there is a hyperlink to many others at their website. Please don't use them. I guarantee you that Mr. Gates and company doesn't understand your projects as well as you do. Using templates created by someone you don't know might help you create a plan faster, but it won't help you make it any better. More than anything else, good project plans come from good work breakdown structures. Starting with anything less than an excellent WBS rigs your project for trouble, not success. See Chapter 5 for more information on creating work breakdown structures.

The Least You Need to Know

- Combining projects into master projects facilitates resource sharing, project prioritization, and reporting.

- The more projects you have, the more important it is to carefully plan each project.

- Successful project portfolios begin with effective project screening.

- Resource pools can ease the burden of resource allocation and overallocation and help manage scarcity.

- Whether they know it or not, all project managers have a limit to the number of projects they can manage.

Project Communications in a Web-Wired World

In This Chapter

◆ Understanding the Microsoft Project 2003 Enterprise Project Management model

◆ Overview of communication and collaboration tools included in Project 2000, Project 2002, and Project 2003

◆ Using the web to distribute static project information

◆ Creating HTML and GIF images for use on the web and in other programs

The importance of effective project communications cannot be overstated. Project success has always required the integration of effort from many contributors, but the trend toward increasingly complex and competitive project environments is driving communication and collaboration requirements to new levels.

Microsoft began using Internet based communications early on. They have steadily expanded Project's communication features from the earliest releases to Project 2000, Project 2002, and now Project 2003 Standard and Professional. Many of the changes in each version have centered around the communication aspects. From simple e-mail messaging to work group communications to enterprise-wide collaborative tools, Microsoft and the web are transforming the way project teams work. This chapter will help you get the most out of your version of Microsoft Project.

Understanding Project Collaboration

Even the smallest project requires an amazing array of skill and expertise. Whether your projects are high tech, low tech, or no tech, these days every project team is in the information business. Back when workers provided more labor than knowledge (as in the industrial age), managers controlled most of the knowledge. Obviously, those days are over in almost every industry. Now (in the information age), workers provide most of the required knowledge and expertise. Project work has transformed from leaders and followers to leaders and experts. The project manager's job has transformed from one of supervision to one of facilitation.

Project success now requires full and authentic participation throughout the entire project team. To be effective, this synthesis of expertise must occur beyond traditional organizational structures. Collaboration must go beyond the walls of the traditional project office, beyond departmental rivalries, beyond profit-center alignments, beyond time zones, and even beyond international borders. It's easy to understand why the Internet is quickly becoming an indispensable project management communications channel.

The catchphrase for this broadening and deepening of project management techniques and team interactions is *enterprise-wide project management* (EPM). As organizations struggle to share resources across projects, unite distributed teams, and standardize effective methods in alignment with corporate objectives, collaboration-enabling technologies have become increasingly important.

Overview of the Microsoft EPM Model

If you're familiar with Project 98, 2000, or 2002, you've probably noticed that each new release has seen modest refinements and improvements in Project's basic scheduling and resource management engine. To the benefit of those who have upgraded, the look and feel of the basic system has changed little. On the other hand, Project has steadily grown easier to use with better access to help files, friendly and effective user guides, and even a few Smart tags that catch common errors.

In pursuit of greater project team collaboration, Microsoft has steadily changed the way Project enables communication. In earlier versions, e-mail was the enabling technology for all workgroup communications. Project team communications improved markedly with the release of Project 2000.

Communicating with Project 2000

In addition to its workgroup e-mail capabilities, Project Central was added which created a web-accessible depository for project information. A user of Project 2000 can publish plans to Project Central (an included program that runs on a server), which in turn can be accessed by authorized stakeholders using Microsoft Explorer. Project 2000's workgroup e-mail features are covered in the next chapter.

Communicating with Project 2002

In Project 2002, the basic scheduling and resource management tool was separated into two versions: Project 2002 Professional and Standard. Project 2000's Project Central was replaced and improved with a separately licensed product, Microsoft Project Server. The Professional version enables users to publish projects to the server, which team members can then interact with via an interface called Web Access. E-mail workgroup features were retained from Project 2000. These features are covered in Chapter 20.

More Good Stuff

Many users were disappointed to find that e-mail workgroup communication features available in previous versions were not included in Project 2003. Moreover, Microsoft has stated that they will no longer support these features beyond their license periods. For Project 2003 users who have grown to rely on these features in earlier releases, you can download and install workgroup messaging features into both Project 2003 Professional and Standard editions. This is described in Chapter 20.

Communicating with Project 2003

In Project 2003, the transformation from e-mail to server-based communications has taken another step as illustrated in Figure 19.1. The EPM collaboration capabilities have grown and now rely on several additional applications. These include Project Server 2003 (running separately on a server), Project Professional 2003 (to publish plans to the server), SQL Server (to store project information in an accessible database), Web Access (for each team member's participation), and Windows SharePoint Services (a repository for project documents).

Figure 19.1

Project Professional 2003 is one of a suite of products that is designed to work together to create Microsoft's EPM solution.

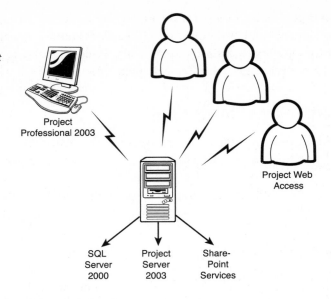

Project Professional 2003

Project Web Access

SQL Server 2000

Project Server 2003

Share-Point Services

How the Microsoft EPM Solution Is Being Used

EPM is still in its infancy, but most industry watchers agree the next few years will see a tremendous surge in its adoption. The promise is alluring. Top management can ensure alignment of organizational objectives, business practices, and project priorities. Resource management can be centralized with an organization-wide resource pool. Project portfolios can be rolled up and analyzed against key performance measures. What-if scenarios can be modeled across projects and departments. And with a centrally located database, project management information can be integrated into existing line-of-business systems.

Simply put, the Microsoft EPM solution provides a technology framework for increasing collaboration between all project stakeholders. Early adopters are reporting improvements in project efficiency, consistency, and capacity. Project management best practices and procedures are more available across the entire organization. Individual contributors are communicating, collaborating, and managing documents from one common, easy-to-use interface.

Prerequisites to Setting Up the Microsoft EPM Solution

For organizations with a mature project management methodology in place, deploying the Microsoft EPM solution is the logical next step. However, it isn't the sort of solution that you can install, learn, and effectively use all by yourself! Nor is it a solution that can be implemented without the principles and practices of project management already in place. Obviously there are many factors, systems, and infra-structure issues that first need to be explored. If you're embarking on this deploy-ment, take a step back and make sure you're following good project management processes in the undertaking. Identify your organization's goals, objectives, stakehold-ers, expectations … well, you get the point. This is a big step for any organization, and it can result in a giant advancement or a major setback.

Don't try to go too far and too fast with an EPM deployment. One of the best ways to drive the initiative is to take a single project and build the systems around its needs. If you start out by promising everyone everything, deployment benefits will be a long time coming! Experience shows that it is better to focus on a representative project and let the deployment grow. You'll need a strong core team with representatives from upper management, information technologies, and project management, and others such as finance, human resources, and operations, depending on the breadth of scope your deployment will encompass. As in all things, it helps if you enlist the experience of someone who has passed this way before. Microsoft has a cadre of certified resource providers who can assist you in the deployment. More information sources are listed in Appendix B.

Publishing Project Information to Websites

Some projects go so well that you just want to tell the whole world; when that hap-pens, there's no place like the web, with or without Microsoft's EPM solution. With the growing reliance on the Internet and intranets for communications, project man-agers are increasingly using the web as a distribution point for all types of project information. Whether you need to keep the boss, the public, or your team abreast of the latest developments, the web provides an inexpensive, multimedia, worldwide information distribution tool.

Microsoft provides easy-to-use information-gathering tools for text or images. When you see how easy they are to use, you'll think of many ways to integrate this informa-tion into your project communications. The caveat is that these methods are static. Unlike the real-time advantages offered with any of Microsoft web-based collabora-tion technologies, after the data is collected or the image is captured, even though your project changes, the published information stays the same.

Exporting Project Data to HTML Format

An easy way to publish text information to the web is to export the data in an HTML (Hypertext Markup Language) format. The data can then be incorporated into pages that can be published on the web by anyone familiar with publishing websites. (Check with your organization's web administrator if you are unfamiliar with publishing web-sites). The information can then be viewed as a table by anyone browsing the website. To export a project's data, click **Save as Web Page** on the **File** menu, as shown in Figure 19.2. Navigate to a location for the file, give it a name, and click **Save.** An Expert Wizard will appear and guide you through selecting the data you want to save in a web page.

Figure 19.2

Project data may be exported in an HTML format by using Save as Web Page.

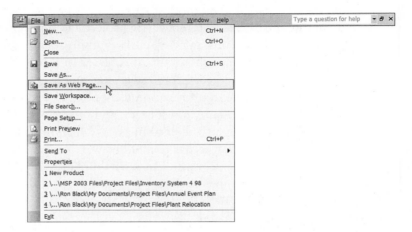

In the dialog box, you can choose to create a new data export map or use an existing one. Before you try to do it yourself, check out the existing maps. It may be easier to modify one than to start from scratch. Figure 19.3 shows the existing map choices. Select one and click **Next** to preview and modify the map as shown in Figure 19.4. Select **Finish** to complete the export operation. The file will be saved in the directory selected earlier.

Figure 19.3

You may select the data you want to export in the Export Mapping dialog box.

Click **Next** to preview
and modify export fields

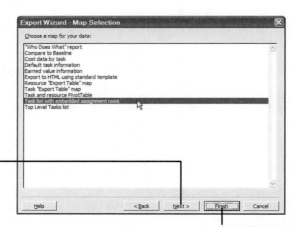

Click **Finish** to complete and save file

Rename output row headers

Limit data to export

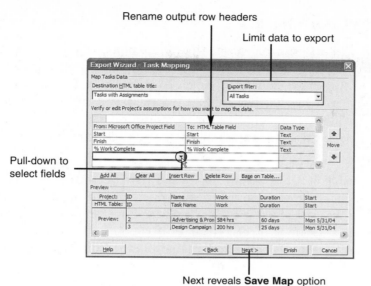

Pull-down to
select fields

Next reveals **Save Map** option

Figure 19.4

The Mapping dialog box enables you to select fields, edit row headings, and apply filters. The preview section is populated with the first few rows of your data.

Opening an HTML Document

After the information has been exported and saved as an HTML document, it can be uploaded to a website or viewed and edited like any other HTML document. To view HTML files before they are posted to a website, go to the folder where the file is stored, right-click the file, and in the pop-up menu select **Open With,** and then choose from the available programs. In Figure 19.5, the file was opened with Word and can now be edited, saved, or posted to a website.

Tasks with Assignments

ID	Task Name	Work	Duration	Start	Finish	% Work Complete
1						
2	Advertising & Promotions Phase	584 hrs	60 days	Mon 5/31/04	Fri 8/20/04	48%
3	Design Campaign	200 hrs	25 days	Mon 5/31/04	Fri 7/2/04	100%
3	*Glenya*	200 hrs		Mon 5/31/04	Fri 7/2/04	100%
4	Design Promotions	160 hrs	20 days	Mon 7/5/04	Fri 7/30/04	40%
6	*Frank*	160 hrs		Mon 7/5/04	Fri 7/30/04	40%
5	Purchase Ad Space	80 hrs	10 days	Mon 8/2/04	Fri 8/13/04	0%
5	*Henry*	80 hrs		Mon 8/2/04	Fri 8/13/04	0%
6	Book Trade Shows	24 hrs	3 days	Mon 7/5/04	Wed 7/7/04	67%
4	*Robyn*	24 hrs		Mon 7/5/04	Wed 7/7/04	67%
7	Set Up Web Site	120 hrs	15 days	Mon 8/2/04	Fri 8/20/04	0%
6	*Frank*	120 hrs		Mon 8/2/04	Fri 8/20/04	0%
8	Adv & Promo Launched	0 hrs	0 days	Fri 8/20/04	Fri 8/20/04	0%
9	Advertising & Promotions Phase	544 hrs	49 days	Mon 5/31/04	Thu 8/5/04	37%
10	Design Campaign	160 hrs	20 days	Mon 5/31/04	Fri 6/25/04	50%
3	*Glenya*	160 hrs		Mon 5/31/04	Fri 6/25/04	50%
11	Determine Media Mix	40 hrs	5 days	Tue 6/22/04	Mon 6/28/04	60%

Figure 19.5

A sample of the project's tasks and assignments as it appears when exported to an HTML format and opened in Word.

Saving Charts and Views as GIF Images

In project management, a picture can describe what words alone cannot. Project makes it easy to create pictures that will help you communicate more effectively in any almost any media. Any information you can get on your screen, you can copy with one click, and save it in a widely recognized file format. You can also copy it to the clipboard and paste it into programs that support this format. To capture a view of your plan as a picture file, click the **camera** icon on the toolbar, as shown in Figure 19.6.

In the Copy Picture dialog box, **For screen** copies and saves the picture to the clipboard in an image format and resolution that is appropriate for the Internet, e-mail, slide shows, and any other use to be viewed on a monitor. To use it in any Microsoft Office application (such as Outlook, Excel, Word, PowerPoint, or Visio), position your cursor at the point of insertion and select **Paste** from the **Edit** menu. The **For printer** selection also copies a picture to your clipboard, but this time the resolution is set for best results on your currently selected printer. Paste this image into any Microsoft Office application. The **To GIF image file**: copies a picture to any file location you select and can be edited by most image editors or included in any Microsoft Office product.

Captures GIF image of current screen

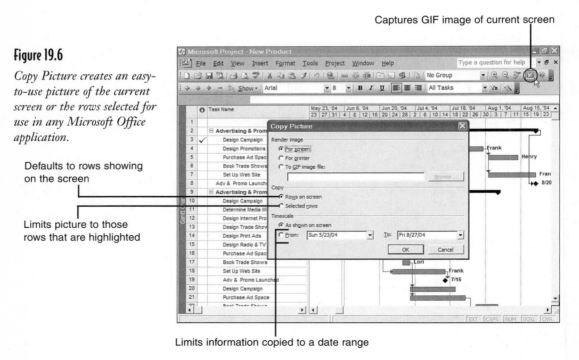

Figure 19.6

Copy Picture creates an easy-to-use picture of the current screen or the rows selected for use in any Microsoft Office application.

Defaults to rows showing on the screen

Limits picture to those rows that are highlighted

Limits information copied to a date range

The Least You Need to Know

♦ Both text and pictures can be easily exported for publishing on the web or use in any Microsoft Office application.

♦ Microsoft Project's Enterprise Project Management (EPM) solution provides a framework for driving project collaboration throughout the entire organization.

♦ The e-mail workgroup messaging capability provided in Project 2000 and Project 2002 is not included with Project 2003 Standard or Professional versions, but it can be downloaded from the Microsoft website and installed.

♦ Additional software must be acquired and installed separately to enable the Microsoft EPM solution. Project 2003 Professional version publishes project information to the EPM solution.

Communicating With Teams via E-Mail

In This Chapter

- ◆ Using e-mail effectively in the project team environment
- ◆ Using workgroup e-mail to assign tasks, monitor project progress, and stay informed
- ◆ Updating the project's progress directly from your team's e-mail
- ◆ Routing a project file for review and comment

It's 10 o'clock. Do you know where your teammates are? In a world of distributed workforces, international companies, telecommuting, and multiple project responsibilities, maintaining effective communications within the project team can be a daunting task.

On even the best-planned project, schedules change, problems arise, and the unexpected occurs. You must keep others informed, and it's essential that they keep you informed. To make good, fast decisions, you need a steady stream of good, fast information. Whether your 10 A.M. is their 10 P.M., or everyone's just down the hallway, this chapter will help you keep the information flowing.

E-Mail Etiquette for Project Teams

The thing I love most about having a computer is access to e-mail. It's great to keep in touch with team members around the world (or across the building) with such speed and convenience.

On the other hand, if there is one thing I hate about my computer, it's also e-mail! It seems the lure of cramming my electronic Inbox with junk is too much for some teammates to resist! I actually dread seeing some of their names appear as the sender (here comes the clutter!) I'm afraid they've buried important information somewhere in all that trivia.

Secrets of Success

In the age of e-mail, cellular phones, teleconferences, faxes, Net meetings, and the Internet, virtual teams are commonplace. Unfortunately, the lack of social contact in these distributed workgroups makes it difficult to build interpersonal rapport, trust, and mutual respect. Workgroups without these basics are virtually teams, not virtual teams. Make it a point to know your teammates as people, not just workers. To be a team, people must stay connected emotionally, not just electronically.

Here are a few tips to make e-mail a more effective project communication tool:

◆ Limit the information you send to what is truly important. The "must-have" content should always outweigh the "nice-to-have" content. The "I-don't-know-if-you-need-it" content should be briefly described and sent only if requested.

◆ Don't bury important information at the end of a long message. The reader may hit the Delete button long before she finds your nugget of wisdom.

◆ Make key points standout with bullets and indentations.

◆ When sending more than one question, number each question so none are overlooked and so that replies can be referenced.

◆ Don't ask for (or send) more detail than you really need. Remember, you're seeking success, not perfection.

◆ Clean up your distribution lists frequently. Nothing destroys credibility faster than sending e-mail to a person who has been gone for several months.

◆ Always place a brief description of the content in the subject area. Help the recipient prioritize their communication workload.

◆ Make your e-mail reader-friendly by using appropriate grammar, capitalization, punctuation, and spelling.

♦ Avoid humorous content. Because e-mail provides no immediate feedback in the way of body language or facial expressions, intended humor may easily become an unintended insult.

♦ Keep your messages professional. Inspirational quotes, promises of chain mail riches, and urban myths are best left to those with free e-mail accounts.

Workgroup Messaging Systems

Workgroup Messaging is a popular and useful feature of both Project 2000 and Project 2002, however in Project 2003 these features have been replaced and greatly improved with Microsoft's EPM solution. (See Chapter 19 for an overview of these features and additional software requirements.) You can enable Workgroup Messaging in Project 2003 (Standard or Professional) as an alternative to the EPM solution. However, Microsoft has notified users that workgroup messaging is no longer supported and will not be available in future versions of Project, so it must be considered an interim solution. Figure 20.1 illustrates how Workgroup Messaging connects the team and the project manager through existing e-mail systems. The files are free to download and the installation is straightforward.

Secrets of Success

Keeping the plan's actuals current can be an onerous chore that frequently doesn't get done. But without actuals, the plan is woefully underutilized—trends remain hidden, problems compound, and the few choices a project manager really has can easily be missed. Current actuals against a good baseline plan provide the knowledge and the confidence needed to act.

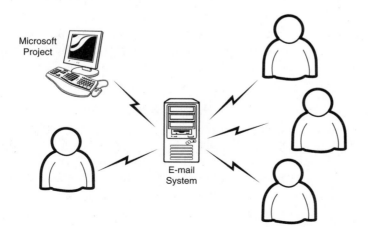

Figure 20.1

Workgroup Messaging is available in both Project 2000 and Project 2002 and can be installed as an interim communication solution in Project 2003.

Microsoft Project

E-mail System

The most useful feature in Workgroup Messaging is the ability to update actuals without entering all the data by yourself. With a few clicks of your mouse, you can send a request for progress information to some or all of the project team and directly update your plan with their responses!

It is also easy to assign tasks, notify the team of schedule changes, and generally keep everyone informed (especially yourself).

Setting Up Workgroup Messaging in Project 2003

In Project 2000 and Project 2002, Workgroup Messaging is a standard feature. To make it available in Project 2003, you must download and install Workgroup Messaging as follows:

1. Download and install the Workgroup Messaging handler files from the Microsoft downloads website.

2. Change your computer's Registry to enable the workgroup features and make them visible on Project 2003.

3. Prepare your plan for e-mail messaging by adding e-mail addresses for resources and by choosing e-mail as the preferred collaboration method.

To get the Workgroup Messaging handler, go to www.microsoft.com/downloads and in the **Search for a Download** section enter "Project 2003 workgroup message handler" in the **Keywords** box. Find and download the WGFiles.exe file from the list of search results, saving it to an easily accessible place on your computer. Others who will be participating in Workgroup Messaging will need to install this file on their computers, so you'll want to place this file in a folder easily accessible to them. Microsoft Knowledge Base Article 818337, "How to turn on the Workgroup Mail feature in Project 2003," provides additional information.

> **More Good Stuff**
>
> If you're using Project 2000 or 2002 and want to further improve communications, consider upgrading to Project 2003. Microsoft's new EPM solution advances communications to the level of enterprise-wide collaboration. If you haven't already deployed Project 2000's Project Central or Project 2002's Project Server, don't. Your time and investment will be better served moving to Project 2003's EPM solution.

After WGFiles.exe has been downloaded, double-click it to extract the Workgroup Messaging handler files, including WGSetup.exe. Close Project 2003 if it is running, and then double-click WGSetup.exe to begin installing the message handler. A dialog box appears, as shown in Figure 20.2. Follow the instructions and click **OK** when completed.

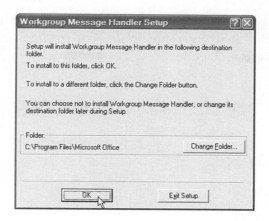

Figure 20.2

Enabling workgroup messaging via e-mail in Project 2003 requires running WGSetup.exe on each participating computer.

You must now edit the Windows Registry file of the computer running Project 2003. From Windows Start select **Run,** type **regedit** in the dialog box, and click **OK.** Navigate to HKEY_CURRENT_USER\Software\Microsoft\Office\11.0\ MS Project\Options. Select **Edit, New,** and then click **Key** and type **Workgroup** as the folder's name. This step is shown in Figure 20.3.

More Good Stuff

Be careful when editing the Registry. It can require the reinstallation of your operating system, so get someone with experience to assist you if necessary. It's always a good idea to make a backup of your Registry before it's modified. From the Registry Editor dialog box menu select **File, Export,** and save a copy to a safe location.

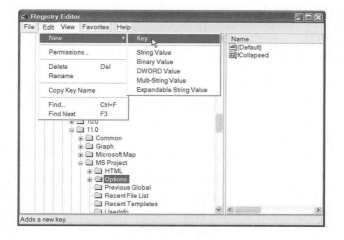

Figure 20.3

Create a key folder in the HKEY_CURRENT_USER \Software\Microsoft\Office \11.0\MS Project\Options registry and name it Workgroup.

Make sure the new folder you've just created is selected. Then on the menu select **Edit, New** and then click **String Value.** Enter **Workgroup Mail** as the value, press **Enter,** and then **Exit** from the File menu. These steps are shown in Figure 20.4 and Figure 20.5.

Figure 20.4

Prepare the Workgroup folder for a string value.

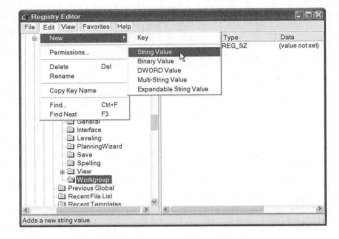

Figure 20.5

Replace New Value #1 with Workgroup Mail and exit the Registry.

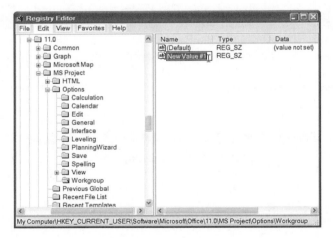

Now all that's left to use Workgroup Messaging is to set up your project plan with e-mail addresses and change your collaboration preferences for this project.

Start Project 2003, and from the Collaborate menu choose **Collaborate Options**. In the Collaborate Options dialog box, select **E-mail only,** as shown in Figure 20.6. In the lower section you can limit when e-mail updates are sent. It's easy to bury your team in a flurry of e-mails if you select the option: **On every save, publish the following to project server,** so make sure this box is not checked. (The option is best for sending updates to the Microsoft EPM solution server when e-mail work-group messaging isn't). Conversely, you can select either of the options under **Publish New and Changed Assignments ....** E-mails are only sent (and both options are available) when you select **Publish,** in the **Collaborate** menu. Click **Set as Default** when finished choosing options, so that you won't have to modify each resource's information separately.

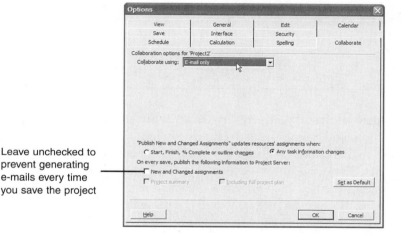

Figure 20.6

*Choose **E-mail only** in the Collaborate Options dialog box.*

Leave unchecked to prevent generating e-mails every time you save the project

While you're in the Options dialog box, choose the **General** tab and make sure that your name appears in the User name box. This is where workgroup e-mail replies will be sent.

Now make sure your resources have e-mail addresses and you'll be ready to go. There are two easy ways to do this. If you haven't yet added resources to your project, you can enter the e-mail addresses automatically from your address book. Open the Resource Sheet view and click **Insert, New Resource From,** and choose **Address Book,** as shown in Figure 20.7 and Figure 20.8.

Figure 20.7

Add resources and e-mail addresses directly from your e-mail address book or Active Directory.

Figure 20.8

*When finished selecting resources, click **OK** and they will be added into your project's resource sheet.*

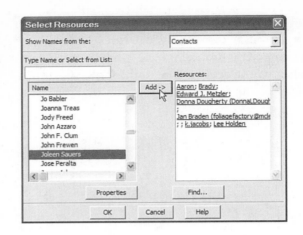

You can also add an e-mail address directly in the Resource Sheet view by inserting the E-mail Address column and typing the address directly into the field. Inserting the E-mail column also makes it easy to check for missing addresses or to modify project-specific addresses. From the Resource Sheet view, select the column header to the right of where you want the new column, right-click and from the pop-up menu choose E-mail Address, as shown in Figure 20.9 (and the results in Figure 20.10).

Don't worry if you miss or forget to add an address for all resources; after the message is prepared, you will be prompted to add any missing addresses.

Figure 20.9

Insert the E-mail Address column into the Resource Sheet view for direct entry.

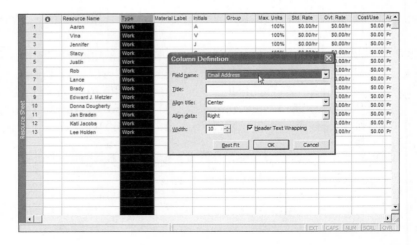

Project 2003 is now set up and ready to communicate with anyone on the team who has access to MAPI-compliant e-mail. This includes Outlook and Outlook Express, Microsoft Exchange Server, Microsoft Mail, Lotus cc:Mail, and Lotus Notes.

	ⓘ	Resource Name	Email Address	Type	Material Label	Initials	Group	Max. Units	Std. Rate
1		Aaron	Aaron	Work		A		100%	$0.00/hr
2		Vina	VS@parkrose.com	Work		V		100%	$0.00/hr
3		Jennifer	Jwagner@IFDS.com	Work		J		100%	$0.00/hr
4		Stacy Green	SBS@UNMPT.edu	Work		S		100%	$0.00/hr
5		Justin	Jharrington@universal.com	Work		J		100%	$0.00/hr
6		Rob	RH@serviceengineering.com	Work		R		100%	$0.00/hr
7		Lance		Work		L		100%	$0.00/hr
8		Brady	Brady	Work		B		100%	$0.00/hr
9		Edward J. Metzler	Emetzler@Accredo.com	Work		E		100%	$0.00/hr
10		Donna Dougherty	Donna Dougherty	Work		D		100%	$0.00/hr
11		Jan Braden	agefactory@mcleodusa.net)	Work		J		100%	$0.00/hr
12		Kati Jacobs	kjacobs@bigpond.com.au	Work		K		100%	$0.00/hr
13		Lee Holden	Lee Holden	Work		L		100%	$0.00/hr

Figure 20.10

It's easy to spot missing information with the E-mail Address column inserted into the resource sheet.

All that has to be done now is to run WGSetup.exe on any computer that needs to be able to receive or reply to workgroup e-mail messages. The program is found on the CD included with Project 2000 and Project 2002. WGSetup.exe may be shared with the project team members with no additional licensing fees. Microsoft recommends that you place the entire WGSetup folder on a drive accessible to the workgroup. If a remote team member needs it, just e-mail it as an attachment.

Using Workgroup Messaging

It used to be an onerous task at the beginning of a project to notify everyone of his or her assignments; with Workgroup Messaging, however, nothing could be easier!

It's always a good idea to save your project before starting a new procedure, so take a moment and save your file before continuing. A fast way to save your file is to press and hold the **Ctrl** key while pressing **S.** When you're ready, select the Gantt Chart view by clicking **Gantt Chart** in the View menu.

> **More Good Stuff**
>
> Using Workgroup Messaging with e-mail in Project 2002 and 2003 is very similar. In Project 2000, Workgroup Messaging works the same way, but the menu selections and dialog boxes have different terminology, such as TeamAssign, TeamUpdate, and TeamStatus. Where Project 2000 is different, it is covered separately later in this chapter.

Publishing All Assignments to the Team

First save a baseline as described in Chapter 13. Then from the **Collaborate** menu select **Publish** and click **All Information.** This selection sends information to all resources without allowing you to change individual messages or limit who will receive them. For more control, you can use the Publish New and Changed Assignments option, as described later in this section. The Collaborate menu shown in Figure 20.11 is from Project 2003 Standard. The Professional edition includes Project Center, Resource Center, Portfolio Analyzer, Portfolio Modeler, Risks, Issues, and Documents. These features are functional only when used with the Microsoft EPM solution.

Figure 20.11

To notify all team members participating in Workgroup Messaging of their individual assignments, select **Publish**, **All Information** *from the Collaborate menu.*

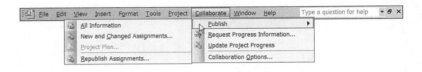

When the message appears that your plan will be saved before publishing, click **OK.** Project then prepares an e-mail message for each individual resource listing his or her assignments. Depending on your e-mail system settings, the messages might not be sent automatically. You'll want to check your Outbox and manually send them if necessary. An icon appears in the Indicator column (see Figure 20.12) advising you that the resource has not yet replied to this message.

Figure 20.12

An icon reminds you that a workgroup message sent to this resource has not yet been returned.

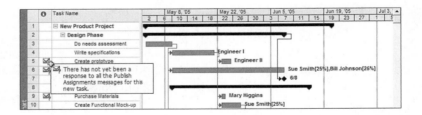

The message each resource receives is shown in Figure 20.13. The resource can accept or reject assignments by clicking **Reply,** editing the Accept? column to a Yes or No, and optionally adding a message for the project manager. The Reply button changes to Send when it is first clicked or when the message is edited. With a final click on **Send,** the message is on its way back to the project manager.

Reply button changes to
Send after clicking or editing

Add comments for
project manager

Enter Yes or No

Scroll for more fields

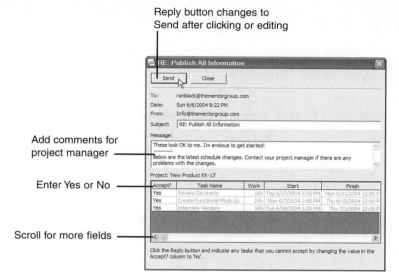

Figure 20.13

*The resource can accept or reject each task, make comments, and return the message by clicking **Reply** and then **Send**.*

Updating the Project with Returned Messages

When received by the project manager, the returned message looks like the one in Figure 20.14. The project manager then has two options. To accept the message as is and update the plan click **Update Project**. To return to the message with additional comments or edits click **Reply**.

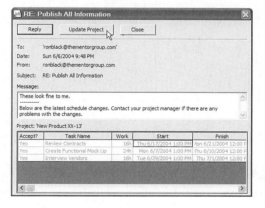

Figure 20.14

*When the message is returned to the project manager, it can be incorporated directly into the plan by clicking **Update Project**.*

Publish New and Changed Assignments

To send schedule or assignment changes to a selection or to all team members, use the **Publish New and Changed Assignments** command from the Collaborate menu. A dialog box will appear, as shown in Figure 20.15, with all resources (those who will be receiving a message). This is a very useful command when you've made several changes to the plan but haven't been keeping track of your changes or how the changes have rippled throughout the plan. An icon appears in the Indicator column to alert you that the plan has changed and notification should be sent (see Figure 20.15).

Figure 20.15

To alert team members whose assignments have changed use Publish New and Changed Assignments.

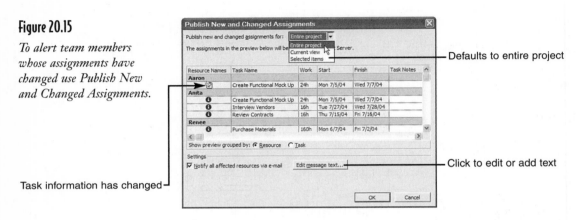

Defaults to entire project

Click to edit or add text

Task information has changed

To change the message that all recipients will see, click **Edit message text,** as noted in Figure 20.15. Change or add to the default message in the Edit message text dialog shown in Figure 20.16.

Figure 20.16

You can change the message that accompanies the resource assignments in this dialog box.

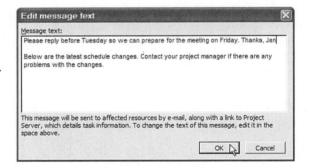

Republish Assignments

When you want to republish assignments to all or a selection of resources, you can use the **Republish Assignments** command. However, Project will send a message to everyone selected, even if you have already received their replies. To prevent sending unnecessary messages, select the tasks in the Gantt chart that you want to resend to, then choose **Selected items** in the **Republish assignments for:** box. The Republishing dialog box looks just like the Publish New and Changed command with two additional options in the lower left of the dialog box. See Figure 20.17. Both of these are applicable only when using the EPM solution.

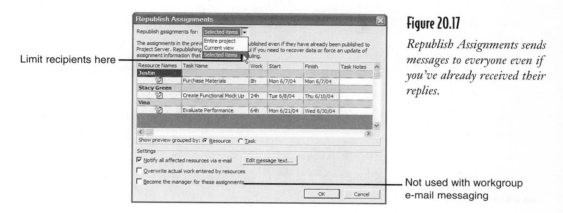

Limit recipients here ⟶

⟵ Not used with workgroup e-mail messaging

Figure 20.17

Republish Assignments sends messages to everyone even if you've already received their replies.

Requesting Progress Information

You probably like knowing how well work is progressing but taking the time to contact everyone and then enter all the actual data is an excruciatingly slow process. With this feature you can request status information and update your plan with just a few mouse clicks. It's easy on the team, easy on you, and helps your project stay on the road to success.

To send a progress request to a selection of resources, highlight the tasks you're interested in the Gantt view. If you don't select any rows a progress request will be sent to the entire team. After you've chosen the tasks, from the Collaborate menu click **Request Progress Information.** A dialog box like the one in Figure 20.18 will appear. You can edit the text that accompanies the message to all recipients. In addition, you can limit the date range for the requested progress report. This is especially useful if you are requesting hours of work and progress over a given reporting period.

Until a progress report has been returned, an icon remains in the Indicator column. When the progress request is returned in your e-mail, the attached message looks similar to all other Workgroup Messaging replies (such as Figure 20.14). You may edit the message and click **Reply** to send it back to the reporting resource, or click **Update** to accept the information and automatically update your plan. Voilà! Now's the time to go to the Tracking Gantt chart and see how you're doing!

Figure 20.18

Updating your plan with actuals is as easy as sending a Request for Progress message, and then clicking Update Plan when the messages are returned.

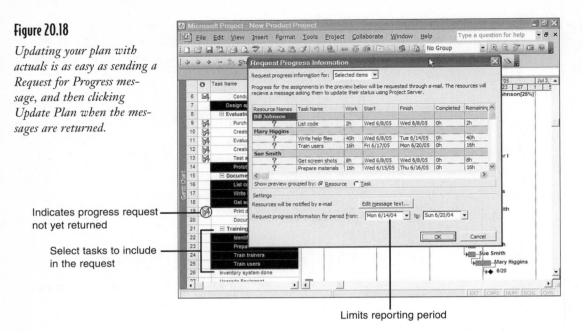

Indicates progress request not yet returned

Select tasks to include in the request

Limits reporting period

Customizing Workgroup Message Reporting Fields

The information in the workgroup message data fields can be modified to track and report on the items that are most important to your project. If you are not tracking hours for example, it's a good idea to remove that field from the message so that team members won't waste time on unnecessary detail. To add or remove fields, select **Customize** from the Tools menu, and then select **Published Fields.**

In the Customize Published Fields dialog box shown in Figure 20.19, the project manager has taken a minimalist approach and is tracking only the actual start, the actual finish, and the percentage completed. You can click **Reset** to return to Project's default settings. When you're satisfied with the fields click **OK** to save the settings.

Figure 20.19

Modify the fields displayed in workgroup messages to fit your project's needs.

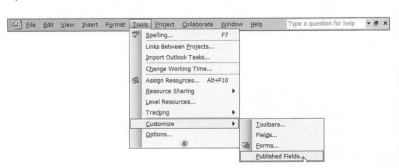

Sending an E-Mail Schedule Note

In Project, you can use your normal e-mail program outside of Workgroup Messaging to send a schedule note to the team, the project manager, or even to others who are not a part of the project's workgroup. If you want to send a note to one or a selection of workgroup members, select them before beginning the following steps. From the File menu select **Send to,** click **Mail Recipient (as Schedule Note).** In the dialog box shown in Figure 20.20, you can designate who will get the message. Choose **Selected tasks** if you highlighted tasks before beginning. To send to recipients who are not members of your workgroup, select **Contacts.** An e-mail message will appear and you can select recipients from your e-mail program's address book or you can type them in. This proves useful when sending updates or a picture of the Gantt chart to stakeholders who aren't working on the project.

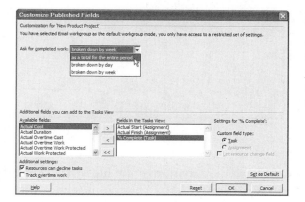

Figure 20.20

Send a picture of the Gantt chart, notes, or the entire project file to workgroup or nonworkgroup recipients with your e-mail program.

The resulting e-mail message is shown in Figure 20.21 as received by the resources. Much of the power of the Send Schedule Note feature is its capability to send a project file or a picture of any current view.

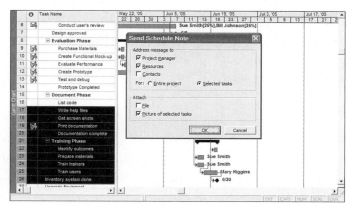

Figure 20.21

Complex workflow relationships can be communicated with ease and accuracy by sending a schedule note.

Routing Project Files

To route a project file to a series of recipients, open the project file in Project 2003. On the File menu select **Send To** and then click **Routing Recipient.** In the Routing Slip dialog box, select the recipients and options, as shown in Figure 20.22.

Figure 20.22

Create a routing slip to send a project file to a series of stakeholders.

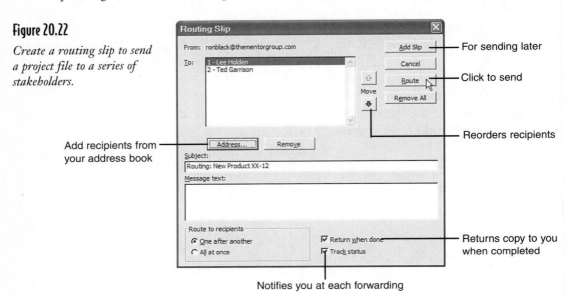

For sending later

Click to send

Reorders recipients

Add recipients from your address book

Returns copy to you when completed

Notifies you at each forwarding

After selecting the recipients and options, send the file by clicking **Route.** If you aren't ready to send the file, click **Add Slip.** The routing slip is stored with the project file. You can then send the file or modify the routing slip later by choosing **Send To** from the File menu and clicking **Other Routing Recipient.**

Using Workgroup Messaging in Project 2000

The Workgroup Messaging features in Project 2000 are very similar to those described above for Project 2002 and Project 2003. However, the menu choices have different names, so the following section identifies menus and terminology. In Project 2000, workgroup e-mail messages are called TeamAssign, TeamUpdate, and TeamStatus.

Using TeamAssign

You may use TeamAssign to notify workgroup members of task assignments. Of course, this presupposes that you've contacted the individuals regarding the project and their involvement on it. Choose the task or tasks that you want to send assignment notifications to. The results are shown in Figure 20.23. On some tasks there may be more than one resource assigned. In this case, each assigned resource is notified.

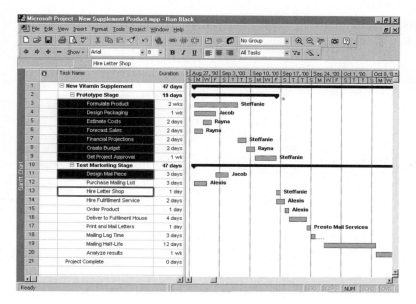

Figure 20.23

Select the tasks you want to send resource notification messages to in the Gantt Chart view.

After the tasks have been selected, select **Workgroup** from the Tools menu and then click **TeamAssign,** as shown in Figure 20.24.

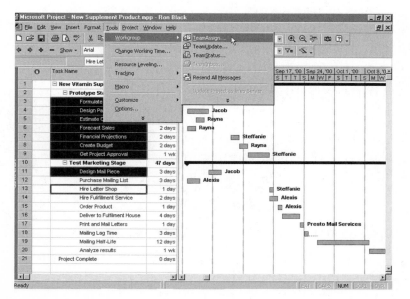

Figure 20.24

Sending assignment notifications to resources is fast and easy with Project 2000.

Modify the subject line and message as appropriate in the TeamAssign dialog box and click **Send,** as shown in Figure 20.25. Your workgroup will be notified of their respective tasks assignments just as soon as they receive their e-mail.

Figure 20.25

The TeamAssign message is ready to send to the workgroup.

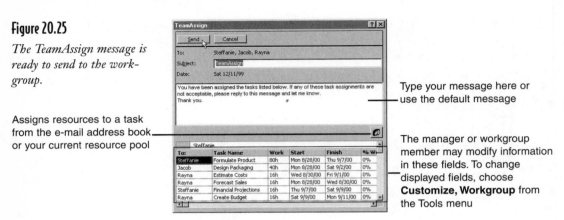

Assigns resources to a task from the e-mail address book or your current resource pool

Type your message here or use the default message

The manager or workgroup member may modify information in these fields. To change displayed fields, choose **Customize, Workgroup** from the Tools menu

When the workgroup members receive the message, they may accept or reject the assignment before replying. After workgroup members reply to TeamAssign messages, the project manager can update the project as shown in Figure 20.26. The task assignment is marked as confirmed and task assignment information is updated.

Figure 20.26

*Replies to TeamAssign messages can be applied to the project by clicking **Update Project.***

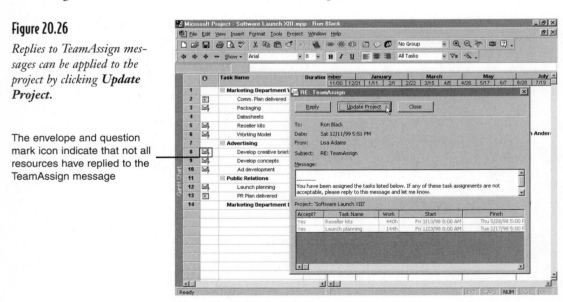

The envelope and question mark icon indicate that not all resources have replied to the TeamAssign message

Using TeamUpdate

TeamUpdate messaging makes it fast and easy to notify resources who are affected by task slippage, changes in start or finish dates, or changes in resources allocations. Sending, replying, and updating TeamUpdate messages follows an almost identical procedure, as described previously in the "Using TeamAssign" section. For example, to send a TeamUpdate message, select **Workgroup** from the Tools menu and then click **TeamUpdate,** as shown in Figure 20.27.

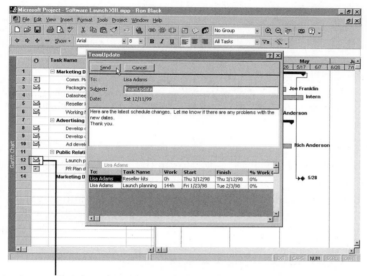

Figure 20.27

Sending a TeamUpdate is the fast and easy way to notify resources when dates slip or assignments change.

The envelope and exclamation point icon indicates that information for this task has changed and a TeamUpdate message should be sent

To update the project after the resource has replied, open the e-mail message and click **Update Task List,** as shown in Figure 20.28.

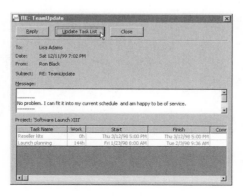

Figure 20.28

*Entering accepted TeamUpdate information into your project schedule is as easy as opening the message and clicking **Update Task List.***

Using TeamStatus

To request a status report from the resources on your project, select **Workgroup** from the Tools menu and then click **TeamStatus.** You may choose to request a TeamStatus from all resources or from a selection. The TeamStatus dialog box is shown in Figure 20.29.

Figure 20.29

Timely status reports can be collected by sending a TeamStatus message.

Fields included in the message are resource, task, work, start, finish, completed work, remaining work, percent of work completed, and comments. Included fields may be modified in the Customize Workgroup dialog box

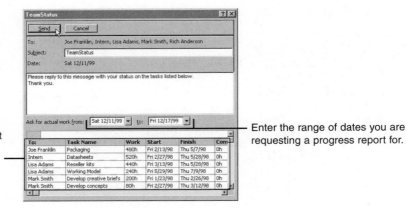

Enter the range of dates you are requesting a progress report for.

The workgroup member enters their work for the period requested and sends the message back to the project manager. The TeamStatus message is shown in Figure 20.30.

Figure 20.30

TeamStatus messages provide a rapid method for collecting the work completed on each task.

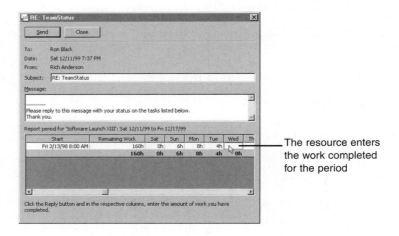

The resource enters the work completed for the period

To update the project's status, open each workgroup TeamStatus message that has been returned and click **Update Project,** as shown in Figure 20.31.

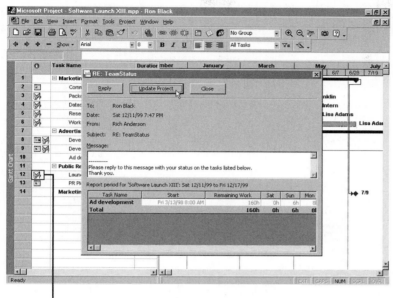

Figure 20.31

Updating project status is quick and easy for the project manager after resources reply.

The envelope, clock, and question mark icon indicate that one or more resources on this task has not yet responded to the TeamStatus message

The Least You Need to Know

◆ When working with virtual teams, strive to establish trust, rapport, and mutual respect with all team members.

◆ Project managers can use workgroup e-mail messaging to assign, check status, and notify team members quickly and easily.

◆ Progress reporting can be automatically entered into the plan from a resource's e-mailed reply.

◆ Schedule notes may be sent to any or all project resources directly from Microsoft Project including pictures of the schedule or complete project files.

◆ Project files can be sent or routed to a list of recipients for review or comment, and a notification can be sent back to the project manager each time the file is forwarded.

Chapter 21

Sharing Information with Other Programs

In This Chapter

◆ Import and export information from Microsoft Project 2003 to word processor, spreadsheet, and database formats

◆ Insert documents and spreadsheets into your project file for viewing or editing from within Microsoft Project 2003

◆ Paste information, graphics, and pictures into note fields

Effective communications among all project stakeholders is essential for project success. No matter how unresponsive, incommunicative, or down-right boneheaded some teammates may be, it's your responsibility to make sure everyone has the information he or she needs. Whenever you hear that mournful whine coming from the rear of the conference room, "But nobody told me …," you know a need has not been met. Worse yet, you know your project's success may be threatened.

Communication is a two-way process. Not only do you have information the team needs, the team has information you need. It therefore benefits you to be receptive to their information in any format they are capable (or willing) of supplying it in. Whether a spreadsheet file, a word processing document, or written on the back of a piece of lumber with a carpenter's pencil, gather every bit of information you can from the team. The more effective you can communicate, the more likely you're project will be a success.

This chapter shows you how to collect, distribute, and analyze information in all popular formats (not including a carpenter's pencil).

Other Project Documentation Needs

Several important project management documents are not implemented in Project 2003. These include the expedite (crash) analysis (Chapter 16), project process documentation (Chapter 2), quotes, contracts, bills of material, payroll time sheets, specifications, and detailed cost estimates. In fact, this lack of coverage is just as well. Not all of these documents are needed or used in every organization. Furthermore, it would be difficult to provide a generic format of each of these that could be used across the many industries served by Project 2003. All these documents (if needed) should be custom created to ensure that your needs and your organization's policies and procedures are well served.

> **More Good Stuff**
>
> One of the driving factors of implementing Microsoft's EPM solution is its ability to interface with line of business information systems. Materials resource planning, cost account, shop-floor control, and many other systems can share information through the Project Server 2003 system. For more information on the range of possibilities, contact the resources listed in the appendix.

It's likely that each of these documents will be easier to create and use in a program other than Microsoft Project. For example, a project-initiation document or specifications are best created in a word processor such as Microsoft Word. Quotes, cost estimates, and the like are best created in a spreadsheet program such as Microsoft Excel. Detailed bills of material and time sheets are best created in a database such as Microsoft Access.

> **More Good Stuff**
>
> The Internet is a powerful tool for the distribution and collection of information. Microsoft Project 2003 has several features—ranging from the simple to the sophisticated—that help you tap into the power of the Internet. The easiest way to begin using the web is to distribute project information. You can easily export both pictures of charts and fields of data into formats that can be posted onto existing websites. These snapshots of information can then be viewed by anyone who has access to the web. For more information about using the web, see Chapter 19.

More Good Stuff

Before you decide to create a specialized program, be sure you shop around. Project is the world's most popular project management program, and as such, many enhancements, add-ins, and tools are available. To look for them, do a little web surfing. If you have access to the Internet, you can start right from Project. Select **Help** from the menu and choose **Microsoft Office Online.** Your browser will connect you to http://office. microsoft.com/home/default.aspx. From there, check out Downloads, Office Marketplace, or search for the item of interest.

Project 2003 is great for scheduling, tracking, resource loading and leveling, and communicating to the project team. Just don't try to use it for bidding, inventory control, accounting, or other tasks that it wasn't specifically designed for. You'll be working too hard! Instead, use the program best suited for those needs. But don't worry, Project facilitates all these other project management requirements by allowing you to easily import, export, and share data in all popular formats. These are described in "Sharing Large Amounts of Information" section later in this chapter. These techniques can help you avoid the tedium of entering and re-entering information in several programs.

Sharing Small Amounts of Information

The easiest way to transfer small amounts of information in and out of Project 2003 is with the copy and paste functions. This works well for a list of task names, durations, resources, or cost fields. For example, if your colleague has prepared a work breakdown structure in Excel or Word, you can copy the information and paste it directly into Project 2003. Be sure that the source and recipient fields are in the same order and format.

To cut and paste information from Excel to Project, open both files and select the area you want to copy in Excel. If the columns or rows to copy are not contiguous or are in a different order than in Project, you can rearrange columns or simply cut and paste one column at time. After the area to copy is highlighted, right-click to open a pop-up menu and click **Copy,** as shown in Figure 21.1.

Now switch to Project and open the sheet view where you want to paste the information. In this case, open the **View** menu, select **More Views,** and then choose **Task Sheet.** Locate your cursor where you want the information to be pasted. Right-click to open the pop-up menu, and select **Paste,** as shown in Figure 21.2. Presto! The information is transferred as shown in Figure 21.3. This same technique works with information supplied to you in a Word document and many other Windows-based applications.

Figure 21.1

Select the information you want and copy it to the clipboard.

The format and layout of the information must be identical in the copied and pasted locations.

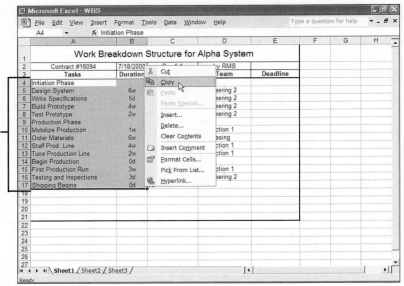

More Good Stuff

You can view any Microsoft Office document or a web page with your browser by inserting a hyperlink into your Project 2003 file. From any sheet view, select **Hyperlink** on the Insert menu and follow the instructions in the dialog box that appears. This is an easy way to place supporting information at your fingertips. The information resides in its original location and format, ready for instant viewing. To access the information, click the **Hyperlink** icon (a small globe and chain link) displayed in the Indicators column. Your browser will automatically load the page for viewing.

Figure 21.2

Place your cursor in the upper-left corner of the area where you want to place the information from your clipboard.

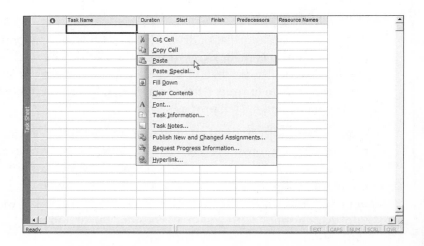

Durations were converted to days when pasted

Start and finish dates were automatically calculated

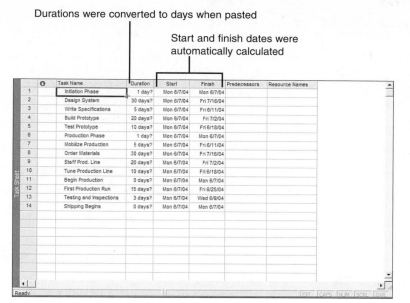

Figure 21.3

A team member's task and duration estimates provided in a spreadsheet is easy to copy and paste into Project 2003.

Don't paste information into calculated fields such as the start or finish dates in the Entry Table view. Pasted start or finish dates into Project 2003 will be interpreted as setting a constraint. As explained in Chapter 10, constraints restrict your schedule and should be avoided unless you specifically want to restrict the workflow sequence and the scheduling options available.

Sharing Large Amounts of Information

If the amount of information you want to share is large, it may be easier to use the import and export features of Project 2003. This method is used by saving or opening a file in one of the supported file formats. Table 21.1 describes these file formats.

Table 21.1   Supported File Formats in Project 2003

Name	Extension	Description
Microsoft Project	.mpp	The file format used by Project to store your project information. When saving Project 2003 files for use in Project 98, use **Save As** and change the **Save as type** to **Microsoft Project 98**.

continues

Table 21.1 Supported File Formats in Project 2003 (continued)

Name	Extension	Description
Microsoft Project	.mpt	Used to save common information for template a given type of project. Several project templates come with Project 2003, and you may add others.
Microsoft Project	.mpx	Used by older versions to exchange project information, Project 2003 can import field data from this format but cannot save to it.
Microsoft Project	.mpd	The standard exchange format that has replaced the .mpx format.
Microsoft Access	.mdb	Used to save all or part of a project's data in the Access 2003 format.
Microsoft Excel	.xls	Project field data may be opened or saved in this file format for use in the Excel spreadsheet program.
Microsoft Excel PivotTable	.xls	A special format used to save field information in an Excel PivotTable. You can't import information into Project from a PivotTable.
HTML	.htm	Field data may be exported to this format for use in HTML documents used by browser programs on the World Wide Web and on intranets. You can't import data from this format into Project 2003.
Text or ASCII	.txt	A tab-delimited file of field data used to export or import information from programs not otherwise supported.
CSV	.csv	A comma-delimited file of field data used to export or import information from programs not otherwise supported.

To use these file formats, select either **Open** or **Save As** from the File menu. When the dialog box appears, select the file type in the **Save as type** field and click **Save** (or **Open**). This process is shown in Figure 21.4.

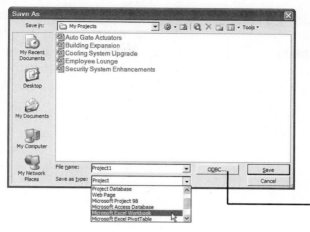

Figure 21.4

*You may import or export project information in several file formats by selecting the file type when using the **Open** or **Save As** commands.*

Data field information may be imported from or exported to ODBC-compliant databases by clicking here

Inserting Documents, Tables, Charts, and Other Items

Another helpful feature in Project 2003 enables you to insert information as an object into the project file. This can be done in several ways, allowing you to view or even edit another program's information from within Project 2003. Objects may be inserted into a Gantt chart and into task, resource, or assignment notes.

For example, you may embed or link an item, such as an Excel spreadsheet cost estimate or a Word project initiation document, into a task's note. The file can be displayed as an icon or as the actual information.

Don't confuse embedding and linking files. There are important differences in how the information is stored and updated. When a file is linked to a destination file, such as a project plan, the linked object is displayed in the destination file (the project plan) as a representation of the actual file. The actual data remains in its original location. If the data is changed, the change is automatically reflected in the destination file. This method keeps the destination file as small as possible and eliminates the risk of multiple file versions. It also enables you to dynamically link files that are not yet complete or that need to be changed throughout the duration of the project.

On the other hand, embedded files become a part of the destination file. If you change the original file, no changes are reflected in the destination file. However, destination file users who don't have access to the original file can view the embedded version and even change it if they have a copy of the source program. Destination files sizes are larger, and the embedded information is readily available to anyone with access to the project plan. To embed or link, the choice is yours.

To insert an object, you can first create and save it, or you can create it during the insertion process. For example, to place an object in a task's note field, right-click the task and select **Task Notes** in the pop-up menu. As shown in Figure 21.5, click the **Insert Object** icon. When the dialog box appears, choose the type of object you want to create or choose **Create from File.** In this case, you can **Browse** to the existing file and select it by clicking on it.

An Excel file is displayed as an icon

Figure 21.5

A wealth of project information can be conveniently stored and instantly accessed by inserting files as objects in Project 2003.

The contents of a Word document can be displayed

Click to insert an object into notes

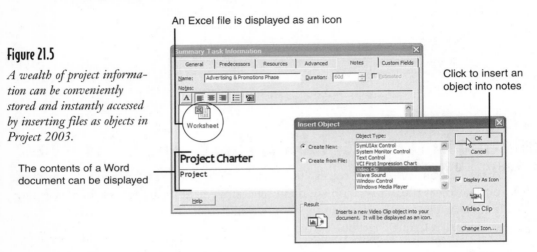

The types of information you can insert this way are almost endless. You can include documents, e-mail messages, spreadsheets, sound files, pictures, presentations, video clips, and more. In this way, you can make every project file a powerful communication tool. You might even be able to prevent that whining from the back of the conference room, "But nobody told me …"!

More Good Stuff

If your team has access to electronic cameras, try these tips on your next project. Some project teams are spread out between buildings or even around the world. They may never see each other. Have each person take a self-portrait on an electronic camera and e-mail the results to you. Insert each photo into the resource notes, and everyone accessing your project file can then see who's on the team.

To access information stored in objects, just open the note and double-click the inserted object. An Excel spreadsheet is shown opened in Figure 21.6.

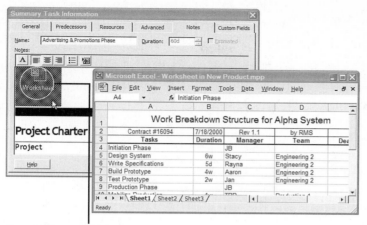

Figure 21.6

Contracts, specifications, estimates, test results, progress photos, and other project-related information can be instantly accessed when inserted as an object.

Open the inserted object to modify or print it by double-clicking

The Least You Need to Know

◆ Project 2003 makes it easy to collect and disseminate information in almost any format.

◆ When sharing small amounts of information among programs, it is easiest to copy the data onto the clipboard from one program and then paste it into the other.

◆ Large amounts of information can be shared by saving the data in a supported file format and then opening it with the recipient program.

◆ Documents, spreadsheets, pictures, and other files are easily inserted into notes where they may be instantly accessed for viewing, modification, or printing.

Presenting Projects with Persuasive Pizzazz

In This Chapter

- ◆ Fast tips and easy tricks to prepare for any project presentation

- ◆ Easy ways to place charts and tables from Project 2003 into Word or PowerPoint

- ◆ Understanding earned value reporting and why it's an effective project status indicator

- ◆ Using Excel to analyze your project's time-scaled data

When pressed, most project managers agree that communicating within the confines of the workgroup, although difficult, is much easier than communicating with upper management or the customer. When communicating with owners and managers, there may be more at risk, fewer chances to recover from mistakes, and a communication environment that is less familiar and perhaps more difficult to master.

This chapter focuses on improving your ability to communicate with greater confidence, credibility, and clout, when it's important to make your best impression.

Two Types of Communications Are Required for Success

As in most leadership roles, the project manager's ability to communicate effectively is based on interpersonal rapport, professional credibility, and persuasive clout. What makes you a good communicator within the workgroup is the same thing that makes you a good communicator with management and customers; you've just got less time to make it happen. Let me explain: You're persuasive within the workgroup not because everyone reports to you, few if any of them do. You're persuasive because you're technically competent; you value and champion contributions to project success; you're knowledgeable, trustworthy, approachable, firm when you must be, always fair, and exceedingly goal driven. In short, you're an effective communicator because you've created a trusting, respectful environment, one of professional rapport.

When dealing with upper management, customers, and other key stakeholders, it is equally important to communicate with credibility and persuasive clout. Ultimately, these are the people project managers serve. In addition, these are the people who hold the power of funding, resources, and who will eventually judge the project's success or failure.

Although it's natural and relatively easy to build rapport with the work group where roles are well understood and there is frequency of contact, it isn't as easy to build rapport with key stakeholder groups. There, roles are less well defined and contact is infrequent. The rules of communicating with credibility and persuasive clout don't change, but the mechanics of communicating does. Formal meetings and written reports outweigh the informal, interpersonal communications common within workgroups. In more structured environments, rapport can be difficult to establish—there's less interpersonal discourse, less time to build understanding, and less mutual history to build on. Worse yet, most project managers simply aren't as comfortable when communicating with upper management or other powerful stakeholder groups as they are within the core team .

The Secret to Communicating with Credibility and Confidence

Any project manager can deliver good news to a friendly group, but sometimes both the news and the group are more challenging. Whether it's a written report or a formal presentation, your confidence, credibility, and clout all stem from one essential element: a genuine respect for your audience and their needs. When the presenter respects the audience and their needs, it shows in the quality of their delivery, and ultimately in the results they'll achieve. This cause and effect is easy to trace. Respect drives a more thorough preparation. Better preparation builds the presenter's ability to communicate on target.

Confidence is important when making formal presentations to a group. The persuasiveness of even the best logic is undermined when the presenter is stressed or ill at ease. When prepared, the presenter is more able to focus on the group rather than what he or she wants to say (or on trying to get a laptop working with a strange projector). Finally, when you show respect to an audience through preparation and genuine attentiveness, they'll naturally be more receptive to your message.

As the project manager, you probably have greater project knowledge and a better vantage point for decision making than any other stakeholder. Your views and opinions are essential to the project's success. But knowing what's best is not enough—you must be able to relate it to others with credibility and confidence. Only then will you have persuasive clout.

Presentation Tips

To make the most of your communication opportunities, focus on the audience and prepare, prepare, prepare. And since you've got plenty of things on your to-do list already, it's important to be able to prepare quickly. Here's how to get good at communicating, fast:

- ◆ Create an outline format for each type of presentation that you do. Thinking in terms of "fill in the blank" takes less time and yields better results. In addition, when presenting to the same group it becomes easier for them to find the information they want next time.

- ◆ Use visual images whenever possible. Many of the key project management documents are charts for good reason: Complex time-phased relationships are difficult to communicate without a visual image. Project already has most of these ready.

- ◆ When presenting with your laptop and PowerPoint, place a hyperlink in each slide linking to more detailed information. If you need more detail or backup information to make a point, you'll look like a whiz! If you don't need the detail, the technique helps keep you from overwhelming your audience with information.

- ◆ When presenting to a group, get there early. You'll need to check the room, the seating, the lighting, the projector, the temperature ... everything. It doesn't matter who forgot what or why it doesn't work, the presenter will be held responsible for everything, even the rubber chicken served at lunch.

◆ When presenting to small groups, meet and greet every participant. With large groups, spread yourself around as much as any good host could. Showing courtesy and your best business manners to everyone sets the tone for respectful communications.

◆ If you're using a laptop and projector, always have a backup plan. Burned-out bulbs, poor room lighting, missing projector screens, and lost files happen. Create a CD of your presentation, and remember that in a worst-case situation you can always present from your handouts. The less you have to worry about, the more attention you'll give to the participants.

◆ When heckled, harassed, or hated, remember the secret to communicating with credibility and confidence. Even when they don't deserve it, you've got to genuinely respect the audience. That's the price of leadership. You don't however, have to dwell on a participant's poor behavior. One good tactic is just to acknowledge the heckler's point of view in neutral terms and quickly move on. Half the audience will think you're a genius, and the other half won't even notice.

◆ Dress slightly better than those you're presenting to. Not only does it show your respect for the audience, but people do judge books by their covers.

◆ In a like manner, dress your ideas for success. The worst plan dressed in full-color charts and graphs, with copious backup detail, spiral bound in a glossy 10-point cover stock, will likely hold sway over a better plan scrawled on a yellow pad.

Fast and Powerful Reports Using Word or PowerPoint

When you need to whip up a presentation that makes a point, pictures and charts are hard to beat. Microsoft Project 2003 has simplified producing pictures or charts of your project with two new features. One quickly exports data to Excel for further analysis or for creating charts and graphs. The other new feature formats, sizes, and sends directly to Word, PowerPoint, or Visio any view of any Project 2003 data you can see on your screen. With these great tools and my ready-to-edit outline, you'll be adding persuasive pizzazz to any presentation in a matter of minutes!

Setting Up the Status Report Outline

The first step in creating fast and effective status reports (or any other presentation for that matter) is to create an outline of the content. After you've established a general outline, it can be used for similar presentations with only minor adjustments. You'll be able to prepare quickly and adequately, even on short notice.

To create the outline content areas, think of your presentation as a mini-project, with goals, objectives, stakeholders and deliverables. The project's triple constraints help you focus your report where issues are most important. Add your favorite Project views and reports to the outline and you'll look like the pro you really are, even to the toughest audience. The outline in Table 22.1 is a general-purpose status report for keeping upper management or the customer regularly informed. The outline can be used in Word as a written report, and in PowerPoint for a live presentation or webcast. Both formats of the outline can be downloaded from the author's website, edited as required, and freely used. Just don't sell or distribute my documents to anyone or the publisher and I will get testy!

Table 22.1   Project Status Report Outline

Report Section	Content
Goals and Objectives	Goal statement; summary of the project's key objectives. (The project initiation documents are a good resource for this information.)
Status Overview	Project status key statistics; schedule status and condition; budget status and condition; resources status and condition; other project-specific items and their status. (Use Project 2003's Project Status box from the Project Information dialog box for content or use the Project summary report as a data source. There is no easy way "export" either of these to Word or PowerPoint, but it doesn't take long to type in the key statistics.)
Workflow and Progress	Network diagram. (Select the **Network Diagram** view, hide details, and zoom to one-page display, and then copy picture to Word or PowerPoint. Multiple pages may be required.)
Timeline and Progress	Tracking Gantt. (Select the **Tracking Gantt** view. Zoom to entire project, copy picture to Word or PowerPoint. Multiple pages may be required.)

continues

Table 22.1   Project Status Report Outline   (continued)

Report Section	Content
Budget	Variance chart for general audiences; earned value for knowledgeable professionals. (Select Variance table and insert or hide columns as required. Copy picture to Word or Power-Point or export data to Excel. Optionally, save project data as a text file for inclusion to Word or Excel, using the Cost Data by Task map. Earned value charts may be created with the Analyze Timescaled Data in Excel Wizard. This process is described later in this chapter.)
Billings and Budgets	Expenditures and payables for the period; cash-flow analysis. (Use your organization's project payables and billings information.)
Human Resources	Staffing levels and current utilization of labor; shortages or conflicts encountered; anticipated future needs. (Use the Resource Usage view with an appropriate table or save as an Excel or text file with an appropriately modified data export map.)
Other Resources	Status of materials and supplies; status of plant, tools, and equipment; other key items.
Accomplishments	Milestones achieved; tasks currently under-way; tasks to start before next report; obstacles encountered and overcome. (Sort the project with Milestones, Tasks in Progress, or Incomplete Tasks filter before using the Copy Picture to Office Wizard.)
Risks and Issues	Identified risks; issues in process.
Closing Remarks	Review of key points; solicitation of comments, concerns, and questions.

Copying Project 2003 Pictures to Word or PowerPoint

To access Project 2003's Copy Picture to Office Wizard, right-click the toolbar area and check the **Analysis** toolbar. The toolbar is shown in Figure 22.1. Select the view you want to copy to Word, PowerPoint, or Visio. On the Analysis toolbar click **Copy Picture to Office Wizard.** Proceed to the second page of the wizard and choose how you want the picture to appear. The options shown in Figure 22.2 will vary depending on the view you have on the screen.

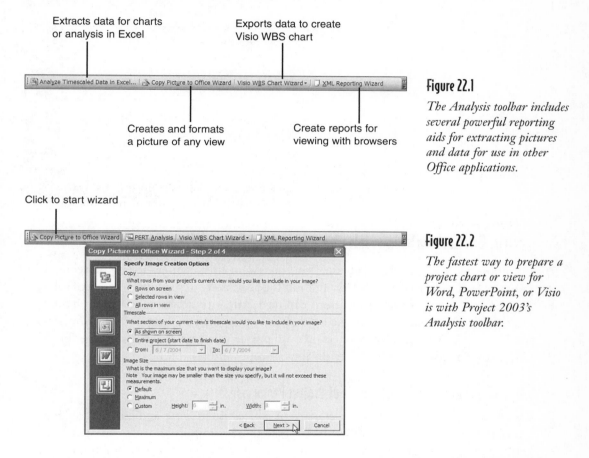

Extracts data for charts or analysis in Excel

Exports data to create Visio WBS chart

Creates and formats a picture of any view

Create reports for viewing with browsers

Figure 22.1

The Analysis toolbar includes several powerful reporting aids for extracting pictures and data for use in other Office applications.

Click to start wizard

Figure 22.2

The fastest way to prepare a project chart or view for Word, PowerPoint, or Visio is with Project 2003's Analysis toolbar.

Click **Next** and on the following screen select the Office application and page orientation. Then click **Preview** to see the results in your web browser. If you need to, you can close the web browser and click **Back** to return the previous page and adjust the your selections. When you're satisfied with the results click **Close.** The picture will be prepared and formatted, and the chosen application will open with the picture inserted. Figure 22.3 shows the result.

Figure 22.3

When you need to prepare for a meeting in a hurry, use the Copy Picture to Office Wizard.

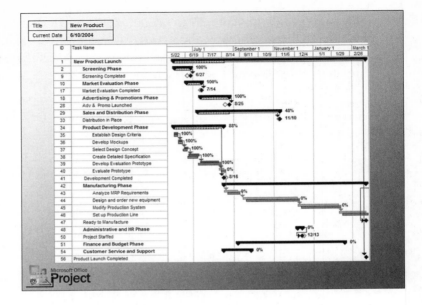

Reporting Earned Values with the Export to Excel Wizard

For a more knowledgeable audience, you may want to use an earned-value report or graph. There simply isn't a better method for accurately describing a project's schedule and cost status. The abbreviations can be a little intimidating to the uninitiated, but after you've used them on one of your own projects you'll understand why seasoned project managers rely so heavily on them. If you have little or no experience with earned value, here's a primer on the concepts and terminology.

Why Earned Value Is a Good Measure of Project Performance

The reason earned value is a useful concept is because judging and communicating a project's real status can be difficult! It's easy to oversimplify the age-old question "How's the project going?" There are five general conditions, and for all but one of these conditions, there is virtually an infinite range of possible values. The project can be …

♦ Exactly on time and on budget (everyone's happy), or to varying degrees.

♦ Under budget and ahead of schedule (we're gloating).

♦ Under budget and behind schedule (we're scrambling).

♦ Over budget and ahead of schedule (we're expediting).

♦ Over budget and behind schedule (we're probably looking for work).

These conditions are more accurately communicated using a common set of terms and a little math that compares planned and actual costs against planned and actual progress. Be careful where and how you use earned value reporting. It can be confusing to the uninitiated. The terms most frequently used and those used in Project 2003 are as follows:

BCWP (budgeted cost of work performed)—This is baseline (planned) cost of the tasks that have been completed.

ACWP (actual cost of work performed)—This is what it has cost you to complete the tasks that have been completed.

These two values are compared to another key measure:

BCWS (budgeted cost of the work scheduled)—This is how much it should have cost to completed the work as it was scheduled.

The reason the BCWS is used as the comparison is because it takes into consider the quantity of tasks as well as the cost of the tasks at any given schedule date. In this way, the project's condition in terms of earned value is affected more by costly tasks than by inexpensive tasks. Pretty cool, eh?

This comparison is described with the **CV** (cost variance) and **SV** (schedule variance). When they're negative, that's bad; when they're positive, that's good. When they're zero, the project is exactly on time and on budget.

One last point, when a chart is used to show earned-value trends, remember that the numbers are history against an estimate. You've got a good understanding of what has happened, but the future may bring surprises. All too often bills are slow to get processed, and problems are put off until the end. Naturally, you don't know the status of the project until it's finished. Some project managers like to use the **EAC** (estimate at completion) to forecast the finished cost. The trend of history to estimate is used to factor how costs are going and used to recalculate the remaining work's cost. The EAC is not deterministic—be careful how you use it!

Using the Analyze Timescaled Data in Excel Wizard

All in all, earned value is a great way to describe a project's condition. But make sure costs and progress are accurately tracked, and that your audience understands the measure. With Microsoft Project 2003, it's easy to include earned-value charts and data in your status reports. Open the project and select any task view. From the Analysis toolbar click **Analyze Timescaled Data in Excel Wizard.** On the first page of the wizard, select **Entire project,** and then click **Next.** Page two of the wizard is shown in Figure 22.4. For a trend line graph add **BCWP, BCWS,** and **ACWP, and remove Work** and any other fields that may be present in Fields to Export window. Click **Next** when you're ready.

Figure 22.4

Choose the BCWP, BCWS, and ACWP to create an earned-value actuals to budgeted line graph.

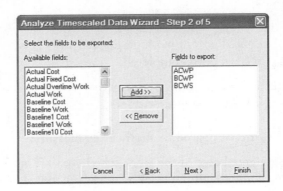

On the next page of the wizard, the start and finish dates of your project appear in the range fields. You may modify them to reduce the period exported, but leaving them as is allows each successive report to be created on the same timescale. In the Units field, select the smallest increment possible while not running over Excel's maximum of 256 columns. Continue to the next page and checkmark **Yes, Please** to create a graph, and then click **Export Data**. Project opens Excel, creates a data table on one sheet, and creates a graph of your data on another. The default 3D view Excel produces has been changed to a simple and more traditional line chart in Figure 22.5.

Modify the chart as you desire, and then save the Excel file. To insert your graph into a Word document, open the document, select **Insert, Object, Create from file,** and then **Browse** to the Excel file, select it, choose **Link to file,** and click **Insert.** The same process is used to insert an Excel graph into PowerPoint.

To create a schedule and CV chart, repeat the process but select only the CV and SV fields to export on page two of the wizard. The result has been formatted as a bar chart and is shown in Figure 22.6. The illustration shows a project that started out under budget and ahead of schedule. In April and May, schedule problems grew; however, late in the project progress quickened, finishing with good news all around.

The next time you have to make a presentation, you'll now be able to do it better, faster, and easier. Just focus on your audience needs and fill in your presentation outline with Project, Excel, PowerPoint, and Word. Then pack up your laptop and grab the projector—you're off to the meeting! You'll be looking good and communicating with credibility and professional pizzazz.

Ahead of schedule   Behind Schedule

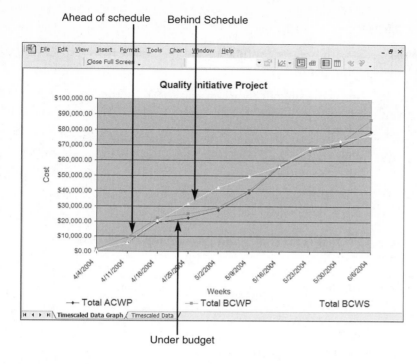

Under budget

Figure 22.5

The completed earned value line graph can be inserted into PowerPoint or Word.

Positive is good

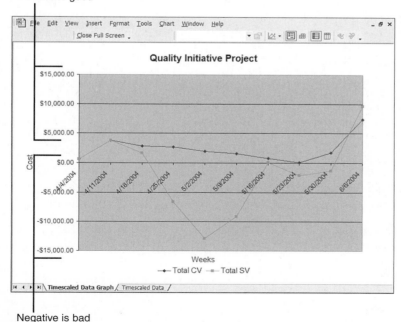

Negative is bad

Figure 22.6

The cost and schedule variance provides a simple and effective view of the project's status over time.

The Least You Need to Know

- ◆ The secret to presenting with greater confidence and credibility is to respect the audience and thoroughly prepare.

- ◆ You can prepare faster and more effectively when you use an outline and a fill-in-the-blanks approach.

- ◆ Earned value status reports are effective when the accounting and progress reports are accurate and up-to-date, and when the audience is familiar with the technique.

- ◆ With Project 2003, you can export timescaled data to Excel for analysis and graphing.

- ◆ The Copy Picture to Office Wizard copies and formats any Project 2003 view for use in Word and PowerPoint.

Appendix A

Words at Work

activity   An element of work that must be accomplished to complete the project. Also known as a *task*.

activity-duration estimating   Estimating the number of work periods needed to accomplish an activity.

activity-on-arrow (AOA)   A network diagramming method that uses arrows to represent activities.

activity-on-node (AON)   A network diagramming method that uses nodes or boxes to represent activities.

actual cost of work performed (ACWP)   The total of all costs incurred during a given time period.

actual finish date (AF)   The date work on an activity was completed.

actual start date (AS)   The date work actually started on an activity.

administrative closure   Formally closing the project in accordance with the organization's documentation procedures.

arrow   The link between tasks in a network diagram that shows the sequence of workflow.

arrow diagramming method (ADM)   A network diagramming method in which activities are shown as arrows.

as-of date   The date the data was collected.

backward pass   Calculating the late finish dates and late start dates of activities by adding the duration of the successor task to the dependent task in a network diagram.

bar chart   A network diagram of activities where the tasks are listed down the left side and activity durations are shown as a horizontal bar scaled to the length of the activity. Also known as a *Gantt chart*.

baseline   The scheduled dates, durations, resources, and costs according to the original plan; used to compare progress.

baseline finish date   The originally scheduled finish date.

baseline start date   The originally scheduled start date.

budget at completion (BAC)   The planned total cost of the finished project.

budgeted cost of work performed (BCWP)   The total value of activities actually completed within a given period according to the planned costs.

budgeted cost of work scheduled (BCWS)   The total value of activities as planned for a given period.

calendar   The methodology used to schedule workdays, shifts, resources, tasks, and the project as a whole. There are four calendar types in Microsoft Project 2003: base, project, resource, and task.

change in scope   A change in the goals and objectives of the project after the project has been planned.

chart of accounts   An accounting numbering system used to relate project costs to the organization's financial control system.

charter   The responsibilities and authorities assigned to the project.

contingencies   An allowance set aside for potential problems to mitigate risk.

contingency planning   A planning technique used to identify and mitigate potential problems.

control   Measuring, evaluating, and taking action based on actual performance compared to the planned performance.

cost estimating   Estimating the total direct and indirect expenses required to achieve project activities.

cost performance index (CPI)   Budgeted costs divided by actual costs (BCWP/ACWP). Sometimes used to predict the project's completed costs.

cost variance (CV)   The difference between actual and estimated costs of an activity.

crashing   Compressing the project's schedule through extraordinary means. Also known as *expediting*.

critical activity   Any activity that is part of the longest sequence of tasks from project start to project end. If the completion of a critical activity is delayed, the total duration of the project is delayed.

critical path   The series of tasks in a network diagram that requires the most time to complete. Activities on the critical path have zero slack or float.

critical path method (CPM)   A project scheduling technique where the duration of the longest complete series of tasks from project start to project completion is used to predict project duration.

cross-functional team   A workgroup that embodies diverse professions, skills, or expertise.

deliverable   Any specific, measurable project accomplishment or outcome.

dependency   Term used to describe the relationship between two or more activities or tasks. See *logical relationship*.

dummy activity   A drafting convention used as a placeholder to show a logical relationship in a network diagram, but where no duration is planned.

duration (DU)   The number of minutes, hours, weeks, or months required to complete an activity or task.

early finish date (EF)   The earliest possible date an activity can be completed based on the schedule.

early start date (ES)   The earliest possible date an activity can start based on the schedule.

earned value (EV)   The total cost of work calculated by comparing planned work for a period against actual work accomplished.

effort   The amount of work units needed to complete an activity.

estimate   A forecast of cost or duration for an activity.

estimate at completion (EAC)   The expected total cost of an activity or project when finished.

estimate to complete (ETC)   The expected additional cost needed to complete an activity or project.

event-on-node   A network diagramming technique in which activities are shown as nodes or boxes and workflow logic is shown with arrows. The original Program Evaluation and Review Technique used event-on-node to diagram workflow.

expediting   Shortening the duration of a task or project by any means available. Usually increases costs. Also known as *crashing*.

fast tracking   Compressing a project's schedule by running tasks in parallel that are normally run in sequence, such as beginning construction before design is complete. Usually increases risk.

finish date   The actual, planned, estimated, early, or late date an activity is to be completed.

finish-to-finish (FF) dependency   The workflow logic between two tasks in which the dependent task may not finish until its predecessor task is finished.

finish-to-start (FS) dependency   The workflow logic between two tasks in which the dependent task may not start until its predecessor task is finished.

float   The amount of time a task may be delayed without pushing out the project finish date. Also called *slack*.

forward pass   The calculation of the early start and early finish dates of all activities in the network diagram.

free float (FF)   The amount of time a task can be delayed without pushing out the start of any immediately following activities. Also called *free slack*.

free slack   See *free float*.

Gantt chart   A network diagram of activities in which the tasks are listed down the left side and durations are shown as a horizontal bar scaled to the length of the activity. Also known as *bar chart*.

lag   Describes the delay of a successor task from its predecessor's start or finish. See also *lead*.

late finish date (LF)   The latest a task may finish without delaying the project's finish date.

late start date (LS)   The latest a task may begin without delaying the project finish date.

lead   Describes the advance of a successor task's start from its predecessor's start or finish. See also *lag*.

leveling   The process of effectively allocating resources to tasks.

link   The arrow that shows the logical work sequence relationship between tasks.

logic   The workflow sequence.

logic diagram   A project's network diagram.

logical relationship   The workflow logic between two project tasks or activities (the predecessor and the dependent tasks) described as a finish-to-start, finish-to-finish, start-to-finish, or start-to-start relationship. Also known as *dependency*.

milestone   A point in the network diagram that shows significant accomplishment.

monitoring   Collecting progress information for judging progress against the plan.

network diagram   A diagram showing the workflow sequence of all tasks required to complete a project.

network logic   The workflow sequence as shown by a network diagram.

network path   Any series of tasks in a network diagram.

overlap   The concurrent period of time two or more parallel tasks share. See *lead*, *lag*, and *parallel task*.

noncritical task   Any task or activity that does not fall on the longest (critical) path.

overallocation   The condition of having too much work for the available resource capacity.

parallel task   A task undertaken during the same time period as another task.

path   A series of activities in a network diagram.

path float   See *float*.

percent complete (PC)   Estimate of progress derived by comparing the amount of work completed with the amount of work planned for an activity or project.

PERT chart   A critical path scheduling method using an activity-on-node network diagram and the Program Evaluation and Review Technique of weighted average duration estimates.

phase   A major subunit of a project's work or set of project deliverables.

planned finish date (PF)   The scheduled finish date of the project.

planned start date (PS)   The scheduled start date of the project.

precedence relationship   The description of two or more tasks' workflow sequence.

predecessor activity   The task which immediately precedes the dependent task.

program   A group of projects that are related and managed in a cohesive way.

Program Evaluation and Review Technique (PERT)   A critical path method of scheduling a project using the weighted average method to estimate durations.

project   The implementation of a strategy to create a specific, measurable outcome.

project charter   The document that authorizes a project manager to use the organization's resources and outlines the intended outcomes of the project.

project management   The process of undertaking and completing a course of action to meet the stated goals and objectives of an endeavor.

project manager (PM)   The person responsible for planning and implementing the project.

remaining duration (RDU)   The amount of time remaining required to complete a task.

request for proposal (RFP)   A solicitation for proposals from potential vendors for good or services.

request for quotation (RFQ)   A solicitation for quotations from vendors for goods or services.

resource leveling   Applying available resources to a project to determine task start and finish dates, project duration, and resource-utilization rates.

resource planning   Estimating the people, equipment, and material resources required to complete a project.

resources   All the people, equipment, materials, and money required to complete a project.

risk assessment   Evaluating potential risks and their effect on the project.

S curve   The graph of cumulative project expenditures plotted against time.

Schedule Performance Index (SPI)   The work performed compared to the work scheduled (BCWP/BCWS).

schedule variance (SV)   The actual versus the planned cost, duration, work, or percentage complete of an activity.

scheduled finish date (SF)   The date the task was to be completed according to the plan.

scheduled start date (SS)   The date the task was to be started according to the plan.

scope   The description of the project's intended breadth and depth.

scope change   Alterations in the project's goals or objectives at any time after the project has been initiated.

slack   The amount of time a task or path can slip without causing the project to finish late. See *float*.

slope   The dependent variables that describe the change in cost and duration when expediting (crashing) a task. Used to compare alternative methods and calculate the total costs required to shorten a project's duration.

start date   The actual, planned, early, late, or baseline date a task is scheduled to start.

start-to-finish (SF) dependency   The workflow logic between two tasks where the dependent task may not finish until its predecessor task has started.

start-to-start (SS) dependency   The workflow logic between two tasks where the dependent task may not start until its predecessor task has started.

successor activity   The activity that follows a predecessor activity.

target schedule   The baseline schedule.

target finish date (TF)   The baseline date work is scheduled to finish.

target start date (TS)   The baseline date work is scheduled to start.

task   An element of work which must be accomplished to complete the project. Also known as an *activity*.

total float (TF)   The amount of time a task or path can be delayed without delaying the completion of the project.

triple constraints   The interrelationship of a project's time, cost, and performance elements. Understanding their relative importance facilitates decision making and problem solving. Usually described as a driver, middle, and weak constraint.

underallocation   The condition of having too much resource capacity for the available work.

work breakdown structure (WBS)   The decomposition of the project's goals and objectives into increasingly detailed units of work, eventually identifying all tasks that are essential to the project's successful completion.

Additional Resources

Within the following listings, you'll find mountains of useful information and opportunities to enhance your project management skills. There are free forms, checklists, and templates so you won't have to reinvent the wheel; service providers to lend hands-on assistance; and hundreds of professional development and networking opportunities. Enjoy!

Author's Website

www.ronblack.com   The website where you can download forms, checklists, worksheets, templates, and presentation outlines described throughout this book. Readers can also sign up for my free e-mailed series of project success tips. To send comments and questions, or to get information on my consulting, coaching, and training services in project management, team leadership, and managing multiple projects, contact me at The Mentor Group. Contact: info@thementorgroup.com; 503-618-8703.

Information and Service Providers

www.accredo.com   A Microsoft EPM solutions service provider who integrates the disciplines of risk management and error-proofing into Microsoft Enterprise Project Management solutions, helping organizations focus on developing and delivering near-perfect internal controls, products, and services. Contact: info@accredo.com; 503-624-2124.

www.allpm.com   An e-zine that features free general-interest project management articles, news, templates, white papers, and other for-fee services.

www.gantthead.com   An e-zine for IT project managers. This is a good source for many free templates, forms, example project documents, stories, tips, news, and forums of interest to information technology projects.

www.pmforum.com   This website provides a library of project management documentation, technical papers, and case studies. It includes links to other project management sites, and commentary by the editors on current issues and concepts.

www.woodyswatch.com/project   Woody's Watch newsletters provide tips for Microsoft Office product users. The free newsletter is brief, covering only one or two problems, workarounds, or patches per issue, and the archives are searchable.

Microsoft Resources

www.microsoft.com/project   Microsoft Project home page with links to templates, assistance, updates, previous version support, discussion groups, and frequently asked questions.

www.msprojectpartner.com   This site contains a listing of worldwide service providers that can help you customize Project 2003 or install an Enterprise Project Management Solution.

www.support.microsoft.com   A searchable knowledge base of articles for troubleshooting Microsoft Office products or to find answers to specific questions.

Organizations

www.aipm.com.au   The Australian Institute of Project Management is the premier professional organization in Australia for the promotion and advancement of project management. Contact: info@aipm.com.au; (02) 9252 7277.

www.apm.org.uk   The Association for Project Management is a professional organization based in the UK for project managers that provides qualifications, standards, accredited training, research, publications, and events. Contact: services@apm.org.uk; (0845) 458 1944.

www.mpug.org   MPUG-Global is the association for Microsoft Project users throughout the world. The organization's purpose is to provide resources for members to improve their understanding of MS Project and to help maintain their investment in the tool. With more than 3,000 members and 34 chapters worldwide,

MPUG-Global is a Microsoft Office Project Partner and a Registered Education Provider (R.E.P.) for PMI. Contact: info@mpug.org; 734-741-0841.

www.mvps.org/project   Microsoft Most Valuable Professionals are volunteers who have been recognized in the online community for their contributions to users of Microsoft products. The Project website includes users tips, discussions and resolutions of common problems and issues, a listing of third-party resources and companion products, and links of interest to users of MS Project.

www.pmi.org   The Project Management Institute is the world's leading professional association for project managers. The organization promotes standards, a professional designation for project managers, research, and the general advancement of the project management knowledge area. Website includes templates, articles, forums, and links to commercial providers. Contact: pmihq@pmi.org; 610-356-4600.

Index

Check Out These
Best-Sellers

Grammar and Style
SECOND EDITION

- Easy-to-understand instructions on writing and speaking
- Perfect punctuation, from the apostrophe to the semi-colon
- Rights and wrongs of sentence structure, word usage, spelling, and much much more

Laurie E. Rozakis, Ph.D.

1-59257-115-8 • $16.95

Buying and Selling a Home
FOURTH EDITION

- What to expect when you buy or sell a home—with or without a broker
- Updated coverage of financing options for buyers, including mortgages and refinancing
- Idiot-proof tips on getting the best possible price when you sell

Shelley O'Hara and Nancy D Lewis

1-59257-120-4 • $18.95

Being a Groom
SECOND EDITION

- Top 10 things to remember on the big day
- Brand-new ideas on last honeymoon destinations
- Idiot-proof advice on breaking the ice between the in-laws

Jennifer Lata Rung and Mark Rung

0-02-864456-5 • $9.95

Learning Spanish
THIRD EDITION

- Easy explanations of Spanish grammar and pronunciation
- Key phrases for travel, hotels, airports, shopping, business, and more
- New and expanded vocabulary lists with English/Spanish and Spanish/English translations

Gail Stein

0-02-864451-4 • $18.95

Personal Finance in Your 20s & 30s
SECOND EDITION

- Savvy advice on getting—and staying—out of debt
- Idiot-proof tips on saving money for the future and still having money to spend
- Down-to-earth advice on making wise investments—especially when you're on a budget

Sarah Young Fisher and Susan Shelly

0-02-864374-7 • $19.95

Organizing Your Life
FOURTH EDITION

- Tips and tricks to getting your house in order—one room at a time
- Filing strategies to help you keep on top of everyday paperwork
- Helpful hints for getting your kids' stuff organized—and how to get them into the habit

Georgene Lockwood

1-59257-413-0 • $16.95

Total Nutrition
FOURTH EDITION

- Food group fundamentals from the dairy, fruit, vegetable, and grain worlds
- Essential information on the good, bad, and ugly of fats, cholesterol, proteins, and carbs
- Healthy advice for people with diabetes, allergies, cancer, and other conditions

Joy Bauer, M.S., R.D., C.D.N.

1-59257-439-4 • $18.95

Positive Dog Training

- Fascinating insights into how dogs learn and communicate
- Proven pointers for training without punishment
- Expert tips for incorporating training into your daily routine

Pamela Dennison

0-02-864463-8 • $14.95

The Bible
THIRD EDITION

- Timeless stories from Genesis to Revelation and all the wondrous tales in between
- Words of wisdom from Jesus Christ's teachings and the epistles of the Apostles
- Illuminating insights into kings and prophets like David, Solomon, Moses, and Isaiah

James Stuart Bell and Stan Campbell

1-59257-389-4 • $18.95

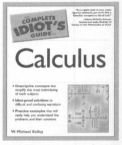

Calculus

- Descriptive concepts that simplify the most intimidating of math subjects
- Idiot-proof solutions to difficult and confusing equations
- Practice examples that will really help you understand the problems and their solutions

W. Michael Kelley

0-02-864365-8 • $18.95

Music Theory
SECOND EDITION

- Essential information on reading and writing music—including basic notes, rhythms, and scales
- Tips on creating your own melodies, chords, and harmonies
- Audio exercises to develop your ear-training skills

Michael Miller

1-59257-437-8 • $19.95

The Perfect Resume
THIRD EDITION

- Winning resume techniques that will convince an employer to call you for an interview
- Expert advice on talking sticky resume issues such as layoffs, employment gaps, and career changes
- More than 100 up-to-date samples of successful resumes and cover letters

Susan Ireland

0-02-864440-9 • $14.95

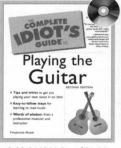

Playing the Guitar
SECOND EDITION

- Tips and tricks to get you playing your own tunes in no time
- Easy-to-follow steps for learning to read music
- Words of wisdom from a professional musician and instructor

Frederick Noad

0-02-864244-9 • $21.95

MANGA
ILLUSTRATED

John Layman and David Hutchison for IDEA + Design Works, LLC

1-59257-335-5 • $19.95

Knitting and Crocheting
SECOND EDITION
Illustrated

- An all-new selection of step-by-follow patterns with step-by-step illustrated instructions
- Crafty tips on choosing the right yarn for your project
- Simple advice for going beyond the basics to create more advanced projects

Barbara Breiter and Gail Diven

1-59257-089-5 • $16.95

More than *450 titles* available at booksellers and online retailers everywhere

www.idiotsguides.com

ALPHA